P9-DMD-085

COMMANDER
WILL CUSHING

ALSO BY JAMIE MALANOWSKI

The Book of Levon:
The Trials and Triumphs of Levon Helm (2013)

And the War Came:
The Six Months That Tore America Apart (2011)

The Coup (2007)

Mr. Stupid Goes to Washington (1992)

The Sinking of the Albemarle

Illustration by C. E. Monroe Jr. (Courtesy C. E. Monroe III)

COMMANDER WILL CUSHING

DAREDEVIL HERO
OF THE CIVIL WAR

Jamie Malanowski

W. W. NORTON & COMPANY
New York   London

Copyright © 2014 by Jamie Malanowski

All rights reserved
Printed in the United States of America
First Edition

For information about permission to reproduce selections from this book,
write to Permissions, W. W. Norton & Company, Inc.,
500 Fifth Avenue, New York, NY 10110

For information about special discounts for bulk purchases, please
contact W. W. Norton Special Sales at specialsales@wwnorton.com
or 800-233-4830

Manufacturing by RR Donnelley, Harrisonburg
Book design by Fearn Cutler de Vicq
Production manager: Devon Zahn

Library of Congress Cataloging-in-Publication Data

Malanowski, Jamie.
Commander Will Cushing : daredevil hero of the Civil War / Jamie
Malanowski. — First edition.
pages cm
Includes bibliographical references.
ISBN 978-0-393-24089-4 (hardcover)
1. Cushing, William Barker, 1842–1874. 2. Ship captains—United
States—Biography. 3. United States. Navy—Officers—Biography. 4.
Albemarle (Confederate ironclad) 5. United States—History—Civil
War, 1861–1865—Commando operations. I. Title.
E467.1.C98M33 2014
973.7'58092—dc23
[B]
2014020493

W. W. Norton & Company, Inc.
500 Fifth Avenue, New York, N.Y. 10110
www.wwnorton.com

W. W. Norton & Company Ltd.
Castle House, 75/76 Wells Street, London W1T 3QT

1 2 3 4 5 6 7 8 9 0

For Rose Marie Malanowski and Matthew Malanowski

"To the outside world we all grow old. But not to brothers and sisters. . . . We live outside the touch of time."

— CLARA ORTEGA

Contents

INTRODUCTION   17

CHAPTER 1   Terrible Excitement   19

CHAPTER 2   Plague and Pride   22

CHAPTER 3   A Talent for Buffoonery   27

CHAPTER 4   Not Recommended   33

CHAPTER 5   Neither Efficient nor Subordinate   35

CHAPTER 6   His Exuberant Spirit   44

CHAPTER 7   The Gosport Debacle   49

CHAPTER 8   The *Delaware Farmer*   54

CHAPTER 9   Baptisms of Fire   59

CHAPTER 10   Twenty-Eight Shells a Minute   62

CHAPTER 11   Original and Speculative   66

CHAPTER 12   Transformations   73

CHAPTER 13   The *Virginia*   77

CHAPTER 14   The *Monitor*   83

Contents

CHAPTER 15   Rising   91

CHAPTER 16   Reenter Flusser   97

CHAPTER 17   Adventures of the *Ellis*   102

CHAPTER 18   Pilot Hunting   108

CHAPTER 19   Alonzo at Antietam   113

CHAPTER 20   In Old Virginia   117

CHAPTER 21   At Gettysburg   127

CHAPTER 22   Alonzo's Glory   132

CHAPTER 23   Grieving   137

CHAPTER 24   The Essence of Impudence   141

CHAPTER 25   Marsh Grass and Cattails   149

CHAPTER 26   High Time We Went   151

CHAPTER 27   Zigzag   154

CHAPTER 28   Letters from Welles   157

CHAPTER 29   The Coming   160

CHAPTER 30   Rampage   164

CHAPTER 31   Too Strong   170

CHAPTER 32   Proceed to New York   176

CHAPTER 33   No One Else   180

CHAPTER 34   In Case of Failure   184

CHAPTER 35   Dead Ahead   187

CHAPTER 36   Now   191

CHAPTER 37   Dead Gone Sunk   194

CONTENTS

CHAPTER 38 Seldom Equaled, Never Excelled   198

CHAPTER 39 Back in Action   202

CHAPTER 40 Secret Weapon   206

CHAPTER 41 Sitting Duck   209

CHAPTER 42 Return to Fort Fisher   212

CHAPTER 43 Slaughter at the Northeast Bastion   216

CHAPTER 44 Endgames   223

CHAPTER 45 Victory   228

CHAPTER 46 On the West Coast   231

CHAPTER 47 Love and Duty   235

CHAPTER 48 Love Letters   240

CHAPTER 49 In the Orient   246

CHAPTER 50 Howard   251

CHAPTER 51 The World Stage   257

CHAPTER 52 The *Virginius*   260

CHAPTER 53 The Butcher   264

CHAPTER 54 Face-off   267

CHAPTER 55 At Rest   272

EPILOGUE   275

ACKNOWLEDGMENTS   283

NOTES ON SOURCES   285

BIBLIOGRAPHY   287

COMMANDER WILL CUSHING

Introduction

I N JUNE 1892, at a meeting of a veterans' organization in Illinois, a man named John Black, who had been a colonel of a volunteer regiment during the Civil War, addressed an audience of former Union soldiers and sailors. To these men, now in their fifties and sixties, Black spoke of youth—the sacrifices rendered, the struggles endured, and the triumphs earned by the men in his audience and others like them thirty years earlier, during the event that would always stand as the great challenge of their era and the greatest victory of their lives.

"Some few of the names of the youth of the war are immortal," said Black.

> *Custer on horseback—a flaming sword in the right hand of Sheridan—won his greatest laurels when but a boy. And Cushing— the darling of the American navy, as Farragut was its glory and its hero,—Cushing, with his little boat amid the swamps and sinks of the Carolina coast, taught the world that the heroic spirit of the American navy survived in all its irresistible force and splendid personal daring, and that there was no danger so great, no darkness so profound, no labyrinth so intricate, no arm so treacherous, that the Boys in the War would not attack, enter, overcome, in the name of the country.*

Immortal? George Armstrong Custer is a name we know mostly because of his ignominious death on the Montana prairie. But Cushing—William Barker Cushing, a native of Wisconsin, a child of upstate New York, the youngest man in United States Navy history to be named a lieutenant, a lieutenant commander, and then commander—is a name that only a few readers will recognize. Yet there was a time when he was the darling of the navy, as Black said; a man whose "glorious achievement and dauntless courage" would "place this beardless Paladin among the veritable heroes of the age," as one fellow officer would put it; "a man who comes next to Farragut on the hero roll of American naval history," as Theodore Roosevelt said, referring to the great Union admiral; "the hero of the war," as David Farragut himself declared.

And yet he is all but unknown today.

There are many possible explanations. The simple passage of time is the most likely culprit, although the Civil War is not exactly a forgotten topic among the American people, and there are plenty of Beauregards and Braggs whose names are known but whose meager accomplishments melt next to Cushing's. Nor is he a dated figure trapped in amber; if there was ever a nineteenth-century figure with a twenty-first-century action hero profile, it is Will Cushing. Good looking, ridiculously young, possessed of a sense of dash and drama and a cool courage and a mischievous antiauthoritarian streak wide enough to get himself expelled from the Naval Academy—not only on the eve of his graduation, but on the eve of war—Cushing would seem to perfectly fit our tastes. But Cushing is more than image; in virtually single-handedly sinking the Confederate ironclad *Albemarle* with a torpedo mounted on an open launch, he performed arguably the greatest single feat of arms in American history. We may not know it, but he is in a great many respects more a hero fit for our times than he was for his.

And to think he might have missed his moment entirely.

CHAPTER 1

Terrible Excitement

O N December 12, 1860, eight days before a convention in Columbia, South Carolina, would decide whether or not the state would secede from the Union, Acting Midshipman William Cushing, a First Classman at the United States Naval Academy, sent a letter to his cousin Mary, back home in Fredonia, New York.

"Here, in Maryland, there is terrible excitement," he wrote.

Men are arming in every portion of the state; all the banks have suspended, and the blue cockade [of secession] may be found in every nook and corner. Within the Academy, where there are representatives from every state in our Union, the huge weight of the crisis has penetrated. Mid[shipmen] are every day resigning. Every Southerner has orders to resign as soon as his state secedes. Secession speeches are made by the South Carolinians and the Georgians, and there is not a southern man but hopes and believes that the world now views for the last time this great Republic. . . . Matters cannot be improved except by a miracle; and unless that miracle happens, the ship of state, which has been so long on a lee shore, must go down, carrying the Naval Academy, which is but a speck on its deck.

If it comes to blows between North and South, I will shed my last drop of blood for the state of New York. If this place does break up, I will get my graduation papers. If it does not, I will get them all the same.

What's remarkable about this letter, apart from the lively description of the turbulence in Maryland during this outbreak of secession fever, is what it tells us about Will Cushing, a freshly turned eighteen-year-old college senior. We see, for example, that Will possessed a fertile gift for embellishment; until years of composing official reports neutered his talents, Will had a fluid, expressive writing style, a vivid vocabulary, and a fiction writer's aptitude for seeing the richness in things and then making them a little richer. "Mid[shipmen] are every day resigning"? In the entire month of December, a total of four men left. "Every Southerner has orders to resign as soon as his state secedes"? Pure exaggeration—even after months of rhapsodic rhetoric, vote rigging, and violence, the secessionists wouldn't even get all the states where slavery was legal to secede; forget about pulling off an elaborate conspiracy to control all southern midshipmen. Not that there's anything wrong with Cushing's overstatements: hyperbole is one way young people express their joie de vivre. We just shouldn't take every word as gospel.

The letter also reveals Will's view of his future. Sharing his thoughts with his adoring country cousin in his best man-of-the-world way, he admits that he doesn't really know what the future holds. Not for his country, certainly not for his speck of a college. What the future holds for him? That's a different story. He's going to graduate, then fight for whatever New York State is fighting for. Could be in a month, could be next June, but graduation? That's a certainty.

Thus does the captain of the good ship Cushing display not an inkling, not an iota of suspicion that within three weeks he would be the recipient of a different sort of letter—one far more concrete, devoid of speculation, empty of hyperbole, official. Written on the twenty-eighth of December by the superintendent of the academy, George Blake, it was a warning shot fired across Cushing's bow.

Sir:

It is my duty to call your attention to the fact that you have incurred one hundred and sixty three demerits during the present academic year. [A midshipman who accumulated two hundred demerits during an academic year would be, in the droll parlance of the academy, "returned to his friends."] Forty five have been removed, in the hope that you might be induced to amend your conduct, leaving one hundred eighteen recorded against you at this time.

The records of the Academy show that in former years, you have been entirely regardless of the regulations. For your first year at the institution, 95 demerits have been recorded against you. For the second, 161. For the third, 158, and among the most prominent of the offenses charged are fighting, disorderly conduct, and for disturbing class in quarters, in recitation rooms, for playing cards, for which you have once been suspended, and for addressing a highly improper communication to the Commandant of midshipmen.

I sincerely trust you will amend your conduct, and be no longer unmindful to your duties to the Academy, yourself and your friends. But I admonish you, that if two hundred demerits are accorded against you, I shall report you to the Department . . . and recommend your dismissal from the service.

This is the sort of letter that causes ordinary women and men to snap to attention. But never in his life was Will Cushing ordinary.

CHAPTER 2

Plague and Pride

B ORN IN DELAFIELD, Wisconsin, on November 4, 1842, William Barker Cushing was the tenth of the eleven children sired by his father, Milton, a judge chronically ill with tuberculosis but evidently blessed with healthy sexual appetites. The judge was forty-seven when he died, possessed of far more respect than wealth; Will was five. Will's mother, Elizabeth, born in 1807, was Milton's second wife (the first, along with one of her children, died before Milton, and the three children who reached adulthood, including the promising Benjamin, who was the law partner of future treasury secretary Salmon Chase, were all dead by 1858).

An intelligent, educated, strong-willed woman, Elizabeth came from a prominent Boston family (standouts include a grandfather who was a congressman and a cousin who was a flag officer) with a distinguished lineage (she was a descendant of John and Priscilla Alden, a cousin to John Adams, and connected to the Hancocks, Madisons, and Phillipses). Fighting against the penuries of widowhood, Elizabeth opened a school in Fredonia, New York, the last place she and her peripatetic husband made a home. With earnings from teaching, and with timely subsidies from her relatives, she raised her brood: the phlegmatic Milton Jr.; the self-sufficient Howard; the earnest, dutiful Alonzo; the irrepressible Will; and the overshadowed Mary Isabel.

She taught them to look out for one another, and they listened. Her boys called her "Little Ma," and the bonds of affection among them were strong. "One trait, was very remarkable in our family," observed Mary Isabel. "That was the respect and courtesy manifested toward each other. I never received a reproof or heard an impatient word from either of my brothers. They always displayed toward each other, and my mother and myself, the same courtesy they would show to a commanding officer. The petting and love I received was enough to have spoiled me for life."

The two children who stood out were Alonzo, who was honest and obedient and conscientious, and Will, who was curious, adventurous, and energetic, as well as headstrong, rambunctious, and heedless. "Dear, darling, mischievous Will," recalled one Fredonia neighbor. "He was the plague and the pride of all who knew him."

The first of his antics to earn the status of legend was performed at the age of three, when he ran away from home, charged off the end of a dock, spent thirty-six unconcerned hours in the custody of the sailor who had fished him out of the Chicago River, and, when asked his name, hampered his own recovery by merrily chirping "Bill Coon," a nickname hung on him by Alonzo.

After that, there was never a shortage of tales about Will. There was the story where Will gets tossed out of church, and the one where he drives the wagon over country roads at breakneck speed, the one where he drives a wagon down and back up a steep riverbank, and the one where his teachers chase him across the school yard after he escaped detention. There's the tale where he loses two teeth when kicked in the head by a horse that he was trying, without bothering to avail himself of any training, to shoe with a new horseshoe, and the one where he's trying to escape the consequences of some unauthorized apple picking, and breaks an arm after he falls off a fence while kicking at a furious pursuer. All of these, in combination with his creativity in thinking up fun things to do, made him invincibly popular. "Will was the ringleader in all the berrying, nutting and fishing frolics," his sister wrote, "and our adventures would fill a volume. He always killed every snake, even pulling them out of their holes." He was always up for anything.

When Will was nine, he and Alonzo formally dubbed their small circle of schoolboys "The Muss Company." Although Alonzo and some other boys were older, Will was the undisputed captain. "Even while very young, he was a daring and willful leader of his young companions," recalled a neighbor. He drilled the gang in marching, and trained them to assemble whenever he blew his whistle. Will attended his mother's school, which had a slightly earlier lunch period than the public school. On more than a few occasions Will went to the public school at the start of his lunch break and blew on his whistle, causing the Muss members to leap up from of their desks, hurtle out of their classrooms, and form up for a quick hike. He kept this up until the public school instructor complained to Mrs. Cushing, who put an end to these antics, but not before admonishing the other teacher for not being able to control his pupils.

Popular, even charismatic, Will was also, as one Fredonian noted, "quick-tempered and always ready to settle disputes with a fight, upon the principle that the best men won the battle." He wasn't ashamed of this, nor did anyone seek to make him ashamed. He wasn't mean, just fast with his fists. After spending a few days visiting cousins in another town, Will received a note from his mother calling him home. "May as well," he said, "I've whipped every boy in town."

One of Will's boyhood friends was David Parker, later to become a lieutenant and superintendent of mail for the Army of the Potomac, a significant job that frequently brought him in and out of Washington, permitting him to meet up with Will on several occasions while Will was on leave. In his memoir, *A Chatauqua Boy in '61 and Afterward*, Parker offers some privileged memories of Will, this one from the time when they were about twelve or thirteen:

> *Cushing was very pugnacious, good-natured generally but very quick to resent an insult, and he would fight any boy or any man*

without the slightest hesitation. On one occasion in front of a grocery store, we came upon a man who had some difficulties with Cushing and who turned upon us and said "I've got you now and I'll give you a good spanking." Will jumped up on a raised platform in front of the store where there was a barrel containing axe handles, hoe handles, and other things of that sort, and seized an axe helve [the handle of a small axe] and struck the man a heavy blow on the side of the head, felling him to the ground. He was not a bully, but he was perfectly fearless.

Will was, in short, the sort of youngster whose exploits might make a person laugh and shake his head, if not simultaneously, then in rapid succession. One could not help but marvel at his nerve, yet also fear that one day he would meet his comeuppance. Wagons do roll over. Hitting a man with an axe handle can result in prison. Dark consequences lurk within every carefree antic. But instead of being punished, Will was often rewarded with a very lucky break.

In 1854, Francis Smith Edwards—the husband of one of Elizabeth Cushing's sisters, the father of Will's favorite cousin Mary—was elected to Congress as the candidate of the American Party, better known as the Know-Nothings. These anti-Catholic, anti-German, anti-Jewish, anti-Negro nativists were a small-minded, provocative bunch, but Edwards was more genial than most, at least to members of his family. He promised Elizabeth that he would try to do something for her boys, and he was true to his word. By the summer, he had wrangled Will a job as a congressional page, and he had begun to work on getting Alonzo an appointment to West Point. It took some time to pull everything together, but early in 1856, Will moved to Washington.

Will spent a year in the icily wintered, swelteringly summered, perpetually muddy, half-built capital. Living some of the time at his uncle's home and some in the Washington House where other pages boarded, he was exposed to a wider variety of people than he would ever see in Fredonia: rich people, westerners, southerners, politicians, prostitutes, entertainers, foreigners, slaves. He got to immerse himself in city life—specifically, life in a city where the people had some ideals and culture and some belief in a larger significance of what they did. If only superficially, Will entered the orbit of serious men, where he could begin to grasp their wants and needs and ordinariness. He got to meet some, too. Among them was another cousin, Commodore Joseph Smith, the chief of the Bureau of Navy Yards and Docks in Washington, an influential, well-connected man who grew fond of his lively young cousin. The experience helped Will grow up a bit, to broaden himself. Still, the job of page involved a great deal of sitting around waiting for a message that needed delivering, and then waiting for a reply. It was often boring, and he didn't like it.

When Francis Edwards lost his bid for reelection in 1856, Joseph Smith took charge of Will and Alonzo's future and soon settled on a plan: in the fall, Will would enter the Naval Academy as a member of the class of 1861, and Alonzo would be admitted to West Point, class of 1862.

CHAPTER 3

A Talent for Buffoonery

WILL ENTERED THE NAVAL ACADEMY IN 1857. He stood 5'4" (en route to a height of six feet), and was not only the youngest in his class, but was and until his third year would remain the youngest in the school. Nonetheless, he took great pride in being an officer, however lowly, in the service. (Once, during his second year, when he was visiting an aunt in Chelsea, outside Boston, a neighborhood boy mocked the short jacket of his uniform, and Will called him out. "The battle raged over the sidewalks and the dusty streets," Will's aunt reported to his mother. "Afterwards [he] walked the streets of Chelsea quite free from comments on his beloved uniform.") But it cannot be said that Will took to scholastic life very eagerly. Life at the academy, as George Dewey, the future admiral and hero of Manila Bay, wrote in his memoirs, was "one endless grind of acquiring knowledge," with no physical exercise or gymnasium to help a young man blow off some energy. The young men took classes in seamanship, gunnery, naval tactics, mathematics, astronomy, navigation, ethics, English, Spanish, French, and drawing. Discipline was rigid, with rules governing a full spectrum of conduct. Two hundred demerits resulted in dismissal. The textbooks stressed duty to country and respect for order and the chain of command.

Will was a popular student; in a school where the students had to make their own fun, his inventiveness and energy made him a leader. He liked to pull pranks—swiping tea from the kitchen, propping buckets of water on half-open doors, sneaking out after dark. Academically, however, he was a consistent underachiever. Seldom exerting himself, he passed his courses with a minimum amount of effort while flirting with the demerit maximum. In only one course did he ever excel: gunnery, ranking third in his class. The rest of the time he was mostly a middle-of-the-pack student, a status he achieved without apparently cracking a book. (As his career would show, Will had the capacity for book learning, but his genius was in improvisation.) He must have been a source of frustration to his teachers; he was certainly a source of great vexation to the commandant of midshipmen, Christopher Raymond Perry Rodgers, the number two man in the administration.

Tall, elegant, and handsome, Rodgers, then forty-one years old, was a full-fledged member of America's naval royal family. On his paternal side, his grandfather was a navy captain who had served during the Revolution and under the first six presidents. His father captained a warship in the War of 1812, and his uncle was a captain as well. His grandfather on his mother's side commanded a navy frigate during the Revolution, and his uncles were Matthew C. Perry, who opened Japan to the West, and Oliver Hazard Perry, the hero of the Battle of Lake Erie, the man whose battle flag was "Don't Give Up the Ship." Known for his dignity and knightly manners, Rodgers in one sense embodied the naval establishment; in another he was its most dangerous opponent.

Alfred Thayer Mahan, the naval historian whose strategies would come to govern naval thinking throughout the world between the Civil War and the Second World War, was two years ahead of Will at Annapolis. In his memoir *From Sail to Stern: Recollections of Naval Life*, he wrote, "It had for some time been recognized within the service that, owing partly to easy-going toleration of offenders, partly to the absence of authorized methods for dealing with the disabled, or the merely incompetent, partly also, doubtless, to the effect of general professional stagnation upon those naturally inclined to worthlessness, there had accumulated a very considerable percentage of officers who were useless; or, worse, unreliable." Most of the leading officers were men deep into their seventh decade, and many were alcoholics, or had other serious physical disabilities; a common evaluation was, "He's a good officer, when he's not drinking." There were also a fair number of officers from prominent families who were lazy or licentious or otherwise corrupt, and who had been deposited in the service in order to obtain a veneer of respectability. The rot at the top created an easygoing, "get along and go along" attitude, which was jealously protected. During the 1850s, the navy establishment fought and defeated efforts to modernize the personnel system and to bring ironclad vessels into the US fleet. Nobody wanted to initiate reform more than Christopher Rodgers, and the most promising place to introduce change was with the new blood at the Naval Academy.

The Naval Academy, founded in 1845, did not enjoy the same esteem as West Point, which was founded in 1805 and was solidly established in the public's mind. By 1860, most of the army's leadership was composed of West Point men who had distinguished themselves during the Mexican war and in Indian conflicts; Annapolis men were just attaining leadership positions (although more would have done, had not the path been blocked by aged officers). The academy, moreover, had struggled since its inception with meager budgets, secondhand facilities, and even scandal involving midshipmen who plotted to commit mutiny, seize a ship, and become pirates. If the Navy was going to modernize, ambitious younger officers like Rodgers would have to bring pressure from below, from Annapolis.

Superintendent Blake wasn't against these objectives. During his years atop the academy, important changes were made to improve the curriculum and facilities. Courses in artillery, seamanship, and topographical and hydrographical drawing were added or upgraded, new textbooks written or adopted, and the size and quality of the faculty expanded. But the fifty-nine-year-old Blake had more sympathy for the struggles of his young students than to become a strictly by-the-book leader. An advocate of strengthening discipline through positive reinforcement, the avuncular Blake had the habit of placing his hand on his round belly and saying, "I can lay my hand upon my heart, and say I have never wronged a midshipman." The academy by itself, with its academic grind and terrible food and rules upon rules, ruthlessly weeded out the boys who weren't officer material. If a young gentleman didn't measure up, Blake had no difficulty bidding him goodbye; but if a student was surviving, Blake wasn't the sort to torque up the pressure to see if he could get a better performance out of the lad. Almost every midshipman knew how to bend the rules, and almost everyone charged with enforcement knew that there were times to look away. As much as Blake may have sympathized with the reformers, he was from an earlier generation, where once a man established his willingness to hold fast on the quarterdeck, a multitude of shortcomings could be forgiven. Perhaps he understood more than others how one jokester in a class might ease the pressure felt by twenty grinders, how the middie nervy enough to pull some pranks could turn out to be a good man to have in a fight.

But Rodgers saw the rot. Rodgers wanted a new commitment to standards, and he wanted to begin at the Naval Academy. He had heard the stories about Will, about his gags and pranks and clowning. The boy glided through, sometimes doing well, sometimes just skimming by, never applying himself, never really doing his best, never being the person the academy could hold up to the country and to the world and say, "This is our man."

On October 17, 1860, Rodgers sent this report to Blake:

Within the last week Mr. Cushing has been reported, once by Assistant Professor Hopkins, and by Professor Roget, for buffoonery at recitation, and for provoking to laughter other members of his section, thus rendering it necessary that they should be reported also. Upon the first occasion I remonstrated gravely and kindly with Mr.

Cushing, but it seems that the warning I gave Mr. Cushing made no impression on his mind or change in his conduct. Two days ago Professor Roget observed him drawing in his Spanish book, looking at his instructor from time to time, as if employed in taking his likeness. Mr. Roget examined the book and found upon one of the blank pages a drawing of a Jackass with the words "drawn from life." Mr. Cushing represents in his defense that he had had no reference to Mr. Roget in the drawing, and that his object in looking at him so frequently was to observe if he was watching him.

It is desirable that this misconduct should be checked for this young gentleman's talent for buffoonery renders him a source of trouble at recitations.

It's important to realize just how swiftly Rodgers was acting against the senior class's reigning demerits leader. School had been in session for just two weeks.

But Will was no buffoon. He was an eighteen-year-old who had spent a year as a congressional page, and if all he ever did was carry messages to legislators, he had with his own eyes seen William Seward and Stephen Douglas and Jefferson Davis and the other leaders of the day, and gained a more privileged view than most of his peers. He was one of the poor relations in his family, but that family was politically connected. He had been exposed to informed discussion at his uncles' tables, and he was surely aware that the 1860 presidential election, just three weeks away, could lead to an outcome where he would be serving in combat. Moreover, he was a midshipman who had no more than two weeks before returned from the academy-required four-month-long Atlantic cruise on the USS *Plymouth*, a sloop that carried twenty guns. This cruise, designed to teach midshipmen the "ideas of the Naval Service afloat," took the midshipmen across the Atlantic, to Spain and Portugal and other countries, and, in this particular year, through the teeth of a major storm. During that cruise, Will, like the other first-class students on board, served as lieutenant of the watch, which required that he exercise real responsibility for the safety and conduct of the ship.

When Will returned from the cruise, his eagerness to begin his naval career was never higher, just as the stakes involved in pursuing that career were never clearer. But he still had to get through one more year at Annapolis, one more year of rules, one more year of recitation, one more year of learning *yo voy, tú vas,* and *él va.* And one more year of Commandant Rodgers.

He handled it poorly. In the fall of 1860, his appearance grew sloppy, his studies suffered, he stopped playing along. In a school where it was against rules to lie on your bed except when sleeping, he hardly bothered to rise. Clearly he did not take Rodgers's admonitions seriously; but no less seriously than Rodgers was taking Acting Midbuffoon Cushing. No martinet, Rodgers was a respected officer whose strict discipline brought out the best in and proved inspirational to many young officers. Will, however, was different, and a different kind of approach from Rodgers might have broken through Will's arrogance and heedlessness and reached the serious boy who had so much to offer. Whatever was actually said between them, whatever was really heard, whatever tone was used, ten weeks after Commandant Rodgers accepted Will's pledge to improve, Superintendent Blake was writing his stern letter of December 28 to Will about his many demerits. But that was hardly the big news in January 1861.

CHAPTER 4

Not Recommended

B Y THE START OF THE NEW YEAR, the challenges to ordinary academic life at the Academy had increased in difficulty and in number. South Carolina became the first state to secede on December 20; by February 1, the total would reach seven. Four acting midshipmen resigned in December; twenty-one left the following month. Others received pressure from their parents. William E. Yancey, a midshipman whose father was the notorious "fire-eating" secessionist, didn't want to go; he received a telegram from his father that said, "Resign or I will disown you." Young Yancey acquiesced, joined the Confederate navy, and was killed at the Battle of Ball's Bluff in October 1861. Robley Evans discovered that his mother in Virginia had submitted a resignation on his behalf, but he defied her, and fought to be restored to the rolls. "It was a time of great suspense for all hands," Evans wrote. Every student and teacher who was from one of the fifteen states where slavery was legal was on tenterhooks, waiting and wondering what would happen. At various moments, war seemed imminent. In January, an unarmed civilian vessel, *Star of the West*, carrying provisions and two hundred US soldiers, tried to reach Fort Sumter, and was fired on by batteries in Charleston. The captain aborted the attempt after sustaining minor damage. Had the ship been more badly damaged, had it sunk, had men been killed, the war almost certainly would have begun right there.

As the winter wore on—as more states seceded, as efforts at compromise failed, as the departed states formed a Confederate government, as war talk intensified—it must have been hard for the students to keep any kind of focus, for none more so than Will Cushing. After missing most of his classes in January, Will managed to pass all but one of his February midterms; he failed Spanish. It's not clear whether or not he suspected or knew that he had done poorly, but if he did, Will doesn't seem to have been burdened by the bad grade. On March 1, he wrote a jocular note to his cousin Mary, full of levity and wordplay; he tells her that he doesn't expect to be in Washington for the inauguration, but will visit not long after.

Soon after writing that letter, Will would learn that he was now free to meet Mary at the time and place of their choosing, for he was no longer bound by the regulations of the Naval Academy. He was out. "Deficient at February semi-annual examination, 1861," Blake wrote in his official report to the Navy Department on March 13. "Midshipman William B. Cushing. Deficient in Spanish. Aptitude for study: good. Habits of study: irregular. General conduct: bad. Aptitude for Naval Service: not good. Not recommended for continuance at the Academy."

At long last, it seems, Will had received his comeuppance.

CHAPTER 5

Neither Efficient nor Subordinate

E VEN AFTER 150 YEARS, Will's expulsion—forced resignation—
seems shocking. Kicked out just three months shy of graduation
for failing Spanish? The punishment seems harsh and arbitrary.
Midshipmen got kicked out when they had amassed two hundred demerits; Will was nearing that total, but just as in his previous two years, when
he flirted with expulsion but each time escaped, he might well have been
able to slam on the behavioral brakes for his final months. Moreover,
while midshipmen were regularly expelled for poor academic results,
ousting a student for a bad grade in Spanish was rather like convicting Al
Capone for tax-code violations. Courses were weighted so that classes in
seamanship, gunnery, and naval tactics counted more than the humani-
ties, and failure in those courses is what would usually get a student
expelled. This seems perfectly reasonable. The young men were being
trained to be naval officers. A certain amount of polish and diplomacy
is required, but a lot of the job is about steering ships and killing people.

And that makes the dismissal all the more inexplicable. Will
resigned from the academy one month before Fort Sumter was fired
upon. Not only had seven states seceded, but they had formed a government, seized federal property, appointed a president, and begun to
organize armed forces. In Washington, the administration was con-

sidering plans to reinforce Sumter; if they were carried out, war would undoubtedly follow. By the end of March, the navy would have lost 222 of its 1,554 officers, with many still on the fence (resignations plus dismissals based on suspect loyalty would reach 373 by the end of 1861). Cushing was a young officer of some aptitude who had been trained at great expense; to toss him out on the eve of war in the face of a man-power shortage seems not only absurd but almost a dereliction of duty.

Most observers agree with Cushing biographer Charles Stewart: so inexplicable was this decision that "one is forced to conclude that some personal resentment entered largely into the motives for prompting summary action in this case." Though irrational, such an explanation is at least comprehensible. But while Stewart and Cushing's subsequent biographers have attempted to explain what happened, none of them seems to have seen letters to and from Blake, Rodgers, and others that we found in the National Archives. These letters show that far from being inexplicable, the decision to force Cushing's resignation was the outcome of a long and ardent discussion about what kind of young man should be tolerated at the Naval Academy and groomed to be a naval officer.

The two culprits usually thought capable of having acted out of spite to get Cushing dumped are the Spanish professor, Edward Roget, and Superintendent Blake. Writing in the magazine *Proceedings* in March 1912, Stewart recounts this story:

> *The head of the Department of Modern Languages was Professor E. A. Roget, a man of distinguished and dignified bearing, gener-ally called "The Don." While the professor was crossing a street of Annapolis in January 1861, he walked in front of a vicious cart horse that severely bit him on the shoulder. Sometime afterward . . . he found his class laughing over a sketch on a fly-leaf of Cushing's book. He demanded a look and found a clever drawing of himself biting the neck of a horse, and the inscription, "The poor old Don, he bit the hoss." The professor excitedly shouted out "I deed not bite the hoss. The*

hoss he bit me," and, when the class roared with laughter, the angry professor rushed over to the superintendent's house and demanded Cushing's immediate dismissal.*

In *Lincoln's Commando*, a 1959 biography, Ralph J. Roske and Charles Van Doren enrich the story with details:

The facts of the matter are that on the 14th of January [Roget] was severely bitten on the left shoulder by a horse. The next day he came into class, his shoulder swathed in bandages, to find his students laughing at a well-executed sketch on the flyleaf of Cushing's text-book. The haughty little professor, his Latin blood boiling, demanded the book and found that the drawing depicted him in the act of biting the horse's neck, with the inscription, in clear, bold capitals, "The poor old Don, he bit the hoss!" He began to wave his untethered arm in the air. "I did not bite the hoss!" he shouted angrily. "The hoss bit me!" The class was of course convulsed with merriment, and remained so throughout the hour; the teacher could find no way of quieting them. When he did get a measure of silence at one time he ended it himself by muttering that it was absurd that anyone should make the stupid mistake of assuming that he would have any interest whatever in biting the neck of a horse. The class was again convulsed.

Roske and Van Doren also include an account of an earlier prank Cushing supposedly played on Roget. "Cushing had often mimicked the professor, a dapper little man who the midshipmen considered an effeminate dandy. Once Roget had dressed in his best clothes to meet a young lady and Cushing had prepared a bucket of water at the top of a doorway through which the swain had to pass on his way to the party;

---

* Published by the private, not-for-profit United States Naval Institute, *Proceedings* is the third oldest continuously published magazine in the United States. Its concern is military and defense issues.

he was deluged and angry. Cushing was not punished, perhaps for want of certain proof."

Or perhaps because it never happened.

There is no good reason to believe that either of these incidents—the "bit the hoss" tale or the bucket tale—is true; no sources are cited. But Rodgers's letter to Blake in October 1860, cited earlier, describes in detail a joke that Will pulled on Roget involving a drawing and another equine mammal, a jackass instead of a horse. That there would be two incidents involving the same person, studded with such similar details, is not impossible, but an incredible coincidence. Moreover, a series of routine notes between Superintendent Blake and Navy Secretary Isaac Toucy show that Will was absent from the Naval Academy between January 7 and February 2. This leaves a very narrow window during which the Stewart version could have taken place, and shows that Roske and Van Doren were mistaken in placing this already dubious story on January 14.

Roske and Van Doren add so many other colorful embellishments that their account veers into the realm of fiction. The evolution of Professor Roget into a comic figure straight out of an MGM musical is especially egregious, and close to defamatory. In *The Spirited Years: A History of the Antebellum Naval Academy*, Charles Todorich describes Roget as "distinguished," "dignified," "a gentleman," and "a protégé of Arsène Girault," who was one of the most beloved figures in the early days of the academy, a man admired for his personal character and intellectual prowess. In the hands of Roske and Van Doren, Roget is described as haughty, little, effeminate, with boiling Latin blood. In the bucket incident, Roske and Van Doren tell us that Roget was on his way to meet a young lady. And so he might have been. One might then wonder where the fifty-nine-year-old Roget stowed Eugenie, his wife of some two decades.

In my opinion, the jackass story is the true one, and in the bored wardrooms of blockade ships, in the raucous alehouses of Washington and New York and Boston, even on starry nights on the decks of

Confederate vessels at Cape Fear, the tale evolved. Details were added, facts changed, the chomping hoss was introduced, the distinguished, gentlemanly Don reduced to a cartoon cliché. It's quite possible that the foremost author of the enlarged tale was Will Cushing. Young Cushing had a habit of embroidering detail, heightening the drama of a situation, and embellishing his part. The habit seems to have diminished over time, but it's easy to believe that on the fiftieth or hundredth time he was asked what he really did to get himself tossed out of the Naval Academy, he shrank from saying "I screwed up," and chose to entertain his companions with the tale of a witty, heroic rebel who deflated a pompous, foreign, effeminate windbag, and paid a heroic price.

The second person suspected of triggering Cushing's surprising termination is George Blake. In January 1861, Blake granted Will leave in order to go to Washington to tend to an "ill and lonely" aunt. That leave was twice extended, once when Will claimed that the aunt was still sick, and a second time when he said that he had caught the disease. According to biographer Stewart, at some point during this month Superintendent Blake ran into Commodore Joseph Smith, Will's influential cousin. Blake, assuming that Smith's wife was the sick aunt Will was visiting, asked about Mrs. Smith's health, and was surprised to learn that she was well. When Cushing returned to Annapolis, Blake accused him of making a false statement regarding his aunt's health. Cushing, his honor impugned, responded hotly, and charged Blake with belonging to "the Ananias class," apparently a reference to a figure in the Acts of the Apostles, an early Christian who lies to the apostles and drops dead.

While perhaps more credible than the Roget tale, it would seem to be highly out of character for the kindly superintendent to be the grudge-bearing kind. In fact, about the same time that Will was supposedly insulting Blake, the superintendent was writing a letter to the academy's surgeon, James Palmer. Noting that Cushing's absence "unfortunately" took place at a period of the academic year "of great importance"—just before the February exams—Blake requested that

Palmer examine Will "and make such an inquiry into his case, as may enable you to state, whether in your judgment, he is entitled to special consideration if found deficient in his studies."

Palmer examined Cushing the next day, and responded with an oddly uninformative letter. He tells Blake he has seen Cushing,

> *who represents that during a late session, he had difficulties for about a week, and was necessarily detained by that cause for about ten days. This is not an unusual period of absence from class by reason of illness: we have at this moment, in Hospital, an Acting Midshipman who has been cut off from his studies for the last ten days, and who tells us that he apprehends no difficulty on that account at his examination, because this is only a period of review of studies supposed to have been completed in December last. This, as I understand, is exactly the case with Mr. Cushing also: he has not appealed to me to recommend him to "special consideration," and I am unaware of any reason sufficient to justify me in volunteering to do so.*

What a peculiar response. Palmer tells his boss nothing about Cushing's condition, but instead says Cushing's case is similar to that of an unnamed midshipman presently hospitalized with an unnamed condition. That midshipman, Palmer reports, says he has no need for "special consideration," and because Cushing didn't ask for "special consideration," Palmer won't volunteer to give it.

Whether Palmer is being dim-witted about his boss's request or just artfully elusive, what's clear is that it is Blake who is trying to create a medical out for any academic shortcomings that might result from Will's twenty-four-day absence from the academy. One can't say that Blake wasn't offended by Will's outburst, if it indeed occurred. But it does seem unlikely that Blake would have been trying to save Will's academic career with one hand while greasing the skids with the other.

The real author of the decision to oust Cushing was the paragon of standards and agent of change, the commandant of midshipmen,

Lieutenant Commander C. R. P. Rodgers. On March 13, he wrote a letter to Blake. It is a response to at least one note from Blake but, more likely, part of a long discussion. Even-handed and lawyerly, the note's very carefulness makes it all the more lethal:

Sir,

In reply to your note this morning, I beg leave to send you a copy of the conduct roll of Acting Midshipman Cushing, by which you will perceive that upon his return from leave of absence of the 2nd of February, his conduct has greatly improved. Your own thorough knowledge of the young gentleman's character will enable you to judge far better than I as to the possible permanence of this improvement. A promise of improvement, given to me, by him, soon after I arrived, was not kept.

In October I had occasion to report Mr. Cushing to you for disorderly conduct in the recitation room. Since his return from leave of absence, I have mentioned to you an instance of similar misconduct, which has not been repeated, though at the time it gave me some concern lest it should lead to the renewal of the disorderly habits of which I had complained.

In answer to your last question, whether if Mr. Cushing should graduate or enter the service, he would, in my opinion, prove to be an efficient or subordinate officer, . . . I would respectfully state that from what I have seen here, and from what I have heard of him from you, I do not think him likely to prove either efficient or subordinate. In my opinion, Mr Cushing has not given that promise of usefulness and correct conduct which would entitle him to go forth into the Navy, stamped with the approval of his school, which is one of probation as well as of instruction.

I am respectfully your servant,
CRP Rodgers,
Commandant of Midshipmen

In other words, *he's not our kind.*

This is a remarkable letter. There is nothing here about the importance of an officer knowing Spanish, nothing about Cushing's academic record at all, although the failure in the exam is the pretext for discussing Will's suitability. There is also the acknowledgment that Will's behavior has improved. Rodgers is reduced to pointing to an incident that wasn't reported.

The most important line is the one where Rodgers responds to a question Blake seems to have posed: if Cushing entered the navy, Blake asked, do you think he would prove to be an efficient and subordinate officer?

This had to have been a loaded question. The standard for an "efficient and subordinate officer" couldn't have been much higher in those days of deadwood than breathing and sensate. Indeed, in the naval services of some countries, a subordinate officer is a specific rank for one who is effectively still in training, raising the possibility that Blake may have been laying the groundwork for a compromise in which Cushing could graduate yet not receive his full rank until he had further proven himself. Blake knew that Cushing, for all his bad habits and high spirits, would be capable of leading a section of swabbies through their gun drills. And Blake also knew how much uselessness currently wore the uniform. He likely expected Rodgers and other administrators (like Captain George Magruder, the chief of the ordnance bureau, who oversaw Will's section) to shrug and acknowledge that Cushing would do nothing to lower the quality of the navy's officer corps.

Instead, Rodgers said no, making sure that his opinion was based not only on his experiences but "from what he had heard from [Blake]." The silken Rodgers had slipped the stiletto into Blake's palm: "Your own thorough knowledge . . . will enable you to judge far better than I." If it is true that Will did rudely erupt when Blake asked him a question in February, this might have been the point where the kindly old captain asked himself, *Do I really know this boy?*

Rodgers wrote that letter on March 13. On the same day, Cushing tendered his resignation. The officers at the academy told him that he'd be better off resigning than being dismissed. It's always a bad day for the fox when he finds himself accepting the advice of the hounds.

CHAPTER 6

His Exuberant Spirit

ORCED TO LEAVE THE ACADEMY GROUNDS, Will went to Washington to stay with Commandant Smith. Cousin Joe was entirely sympathetic to the idea that Will had been unfairly handled—he sneered at the notion that a midshipman would be dismissed for reasons "scholastic rather than naval"—and he began a campaign to get Gideon Welles, Lincoln's new navy secretary, to review the case and restore Will to the academy. Joe's son, Alfred Smith, a prominent attorney in Washington, worked up a memo for the secretary on Will's behalf:

> *He has never been accused of an act of meanness or dishonesty.*
> *His classmates accord to him a character of honor, generosity*
> *   and chivalry.*
> *His physique and personal bearing are remarkably fine.*
> *His mental capacity is excellent.*
> *He is not a "drinking man," nor inclined to any sort of*
> *   dissipation.*

Along with the Smiths, twenty-one of Cushing's classmates wrote to Welles protesting the administration's decision, as did Congressman

Alfred Ely, who represented a district in upstate New York that probably included Fredonia.

While in Washington, Will stayed with Charles Flusser, his former gunnery instructor at the academy, now a lieutenant in between posts. "A little below medium height, sparsely built, of light complexion bronzed from exposure," Flussser also had "a long tawny moustache the ends of which he sometimes unconsciously pulled while talking." He and Will had a lot of long, soul-searching talks, and their friendship deepened. Charles, not yet twenty-nine, was a young officer thought to have a brilliant future. He had his own predicament: a native Marylander, appointed to the academy through Kentucky, Charles was torn about what he would do if one or both of these slaveholding border states decided to secede. Will, too, was tempted to go south. Some erstwhile classmates were heading back to Dixie, and invited Will to join them. What better way to make the navy regret its decision? they challenged him. The idea never traveled far; Will would never be able to desert the Union, and Flusser came to the same conclusion, as he eloquently explained in a letter to Captain George Hollins, a fellow Marylander, who left the navy at an advanced age to join the rebels.

Dear Cap—I shall never do it. What! Be one of the very first to fire on the flag? Not I. I have no appetite for argument tonight, my heart is sick. Is it not enough to drive an honest man out of his senses to find thieves making a great nation destroy itself? Where are your wits, man? Where can this business end? In "peace" and "slavery"? The end may bring the death of both, forever, and worse. Inaugurate a period of bloodshed unparalleled. Will the South be whipped by the North? Not while one southerner lives. Will the North be whipped by the South? Not while the Alleghenies rise above the land. Just look, then, at the prospect. Blood, rapine, deso-

*lation, war. Hollins, "thou canst not shake thy gory locks at me,
and say I did it!"**

> *Yours in union,*
> *C. W. Flusser*

While Cushing bunked with him, Flusser gave him a book to read.
It was called *Naval Enterprise, Illustrative of Heroism, Courage and Duty*.
Published by Frederick Warne and Co., a British house that in the
second half of the nineteenth century enjoyed enormous success publishing the Beatrix Potter books. *Naval Enterprise* runs 250 pages and
is jammed with about 150 stories of intrepid exploits of arms and many
eye-catching color illustrations. The tales run from ancient to modern,
but specialize in the thrilling feats of the British Navy, including such
heroes as Howe, Pellew, Earl St. Vincent, the great Nelson, and more.
Will drank them in.

At some point Secretary Welles, though resentful of pressure,
succumbed to the entreaties made on Will's behalf and decided to at
least meet with the young man who had inspired such ardently held,
diametrically opposed impressions. When Will went to the Navy
Department's offices on March 23, his head was full of stories of courage, valor, and daring.

Gideon Welles, a fifty-nine-year-old Connecticut editor and anti-
slavery man, had been secretary of the navy for sixteen days when he
first met William Cushing. A level-headed man with a fearsome, patri-
archal appearance—he had a large head with a full white bushy beard
on his chin and an even fuller, curly, defiantly fraudulent wig on his
pate—Welles was more than a little busy: the seven seceded states were
absorbing navy property, gangs of armed brigands were seizing federal

---

* An approximation of the line from Act 4, Scene 3, of *Macbeth*, where Macbeth denies
responsibility for Banquo's murder, saying to Banquo's Ghost, "Thou canst not say I did it.
Never shake thy gory locks at me."

vessels, the Naval Academy might need to be moved out of Maryland, and, most pressing, Fort Pickens in Florida and especially Fort Sumter, where the men were down to just about three weeks' rations, faced a threat of attack. Welles was coming to the realization that he headed a navy whose vessels were fewer in number, more widely scattered, and less prepared for war than he had imagined; a naval officer corps filled with southerners whose loyalty was at best questionable and at worst wholly unreliable; and colleagues in the administration whose pride, ambition, and ignorance would have created conflicts even in peaceful times.

Writing years after the war ended, Welles's recollection of that meeting was sharp. "I first encountered Cushing soon after entering my duties as Secretary of the Navy," he wrote.

He had just been dismissed from the Naval Academy for reasons which his kinsman, Admiral Joseph Smith, pronounced scholastic rather than naval—not essential to the profession, and wholly insufficient to justify such treatment. But the Superintendent, Captain Blake, and Capt Magruder, chief of the ordnance bureau who had special charge of the School at Annapolis, declared it was not his first failure, that he was inattentive to certain studies, was boyish and wayward, was wanting in essential elements which were requisite to the make-up of a good naval officer, and that to reinstate him at the academy would be detrimental.

In March 1861, Welles was meeting for the first time a young man whom those officers had known for years, but Old Neptune, as Lincoln would come to call Welles, just wasn't buying their assessment. "The truth is," Welles wrote after the war, "with his exuberant spirit he had too little to do; his restless, active mind was filled with zeal to accomplish something." But regardless of what Welles thought about the crime or the punishment or the appellant, he believed that he had to support the decision of Blake and the administration. "Under the emphatic protest and remonstrance of those officers, he could not well be restored," said Welles. "But I remember the expression of saddened disappointment and grief which shadowed his juvenile face when informed of the fact."

Not three weeks later, however, the rebels bombarded Fort Sumter. The long-threatened war had begun at last, and Cushing applied for permission to reenter the navy. Flusser spoke to Major General Benjamin Butler, a politically influential general he had met in Annapolis, who would earn the nickname "the Beast" when he headed the Union occupation of New Orleans in 1862, and Butler spoke to his college roommate, Gus Fox, who was now the assistant secretary of the navy, who spoke to Welles. "In the emergency of that moment," recalled Welles, "it became necessary to immediately increase the naval force, and one of the earliest appointments I made was that of young Cushing. Sympathy for the youth, whose perseverance, enthusiasm and zeal impressed me, had probably as much influence as the recommendation of his friends in this selection. His gratitude for the appointment was earnest. He said he considered it his first step, that he would gain position, and that I should never have cause to regret his re-instatement." In an appointment backdated to April 1, Welles named Cushing an acting master's mate, and assigned him to the USS *Minnesota*.

CHAPTER 7

The Gosport Debacle

A T 4:30 A.M. ON APRIL 12, 1861, Lieutenant Henry S. Farley, late a cadet at West Point, accepted an order from Captain George S. James, and fired a single ten-inch mortar round from a battery on James Island in Charleston harbor toward Fort Sumter. With that, the war was on. Sumter surrendered the next day, and on the fifteenth, President Lincoln issued a call for each state to recruit volunteers to subdue the rebellion. This decree had a polarizing effect; many southerners who were pro-Union were less horrified by the thought of secession than by the idea of northern battalions roosting in their states. In no state did the secessionist cause benefit more from the order than in Virginia. Until Lincoln's call to arms, pro-Unionists in the state legislature were holding the line; afterward, secessionists took control. Virginia, the South's largest and most influential state, which had only two weeks earlier rejected calls for secession, galloped into the rebels' embrace.

The Lincoln administration was seemingly unprepared for this turn of events, but that was at least partially by design; Lincoln feared that if he prepared for war, he would be accused by the secessionists of provoking war. Consequently, he did nothing, and got war nonetheless, except that now he was less equipped to wage it. Washington sat undefended across from hostile Virginia (and surrounded on the other side by conflicted Maryland and its many slaveholding firebrands). For almost two weeks, panicked Washingtonians expected to see rebels riding across Arlington Heights. Not until April 25, when the Eighth Massachusetts Regiment arrived, did residents begin to calm down.

But more tangible losses resulted from Virginia's departure. These included the federal arsenal at Harper's Ferry, one of only two in the country. Sitting at the confluence of the Potomac and Shenandoah rivers, on a floodplain at the bottom of three steep hills, the arsenal was utterly indefensible once Virginia left the Union. Anybody who could put a cannon on one of the hills could blow the town to pieces. The forty federal soldiers stationed there chose not to mount a defense; instead, using kegs of gunpowder providentially left behind in 1859 by John Brown, the troops set fire to the two arsenals and twenty armory buildings and headed north to an army post in Chambersburg, Pennsylvania. The blaze destroyed more than 15,000 rifles that would surely have ended up in the hands of Virginia militia men who had taken the train up from Richmond in time to see the arsenal go up in smoke.

But the most serious—indeed, catastrophic—loss was the Gosport Navy Yard in Norfolk. Located on the Elizabeth River, which empties into the lower Chesapeake Bay, Gosport was one of the premier shipyards in the country. It featured a granite dry dock (the only other one in North America was at Boston's Charlestown facility), foundries, machine and boiler shops, the navy's biggest arsenal, a powder magazine, gun-carriage works, other facilities vital to building and refurbishing ships—in short, everything necessary to construct and maintain a modern navy, including 2,000 pieces of ordnance among which were 300 state-of-the-art smoothbore Dahlgren guns. Gosport routinely played host to a large number of ships that had come in for refitting and refurbishment, but April 1861 brought an unusually impressive collection of tenants: among the vessels on hand were the *Cumberland*, flagship of the Home Squadron; the smaller steamers *Germantown* and *Plymouth*; and the formidable forty-gun steam frigate *Merrimack*, one of the newest and most advanced ships in the fleet.

During the nerve-wracking days prior to the bombardment of Fort Sumter, the Navy Department took no steps to reinforce Gosport, hoping such reserve would calm disunionist fears. Once Virginia seceded, however, the administration began the process of removing its ships from the vulnerable navy base, only to discover that it lacked the men to do so. With most available seamen already assigned to missions involving Fort Sumter and Fort Pickens, the navy no longer had enough sailors on the eastern seaboard to form even skeleton crews who could sail the ships to safe harbors.

While Welles worked on that problem, around six hundred members of Virginia militia units arrived in Norfolk. They were poorly armed, but they began building breastworks on Craney Island, a choke point on the Elizabeth River about four miles from Gosport. Fearing that Gosport's sixty-eight-year-old commander, Captain Charles McCauley, a fifty-two-year veteran of the service, might not be up to the challenge of dealing with this opposition, Welles sent Commodore James Alden, forty-one, to Gosport to take command of the *Merrimack* and steam her to safety.

Over the next days, Alden drove mechanics to get the engines reassembled. He managed to scrape together a crew of thirty men (it usually takes six hundred) that could get the ship out of Gosport. After frantic negotiating—Alden dramatically offered $1,000 cash to any civilian pilot who would take the ship down the Elizabeth and across Hampton Roads to Fort Monroe—Alden was prepared to cast off. Instead, he was shocked to hear that McCauley had cancelled the departure. Furious, he went to McCauley's quarters to demand an explanation, only to find the captain in a state of "complete prostration," incapable of explaining his reasoning beyond saying "that nothing should be done to inflame the locals." Alden later said he contemplated taking the *Merrimack* out on his own authority, but having spent thirty-two years in the service, he did not find within him the initiative to countermand an order.

Friday the nineteenth was a momentous day for the Department of the Navy. President Lincoln ordered the service to institute a blockade of the entire coastline of the Confederacy, all 3,500 miles along the Atlantic and the Gulf of Mexico. He also ordered the closing of a dozen ports, including New Orleans, Mobile, Richmond, Charleston, Savannah, and Wilmington, in an effort to prevent the importation of war matériel and to disrupt the export of cotton, the pillar of the South's economy. Needless to say, the government anticipated needing the vessels docked at Gosport, but even more it was going to need Gosport itself. Any government that aimed to break such a blockade would feel the same.

The nineteenth was also the day that Welles finally decided to relieve McCauley of command. Captain Hiram Paulding, sixty-four years old and a veteran of nearly fifty years of service, replaced him. Welles ordered Paulding to repel with force any attempts to seize the navy yard to prevent anything from falling into rebel hands and, as a last resort, to destroy the navy yard and everything in it. Paulding departed immediately on the steamer *Pawnee*, accompanied by a group of senior officers who were carrying orders to take command of the various ships in Gosport. When they arrived on the twentieth, however, they were horrified to discover that not three hours earlier, McCauley, panicked by the rebel presence outside the shipyard and convinced that he could no longer depend on the loyalty of anyone in his command or employ, ordered that every ship except the *Cumberland* be scuttled. Seeking an explanation, Paulding summoned McCauley, who arrived "armed like a Brigand—swords and pistols in his belt, and revolvers in his hand," and so drunk that he could no longer walk.

After ascertaining that the ships were beyond rescue, Paulding concluded that he could not hold the navy yard until reinforcements arrived. McCauley could at least argue in his defense that he was drunk when he arrived at that conclusion. Paulding, apparently sober when he affirmed the order, somehow ignored that he had at his disposal a thousand sailors and marines and all the heavy guns aboard the *Cumberland* and the *Pawnee* to counter six hundred lightly armed militia.

In short order they scuttled the ships, burned the shops and guns, and packed the dry dock with gunpowder. Fueling the fire with turpentine, Paulding's men put everything to the torch, and before long, sheets of flame painted the night sky. At that point, the pathetic McCauley refused to desert his post, and Paulding had to send a party of men to drag the stupefied officer onto the *Pawnee*. Under the cover of smoke and fire, the Union vessels slipped down the Elizabeth, with the men on deck awaiting what promised to be a breathtaking explosion, the detonation of the gunpowder in the dry dock.

It never came. Someone or something interrupted the burning of the fuse, and in the morning the rebel militia took possession of the charred facility. The damage seemed to be catastrophic, but the invaluable dry dock was intact. Nearly 1,200 guns were also found to be in working order. Shops were burned, but the machinery inside still functioned. And salvage crews were soon at work on the hulks of the scuttled vessels, optimistic that they could be recovered.

With the recovered powder, shot, and gun carriages, the abandonment of Gosport was undoubtedly the most lopsided Confederate victory of the war. Without suffering a casualty, without firing a shot or receiving one, lightly armed Virginia militia men had routed the United States Navy, sunk its vessels, captured its guns, and seized one of its prized facilities. The drunken McCauley remained with the navy until the end of the year, when he was put on the retired list and promoted to commodore.

The events at Gosport took place in the days just after Will Cushing was restored to the navy. It's unlikely that the hectic, pressured Gideon Welles gave a fig about Will during that time, but already his decision to reinstate Cushing was being proved correct. One after another, the chieftains of the navy had proved to be incompetent, indecisive, and feebleminded. If the North was going to win the war, the navy was going to need new blood—young men of vigor and determination, with an appetite for risk and a will to win. And though it would take a while, the service would come to realize that the expendable youngster Gideon Welles saved from the scrap heap was just such a man.

CHAPTER 8

The *Delaware Farmer*

"I AM AN OFFICER ABOARD the splendid steam frigate *Minnesota*," Cushing wrote to his cousin on May 8, 1861. He had just spent his first five weeks of service in the muddy Charlestown Navy Yard, where he joined the three-year-old ship after it had cruised to the East Indies and was found to be "rotten as a pear." But now the repairs were finished, the training complete, and the ship, along with its 47-gun, 540-man crew, and a master's mate named William Cushing, was at last off to war. "We have just left our moorings, and as I write we are moving under steam and sail out of Boston harbor." It had been a glorious morning. A great crowd had gathered to witness the *Minnesota*'s departure, packing the wharves and bobbing around the harbor in small boats. When she slipped her cables and headed out past the cheering, waving spectators, cannons fired, whistles sounded, and the crews aboard other navy vessels offered their salutes. The men of the *Minnesota* themselves had clambered up the rigging and stood high on the shrouds, receiving the outpoured acclaim. "I am going to fight under the old banner of freedom," wrote Will. "I may never return, but if I die, it shall be under the folds of the flag that sheltered my infancy and while striking a blow for its honor and my own. . . . Wherever there is fighting, there we will be, and where there is danger in the battle, *there will I be*, for I will gain a name in this war." Very audacious; shockingly prescient.

Lincoln ordered the blockade of the seceded states on the recommendation of the ailing Winfield Scott, the 6'5", 300-pound, seventy-five-year-old Commanding General of the Army. Old Fuss and Feathers began his military career in 1807, commanded troops in battle against armies British, Black Hawk, and Mexican, and had served with honor and distinction. Though a native Virginian, he was staunchly pro-Union. Indeed during the weak-kneed months of James Buchanan's presidency, he had been a towering symbol of Unionism. In February 1861, when Congress met to give its official stamp on the results of the 1860 election, rumors were rampant in panicky Washington that the secessionists might try to stage a disruption that would forestall the election's ultimate validation. Scott called out the army and lined the streets with cannon, vowing "to manure the hills of Arlington" with the intestines of anyone bent on disturbance.

Now the gouty warrior offered one more contribution: a strategy for winning the war. The plan consisted of four elements: split the Confederacy along the line of the Mississippi River; engage the rebel armies in Virginia; use combined army-navy operations wherever possible on coasts and rivers; and last but hardly least, employ a tight naval blockade to strangle the seceded states. The South did not have the industrial capacity to fight toe-to-toe with the North. It had to trade its most valuable commodity, cotton, for guns, ammunition, food, and most other goods. Stop the cotton from going out, and stop the goods from coming in: that was the principal job of the navy. The plan was derided by a mocking newspaper as Scott's Anaconda, after the South American snake that encircles its victims and squeezes the life out of them. But that plan, diligently executed, eventually won the war.

The actual execution of the plan fell to an ad hoc group called the Blockade Board. It was made up of four men: Commodore Samuel du Pont; professor Alexander Bache, who was superintendent of the Treasury Department's nautical mapping agency; Major John Barnard of the Army Corps of Engineers; and Commander Charles Davis, a Harvard graduate, who served as secretary. Bache possessed detailed maps of the American coasts—more pertinently, detailed maps of all 189 harbors and river openings along the 3,549 miles of shoreline between the Potomac and the Rio Grande. Equipped with that knowledge, the group could figure which routes could be taken to which ports, and how to lock them down. The Blockade Board's first targets were Hampton Roads, in the lower Chesapeake Bay, and Key West, Florida. The *Minnesota*, carrying young Mr. Cushing, was sent to Hampton Roads. Her trip took five days; on the sixth, the ship saw her first action.

Once in Hampton Roads, the *Minnesota* became the flagship of the squadron's commander, Flag Officer Silas Stringham, sixty-three years old, a man who during the course of a fifty-one-year-long career had seen action in the War of 1812, against the Barbary pirates, and during the Mexican-American War.* Joining the other members of the blockading squadron—the sloop of war *Cumberland*; the steamer *Monticello*; and the side-wheel steamer *Quaker City*—the *Minnesota* had been on the scene for scarcely a day when, quite nonchalantly, a trio of schooners floated into the bay. Manned by a crew that Will described as "unarmed, ungrammatical and dirty," the ships were bound from Richmond to Baltimore loaded with tobacco, and the navy seized all three. Short of the lieutenants who would normally be charged with taking prizes back to a friendly port, Stringham assigned Will to captain one of the vessels, the *Delaware Farmer*, and take it to Philadelphia.

Cushing was over the moon to have been chosen, but his little command soon turned challenging. Once in the Atlantic, a storm blew up, cutting visibility. The boat sprang leaks, and the pumps were overwhelmed. Thanks to a flash of lightning, Will glimpsed a large vessel about to hit the *Delaware Farmer*. He turned his wheel and the ships

---

* From the time of the American Revolution, the highest rank in the navy was captain. In 1857, Congress created the title of "flag officer," which was bestowed on senior navy captains who were assigned to lead a squadron of vessels in addition to commanding their own ship. By 1862, Congress recognized that the navy needed a rank equivalent to the army's general, and created the rank of admiral. David Farragut was the service's first admiral, although Stringham and other flag officers were quickly elevated.

collided, but thanks to Will's last-second action, not bows on. Having survived the first narrow escape of a career that would be full of them, Will continued on to a grand reception in Philadelphia, where crowds lined the wharves to get a look at the first captured southern vessel to be brought to the port. Will received endless backslapping. It was the sort of thing a man could get used to.

Almost immediately after hitching a ride back to the *Minnesota*, Will was entrusted with a second prize. This assignment was more dangerous. He and Master's Mate Harrington of the *Cumberland* were ordered to take a bark called the *Pioneer* all the way to New York, four or five days away, with just the two of them to manage the vessel and the sixteen prisoners of war who were members of the original crew. The two youngsters took turns guarding their captives, brandishing a pair of loaded revolvers to disincentivize any acts of bravery. "As I write, I feel the weight of a brace of revolvers in my belt," Will wrote to his mother, apparently during the prisoners' nap time. "I know not at what moment the crew may try to retake her, but your boy is ready." The prisoners were compliant, and Stringham personally commended the two junior officers when they got back.

Quite some time passed, however, before Stringham had the opportunity to bestow that praise. The *Minnesota* left Hampton Roads to join the blockade of Charleston harbor, and Will had to go to Boston to catch a ride to Charleston with the *Colorado*, which wasn't due to depart for several days. Will got to spend some time with his mother's family, including some pretty young female cousins who couldn't stop fluttering over the handsome officer—but by the time the *Colorado* weighed anchor and reached South Carolina, the *Minnesota* had gone back to Hampton Roads. Cushing was temporarily detailed to one of the *Minnesota*'s sister ships, the *Wabash*, which blockaded Charleston for several weeks.

Will hated blockade duty—the boredom, the routine, the tedium. Daily life involved an incessant repetition of basic tasks like cleaning and drilling, and centered on the high point of the midday meal. Very occasionally the chores were interrupted by the opportunity to chase a blockade runner, go on leave, or go into battle. Taking on coal broke the routine but was a filthy job, and ridding the ship of the resilient dust took weeks, or about the time until the ship had to take on coal again. One sailor summed up the blockade experience in a letter to his mother, telling her that if she wanted to know what his life was like, she should "go to the roof on a hot summer day, talk with a half-dozen degenerates, descend to the basement, drink tepid water full of iron rust, and repeat the process at intervals until [you are] fagged out, then go to bed with everything shut tight."

CHAPTER 9

Baptisms of Fire

J UST AS AT THE NAVAL ACADEMY, secession had a searing impact at the United States Military Academy at West Point. Leaving the academy, of course, was never a question for Alonzo Cushing, but the cadets brought their sympathies to the academy, and as feelings tightened throughout the country, opinions grew more heated at the school. There were arguments and occasional fistfights. A cadet from Virginia hung an effigy of John Brown's body from his window, and students from northern states claimed a mock presidential election was rigged after John C. Breckinridge, the slaveholders' preferred candidate, won the most votes; Lincoln finished last in a field of four. (In reality, of course, Lincoln was elected, while Breckinridge finished third in the popular vote, second in the electoral college tally.)

Not two weeks after Lincoln won, Henry Farley of South Carolina became the first cadet to resign, a full month and a day before his state led the secession parade (Farley, recall, went on to fire the first shot at Fort Sumter). In the days and weeks that followed, a steady trickle of students and instructors departed, including the school's new superintendent, Colonel Pierre Gustave Toutant Beauregard; he served just five days until his home state of Louisiana seceded, at which point he was promptly relieved by Secretary of War Joseph Holt. The resignations came to an end in May, when a loyalty oath was instituted. By that point, 65 of the 86 southerners among the 278 members of the Corps of Cadets had departed.

After Fort Sumter was fired upon—by gunners under the command of General Beauregard, CSA—the forty-five remaining cadets of the class of 1861, eager to contribute to the war effort, successfully petitioned the administration to graduate early; they received diplomas on May 6, several weeks early. At that point, the thirty-four cadets still in the class of 1862, Alonzo Cushing* among them, requested that their graduation be advanced as well. The administration accommodated their request, too, but not before putting them through a demanding senior year that was compressed into forty-nine days. "We have to study exceedingly hard now," Lon Cushing wrote. "I have to study from 5 AM to 11 PM. . . . Only three or four weeks ahead of us now and we are willing to study hard for this length of time for the sake of graduating so soon. Then hurrah for a brush with the Rebels. In less than six weeks I shall undoubtedly have the opportunity of smelling gunpowder."

Lon survived the final rugged weeks, and finished his studies ranked twelfth of thirty-four in his class, and a captain of cadets. In childhood, he had been a good boy, obedient, reliable, considerate, conscientious; at twenty-one, he knew no deviation from that path: tall, good-looking, modest, outgoing, studious, and responsible, still reliable, still conscientious, but not sanctimonious or self-righteous. He was earnest but not a prig, his character strong enough that he could be both respected by his teachers and admired by his peers. On June 24, without the pomp of a ceremony, he was commissioned a first lieutenant in the Fourth United States Artillery, and ordered to report to Washington on July 1.

Alonzo's prediction about smelling gunpowder was off by about three weeks. On July 21, he fought in the first large engagement of the war, the First Battle of Bull Run, in the pastures of Virginia's Prince

---

* Due to a longer undergraduate program at West Point, Alonzo was in the class behind Will, even though Alonzo was twenty-two months older and started college at the same time.

William County west of Washington. Alonzo's unit, part of Greene's Battery, was deployed on the left of the Union lines, and while the heaviest action was taking place to his right, west of his station, Alonzo and his men still had their baptism of fire. Their most intense action came when a column of Virginians emerged from the woods in front of Alonzo and crossed in front of his battery, prompting him to open up on them with canister, a shell packed with shot, nails, and scrap metal. "I fancy I did some of the prettiest firing that was done that day," he wrote later, and he may have been right.

Bull Run was a pell-mell affair, fought by inexperienced troops, full of sudden reverses caused by surprise appearances of badly coordinated, frequently terrified reinforcements. The artillery units where the fighting was heaviest suffered terribly; one battery lost twenty-seven cannoneers and all six of its guns, another also lost twenty-seven men and fifty-five horses. The federals fled the field in panic and soon overtook a gaggle of civilian sightseers, who in their incredible naïveté had driven their carriages out to Manassas to see the show. The beaten, undisciplined soldiers fell in among the now-horrified picnickers, and the whole shocked and sickened crowd did not stop retreating until they reached Washington, where many of the soldiers just collapsed and slept on the sidewalks. Alonzo and his guns did not flee, but pulled back in good order, covering the Union withdrawal.

Will returned to the *Minnesota* at the end of July in time to hear about Alonzo's exploits, and to get a sniff of gunpowder himself. Stringham had learned from General Benjamin Butler that the rebels were accumulating supplies at a depot on the Back River in Hampton Roads. Stringham ordered an attack, sending five launches under the command of Lieutenant Pierce Crosby. Will managed to get himself in the first boat. The raid was entirely successful; ten rebel boats were burned, and a schooner full of provisions was captured and brought back to the fleet. "In this action I had the supreme pleasure of burning one of the vessels with my own hands," he wrote to cousin Mary. An artist was discovering his métier.

CHAPTER 10

Twenty-Eight Shells a Minute

N O OTHER PART OF THE CONFEDERATE coastline posed more problems for the blockade squadron, or more opportunities for blockade runners, than did North Carolina. Fractured by wide, navigable rivers, limned by bays and marshes and islets, and shielded by two hundred miles of Outer Banks providentially severed by well-placed inlets, the landscape and seascape provided innumerable nooks and niches to hide in, slip through, or shoot from. Most important, once a ship slipped through the littoral islands into the Albemarle or Pamlico sounds and up the Plymouth or Neuse rivers, there were towns—Plymouth, New Bern—that were connected by railroad to Richmond, enabling smuggled guns and ammunition to reach rebel brigades.

In midsummer, Stringham, the Blockade Board, and General Butler simultaneously realized that capturing the Hatteras Inlet, located by Cape Hatteras, slightly more than halfway down the Outer Banks, would provide the blockading squadron a base of operations from which to disrupt the smuggling. Guarding the inlet from opposite shores were Fort Hatteras and Fort Clark, a pair of sand redoubts that had been built by slaves. Clark and Hatteras were capped by guns captured at Gosport and manned by 580 militia men from North Carolina. Not for the last time in the war, Butler proposed a joint-forces operation, and

Stringham agreed on a plan: the navy would bombard the forts while landing Butler's soldiers nearby. Once the defenses had been significantly reduced, the army would sweep in and seize the sites, and with them, control of Pamlico Sound.

On August 28, 1861, Stringham led fourteen ships—at the time the largest fleet ever assembled under the American flag—to the Hatteras Inlet. Among them were four transports carrying 860 men under General Butler's command. An ambitious Massachusetts politician who had won his generalship through political horse trading rather than by displaying any military ability, Butler was very keen to have a success. He had already been recorded as the losing general at Big Bethel, the first battle of the war. Now he wanted a victory.

The *Wabash* opened fire for the fleet at 10:15 a.m., and soon the rest of the ships chimed in. Rather than order his ships to form a line and bombard the forts from a relatively stationary position, Stringham told his captains to discharge their broadsides and then form a constantly moving loop that would bring them around to fire again in turn. This tactic had been used by the British and French at Sevastopol during the Crimean War, but it had never been tried by the navy. As advertised, the maneuver enabled Stringham's ships to discharge their broadsides, circle back to reload, and come around to fire again. This hampered the ability of the gunners in the fort to get their range against the ships.

With each shell that gracefully arced across the water and smashed into the long rows of white tents and small wooden buildings of the rebel camp, the superiority of federal ordnance was made clear. Commanding eight eight-inch guns as the officer of the quarterdeck division of the *Minnesota*, Cushing enjoyed himself immensely. "This was a great moment for me," he wrote some years later, "a youngster who had never been fairly under fire—and I shall never forget or again experience the wild pleasure and excitement that I felt, as the stern challenge and response passed over the blue water on that sunny August day."

Will wasn't the only one enjoying himself. Cushing offered this vivid description of Silas Stringham: "I remember well our gallant old captain's look as the first whiz of Rebel iron came to our ears. With flushed face and sparkling eye he straightened his tall form, and with gray hair bared to the sun, stamped his foot upon the bridge and impulsively exclaimed, 'Glorious! Glorious! Closer! Closer!'"

The shelling lasted for five hours. At three p.m., with the flagstaffs of each of the forts shot away, the rebel troops in Fort Clark, the smaller of the two, left the pocked berm and high-stepped it across the beach to what they wrongly assumed was the safety of Fort Hatteras.

Meanwhile, about two miles north of the forts, Butler was trying to land his troops and, not for the last time in the war, was having trouble. The breakers were so intense that only about three hundred men had reached the beach; before sundown the effort was called off. The small, sopping force nonetheless took charge of the abandoned Fort Clark, and proudly raised the Stars and Stripes. Action was then suspended for the evening.

Stringham resumed the bombardment at four a.m. After lobbing a few shells in return, none of which found the range of the navy's vessels, the Confederates hunkered down until around eleven. At that point, a shell hit the rebels' magazine; their ammunition was devoured in one massive explosion, and they gave in. Will was pleased to have a ringside seat when Commodore Samuel Barton of the Confederate navy surrendered his sword on the quarterdeck of the *Minnesota*. "I have been informed by the rebel officers, that no less than *twenty-eight* bomb shells exploded in their fort in one *minute,* such was the intensity of our fire," Will later wrote, barely suppressing his glee. "They say that we made the place a 'Hell upon Earth.'" He sent a tattered shred of a Confederate flag home to his mother as a souvenir.*

---

* General Butler knew that just as a messenger is blamed for bad news, a carrier of good news gets the credit. After the surrender, Butler headed straight for Washington. In his memoirs, he describes how he and Gus Fox of the Navy Department delivered the news of the victory to the White House: "The President was called and when our errand was hinted to him he immediately came in his night shirt. Everybody knows how tall Lincoln was, and he seemed very much taller in that garment; and Fox was about five feet nothing.

At the time, the operation, during which the northern forces suffered only a single casualty, was chalked up as an enormous success, and indeed the victory closed the Hatteras Inlet for the duration of the war. Were the Yankees not so busy patting themselves on the back, however, they might have acted more aggressively and gone through the inlet and established a force in Pamlico Sound, or captured Roanoke Island and effectively ended traffic from the north, or gone up the Neuse River and cut the railroad at New Bern. Instead they did nothing more, and soon enough Confederate soldiers came down from Virginia and foreclosed on the possibility of capturing those positions on the cheap. "The enemy made a mistake," said a Confederate navy lieutenant; three years later, after much killing and destruction, Will Cushing was earning glory for exploits that might never have happened had Union forces been more aggressive that day.

In a few hurried words, not waiting for any forms or ceremonies, Fox communicated the news, and then he and Lincoln fell into each other's arms. That is, Fox put his arms around Lincoln about as high as his hips, and Lincoln reached down over him so that his arms were pretty near the floor apparently, and thus holding each other they flew around the room once or twice, and the night shirt was completely agitated."

CHAPTER 11

Original and Speculative

FTER THE BATTLE, the *Minnesota* went to New York to deliver the 715 prisoners taken in the battle, and Will had another fine day. But such experiences soon became rarer as the *Minnesota* returned to Hampton Roads and resumed the boring routines of blockading, and Will once again took up the inglorious labors of a junior officer. Chafing under the extreme punctiliousness that was required of all hands stationed on the commanding officer's flagship, Will grew irritable and morose and complained of headaches. He read Alonzo's account of the Battle of Bull Run and envied the action his brother had experienced, although it's arguable that between his prize commands and participation in the Back River raid and the bombardment of Fort Hatteras, Will had seen more action. Will began to fantasize about teaming up with Alonzo. He wrote:

I don't know but I may resign before long and go into the land service. "I have no doubt but that I can procure a captain's berth in the volunteers. I so long to be near Allie. It seems I might be some protection to him in a time of action. If the rebels should kill him, I don't think I should be a man any longer. I should become a fiend. I love that boy better than I do my own life; and I would not live without my brother. For myself, I care nothing. I am drifting about the world

*with every wind and tide. I take my fate with me, and whatever it
may be, I hope to meet it like a man.*

Cushing's prose naturally tended toward the purplish, but the
melodrama in this passage is thicker than usual. Will didn't always mix
his sadness with so much self-pity. He and Alonzo were quite close, but
they had been substantially separated for nearly five years. Even so, that
Alonzo was now living directly in harm's way clearly amped up Will's
worries. However, the thought that Will could join the army and be
deployed in such a way that he could save Alonzo from being killed or
wounded seems sweetly naïve.

Perhaps concern about Alonzo aggravated Will's other feelings,
including loneliness. So many of the officers on the *Minnesota* were
older; Will may have lacked for real friends. Plus he had that rebellious streak. He squabbled with at least one other officer, an especially
harsh lieutenant who was his immediate superior and was widely
regarded as obnoxious. One night the lieutenant fell asleep during
watch, a major infraction aboard ship. Will did not theatrically clear
his throat or poke the man's ribs to rouse him, the sort of thing one
might do as a favor for a friend. Nor did Will do the stiff-backed
but entirely correct thing, which would have been to report the man.
Instead, with typical mischievousness, Will collected witnesses, then
made a great show out of waving a lit lantern in front of the sleeping man's unresponsive eyes. No doubt Will and his fellow witnesses
found this highly comical.

The lieutenant's exact response has been lost, but it was sufficiently
dramatic to inspire Will to challenge the man to a duel. Though
entirely against the law, dueling was occasionally accepted by the navy
as the most expedient way to handle a conflict; in fact, the text of the
Code Duello was included in the midshipmen's handbook until 1862.
In an article called "Dueling in the Old Navy," published by the U.S.
Naval Institute in 1909, Charles Oscar Paulin wrote, "Of the 82 duels
of which I have obtained a more or less definitive account, midship-

men had participated in fifty-two. . . . The middies, not having much rank, were wonderfully jealous of what little they had, and woe betide the careless shipmate who cast a shadow of offense upon it." Among the events that incited duels: a midshipman objected to another entering the mess room with his hat on; a midshipman objected to being called a "boot-lick" and "curry-favorer" by another; a midshipman told the girlfriend of another that her sweetheart was "intemperate" and unpopular with his fellows. The eighty-two duels Paulin examined took place between 1798 and 1848; they cost the lives of thirty-six naval officers, a full two-thirds of the number of naval officers who were killed in action during that time.

The lieutenant refused Cushing's challenge. Under the navy's code, a senior officer could rebuff a junior officer's challenge with no loss of honor, unless the junior officer resigned. Which is just what the tempestuous Will did. "As long as I live," he wrote to his cousin, "*no man of any rank* shall insult me with impunity." His career plan—once the duel was fought—was to come back to the navy as a midshipman; having proven his worth, he expected they would return him to his class and rank. If that didn't work, he was willing to go to West Point (with no assurance that West Point would want him). "It seems foolish," he wrote his cousin, "but I have got to like the army better than the navy, because . . . Lon is in the land service." If he came to the conclusion, he wrote, "that I prefer to be a lieutenant in the army, at twenty-two, to be a Lieut, in the navy at thirty—I shall act on that conclusion."* Less than two weeks after jubilantly participating in the victory at Fort Hatteras, Will Cushing annoyed a superior officer, challenged him to a duel, and resigned from the navy for the second time in six months. Perhaps it is important to recognize how the incidents differ. The first time, the resignation was the consequence of heedless behavior. The

---

* Captain in the navy is a higher and more responsible rank than captain in the army; a navy captain's equivalent is an army colonel. A navy lieutenant is equivalent to an army captain.

second time, the resignation was itself the heedless action, performed without regard for the consequences. Will was an eighteen-year-old master of heedlessness.

Resignations from the navy followed a multistep process: after one had been submitted, a commanding officer had to endorse it. When Cushing's letter came to his desk, Silas Stringham made no effort to stand in his way. In flowing cursive he wrote:

Sirs,

 I have the honor to enclose herewith the resignation of M.Mate W.B. Cushing, and to recommend that it be accepted.

 His original and speculative turn of mind makes him unfit for the naval service.

 Your obdt. Servant,
 S. H. Stringham.

Cushing later called it "a cruel endorsement." From a twenty-first-century perspective, it seems less cruel than hilarious. An "original and speculative turn of mind" is the kind of phrase an applicant for almost any kind of job today would welcome on a letter of recommendation; Stringham's words would seem to indict himself and the navy far more than they cast aspersions on Cushing. But perhaps Stringham had personal reasons for accepting the resignation. Cushing had lately taken to calling Stringham Old Sting 'em, apparently with some fondness. Did Stringham take it as mockery? Surely Stringham had encountered both nicknames and hotheads in his long years of service; a man of his experience should be equipped to deal with such outbursts of emotion with greater equanimity.

Or maybe Stringham was just losing his touch. Despite his tactical innovation at Hatteras, his reputation did not long survive his victory there. A year later he resigned his commission amid criticism that he had not put his ships in close enough to the fort and that he had prematurely called off the attack. Following its own peculiar logic, the navy promoted him to admiral, placed him on its retired list, then put him in charge of the Brooklyn Navy Yard.

Whether Will had had a change of heart (nothing more was heard about the duel), or whether his challenge had always been a gambit to get the attention of his superiors (successfully done), by the time Will learned that his resignation had been accepted, he no longer wanted out of the navy. He immediately went back to Washington and once again threw himself on the tender mercies of Gideon Welles. As it turned out, Alonzo was also in town. After Bull Run, Lincoln had named General George McClellan to head the Army of the Potomac, and tens of thousands of men had enlisted. Alonzo had spent months training new recruits, and was then promoted to the temporary rank of captain and assigned to the staff of General Edwin V. Sumner. Unfortunately he fell ill with "a remittent fever." The doctor recommended a good long rest and gave him a leave of absence. Alonzo chose to pay an extended visit to his brother Milton, a pharmacist who was living in a rooming house at 458 Twelfth Street West in Washington. Will joined them, and illnesses and career troubles notwithstanding, the three unmarried brothers had all the fun wartime Washington could provide.

Having resigned as a master's mate, Will turned around and lobbied to be reinstated to his Naval Academy class and returned to the navy as a midshipman. He began by writing to Stringham, asking him to comment on his service, reminding him of "when I went north with the prize vessels" and "had command of the quarter-deck division of guns immediately under your eye." A flag officer's flagship customarily has its own captain, and Stringham tried shuffling Cushing onto the actual commander of the *Minnesota*, Captain G. J. Van Brunt, "as you were more immediately under his command." In the end, he threw Will a bone. "As regards to the time that you refer to, I am happy to say your conduct was meritorious."

The decision about what to do with Will was back in the lap of

Gideon Welles, who could not have been happy, after Will's earnest promises of fealty and devotion to the service, to find the young man asking for another shot. Still, there was a war on, and the lad had an Annapolis education and three months of practical, successful experience. One couldn't just toss aside such an asset. More to the point, Welles saw something in Cushing.

Years after the war, in a letter to a historian from Buffalo, Welles discussed what he was thinking: "[Stringham] thought Cushing too full of levity, too full of fun and frolic to make a valuable officer. The truth was with his exuberant spirit, he had too little to do; his restless, active mind was filled with adventure and zeal to accomplish something that would do himself credit and the country service."

It's worth noting that Welles and his wife had raised three sons and had lost three other children. He knew something about the mercurial, irrepressible spirits of young men, and perhaps had a soft place in his heart for the earnest boy who had never known his father. It didn't seem necessary to impetuously terminate the career of a young man who possessed so many positive attributes.

SURPRISINGLY, WELLES SOUGHT out the opinion of George Blake, the commandant who had recommended Will's dismissal from the Naval Academy. With Cushing now safely extracted from Annapolis, Blake had a more nuanced view. "In my opinion, the abilities of that young gentleman are very good," Blake wrote to Welles. "While at the Naval Academy he was at times very idle and insubordinate, and his failure in his studies was due to the former course alone. I am certain, however, he can become a good officer, and as his services on board the *Minnesota* have been satisfactory to the department, then I respectfully suggest that he be restored." If Blake ever held a grudge against Cushing, it had dissipated.

On October 19, Welles ordered that Cushing be warranted a midshipman, the order to be dated from June 1, with his class rank standing twenty-first out of twenty-six members of the class of '61 (though by some peculiarity, he is not considered a graduate of the academy). Welles assigned Will to the *Cambridge*, a much smaller ship than the *Minnesota*. Small enough, in fact, to use the rivers of the South to penetrate rebel defenses, and operate behind enemy lines.

CHAPTER 12

Transformations

C LOAKED DEFIANTLY IN TRADITION, the Confederacy was a society that reveled in its eighteenth-century ways. With an agrarian economy based on slave labor, and far more interest in sport, leisure, and lifestyle than in education, commerce, or industry, the South was at a distinct disadvantage, economically and culturally, when pitted against the more powerful, more populous North. As it happened, however, one of its most forward thinkers was its secretary of the navy, Stephen G. Mallory. A Catholic who owned no slaves, Mallory had a more amalgamated background than most of his nouveau countrymen—he was born in Trinidad of a Connecticut father whose early death left his Irish mother to raise him in the mosquito trap of Key West, Florida. Young Mallory prospered, becoming first a maritime lawyer and then a United States senator, leading the not always successful fight to modernize the United States Navy.

When he was appointed by Jefferson Davis in February, Mallory became the secretary of a navy that had precisely no warships. Nor did he have a powerful patron in Davis; the president had graduated from West Point, soldiered in Mexico, and served as US secretary of war. He had little interest in or appreciation for naval warfare or strategy, nor did he particularly want to invest in building ships. Still, Davis was smart enough to understand that the survival of the newborn Confederacy depended on breaking the blockade and trading its abundant cotton for scarce guns and food.

Mallory was never going to match the US Navy vessel for vessel, so he turned necessity into a virtue and became an advocate for asymmetrical warfare. Under his administration, the Confederacy led in the development of underwater mines and also the construction of a submarine. These weapons did some damage over the course of the war, but not enough. He also pursued a strategy of encouraging Confederate raiders to attack US shipping on the high seas; in doing so, he hoped to draw the navy out of the blockade to defend merchant shipping. This tactic failed when Lincoln and Welles chose to accept shipping losses rather than loosen the grip the navy had secured.

Mallory's boldest move was to back the construction of ironclads—that is, ships built of, or more commonly encased in, iron or steel of sufficient thickness to stop enemy shells. When he was secretary of the US Navy, he was fascinated by the advance the French had made in ironclad ships in the Crimean War, but he could not get the navy's bureaucracy to give up its beloved frigates. Once he was tapped to head the Confederacy's navy, he assigned an officer, Captain John Brooke, to design an ironclad vessel. Brooke's original designs showed an oblong casemate (a term meaning a fortified structure or emplacement from which a gun is fired) resembling a slanting roof, encased in sheets of iron attached to a submerged hull. Two other designers, constructor John Porter and engineer in chief William Williamson, made some changes, and Mallory, having failed to buy an ironclad in Europe, approved the idea and told them to build the thing. Progress was meager until Engineer Williamson had an idea. The hull of the *Merrimack* was sitting in dry dock in Gosport. Her understructure was sound, as was her engineering plant, despite having spent weeks underwater. Build the casemate on top of what's left of the *Merrimack*, Williamson suggested.

There were ample reasons to reject the idea, mostly predicated on the *Merrimack's* well-documented deficiencies. Although only six years old, and envisioned as a state-of-the-art ship, she had proved to be beamy, hard to navigate, a profligate coal burner, and mechanically unsound. In short, she was a lemon. But there was no faster way to put an ironclad into Confederate hands, and certainly no cheaper way. By September, the Tredegar Iron Works in Richmond was rolling out iron plate, and the *Merrimack* began to undergo her transformation. Among the first changes was a new name, the CSS *Virginia*, although many people on both sides of the conflict continued to use her original name.

CUSHING REPORTED TO the *Cambridge,* a screw steamer with six guns and a crew of ninety-six captained by Commander William Parker. The ship spent most of the rest of the year on the Rappahannock River, looking for blockade runners, shelling rebel positions, and conducting routine patrols that were occasionally disrupted by bouts of combat. "We were heartily congratulated upon our safe return by the officers who had remained on board," Will wrote to his mother after he participated in a mission in which sailors burned a blockade runner, then escaped in a running artillery battle. "I returned safely, although my coat did not, for a splinter torn off by a round shot struck that useful garment, and knowing that it was impossible to wound a midshipman, much less to kill one, it only tore the coat and lodged in the vest, where I found it when the action was over. It was not a large one, not larger than my fist, and I have kept it." One wonders if Will took a perverse pleasure in tormenting his mother with tales of his dangerous exploits; certainly he sent her no consoling lies about the safety of his duties. In fact, the embellishments might have gone in the other direction: one would like to see the piece of shrapnel, big as a fist, that would put a hole in a man's coat without harming him.

The mere appearance of the *Cambridge* on the Rappahannock had a beneficial effect: a number of slaves saw her and were sufficiently encouraged just by her presence to liberate themselves. It's well documented that throughout the war on all fronts many men and women fled from bondage to the protection of the Union army; on some occasions, a gunboat could serve as well as a trench. "In the short time we have been here, we have received on board over one hundred contrabands, all stout and healthy, and valued in good times at over one hundred thousand dollars. I have got one of them for my servant," wrote Cushing. "They are as happy as flies in a sugar bowl. They dance and sing every night, till my sides ache with laughter." There is, alas, no evidence that Cushing, a man of great bravery, ever appreciated the courage it took for the "imps of darkness," as he sometimes called runaway slaves, to risk their lives in that dash for freedom. Nor do we see evidence that he was very disapproving of slavery itself. In fact, as a midshipman, he wrote in a letter during the secession winter, "I believe that the South has been deeply wronged, and unless it can procure security for the safety of its slave property, that it would be cowardly for it to stay in the Union." One can only hope that Cushing, a man from a nativist family, eventually began, or would have begun, the same intellectual and moral journey as the man who became one of his heroes, Abraham Lincoln, undertook at a more advanced stage of maturity.

With the coming of winter, the *Cambridge* was removed from the Rappahannock and redeployed to blockading duty off the Virginia capes. As one of the low men on the totem pole, Midshipman Cushing frequently drew the dreary, arduous duty of boarding officer whenever the *Cambridge* stopped a suspicious vessel. "I was frequently out in open boats," he wrote in his memoirs, "for five and six hours at a time with the icy seas and sleet dashing over me continually. Several times I was too stiff upon return to step over the ship's side and had to be hoisted on deck." This "very severe" duty "caused a sickness that sent me home and very nearly cost me my life," wrote Cushing, who was seldom given to complaint. Cushing would suffer bouts of sickness for the rest of his life; it is not impossible that they originated with this icy duty in the Chesapeake off Yorktown.

CHAPTER 13

The *Virginia*

WITH THE ARRIVAL OF SPRING, the second year of the war began. Neither side could campaign much in the cold and the wet and the snow. But with spring, the large armies that had been assembled and trained all winter would be loosed from their hibernation and released on the land. In March, General McClellan began his Peninsula campaign, in which he would ferry 100,000 Union troops, Alonzo Cushing among them, down the Chesapeake to Fort Monroe, where they would re-form and begin what was assumed to be a war-ending assault on Richmond. The plans called for the navy to play a key role.

On March 8, 1862, part of the North Atlantic Blockading Squadron—twenty-eight vessels including the *Cambridge*—was in Hampton Roads, that point on the water where five rivers empty into the Chesapeake and it invisibly turns into the Atlantic Ocean, to help and support this campaign. It was a Saturday, by tradition the navy's laundry day, and ships across the basin were festooned with blouses and pants, whites hanging from the starboard rigging, blues from the port. About two p.m., lookouts on ships across the fleet noticed something emerging from the Elizabeth River, oblong in shape, bristling with guns and fronted by a menacing iron beak. The ship was escorted by a pair of smaller vessels, and flying the rebel flag. They had never seen anything like it before, but they knew exactly what it was: they had been hearing of its coming for months now, from runaway slaves and gabby oystermen and captured soldiers. It was the *Virginia*, ghost of the *Merrimack*, reborn and clad with Confederate armor, arisen from Gosport to kill them.

The ship that Brooke, Williamson, and Porter built for Mallory was a beast, 260 feet long and 50 feet wide, with a draft of more than 20 feet. It had three inches of iron bolted to twenty-two inches of pine attached to a scaffold built onto the hull of the salvaged *Merrimack*. It bore ten guns and, as an afterthought, a 1,500-pound cast-iron ram protruded from its bow. Most everybody thought the ship would be too heavy to float, and most everybody was wrong; when they put her in the water in February, it became clear that she actually had a high center of gravity. This made her difficult to turn; worse, it meant that the iron plates that protected her did not extend very far below the surface— only a foot or so—leaving her highly vulnerable to a shot landing just below her waterline. Immediately, two hundred tons of pig iron was added to her bilge to settle her, but she was still hard to steer, still rode high in the water, and now had a deeper draft. No matter; the Yankees were coming to the peninsula, so the *Virginia* was going to war.

ON FEBRUARY 24, the ironclad received her master, Captain Franklin Buchanan, sixty-one years old, one of the most popular and respected figures in the old navy. A Marylander by birth, Buchanan resigned his commission in the tumultuous days around the time Fort Sumter fell, believing that Maryland, a slave state, would follow Virginia out of the Union. But pro-Union forces in Maryland were too resilient, and when it became clear that the Old Line State wasn't going anywhere, Buchanan applied for reinstatement, which Gideon Welles adamantly refused. There was no room for mixed emotions in the United States Navy.

So Buchanan went south, where he was welcomed with the Confederate navy's most prestigious command. When he took charge, the ship that was once the property of designers and engineers now belonged to a fighting man. Asked how he planned to treat the *Virginia*'s lingering problems, the old salt replied, "I mean to try her against the enemy, sir! There will be time to complete the shutters and armor after we have proved her in action!" He fixed the *Virginia*'s maiden voyage for the night of March 6.

It didn't happen. The ship needed to be navigated down the twisty, tricky Elizabeth River to where the federal navy waited at Hampton Roads, and none of the local pilots were willing to try to negotiate the river in the dark. Very well, the impatient Buchanan allowed, first thing in the morning. Sorry, the chief pilot told him, but this ship draws twenty-three feet; you won't be going anywhere until high tide, which will be about two p.m. on Friday the seventh. But that afternoon arrived with rain, heavy winds, and roiling water. The ungainly *Virginia* took half an hour to make a half circle, and the frustrated Buchanan put the ship back into port.

Saturday the eighth dawned bright and clear, and Buchanan at last got his ship in the water. The plan had always been to take her on a traditional trial run, and give the *Merrimack*'s old boilers a good blowout. Buchanan treated the first part of the trip down the Elizabeth River as a trial run, but after ten miles of reliable performance, he hadn't learned anything he didn't already know or suspect: she was slow, had a deep draft, and handled badly, but her engines performed well and she made good time, better than ever. When she got to Craney Island a little after noon, every man on board knew that the next stop would be Hampton Roads, and the federal flotilla.

Emerging from the Elizabeth, Buchanan could look to the northwest, to his left, and see the mouth of the James River, sitting under the protective Union batteries on Newport News Point; in the six miles in between sat the federal fleet, comprising five large federal warships and their support vessels, all made of wood. Among them were the *Cumberland*, a thirty-gun sloop; the *Congress*, a fifty-gun frigate; Cushing's erstwhile ship, the *Minnesota*, now the flagship of Flag Officer Louis M. Goldsborough; and her sister ships the *Roanoke* and the *St. Lawrence*, both fifty-gun frigates, the latter being attended to by Will Cushing's ship, the *Cambridge*. The leviathan prepared to feast.

Buchanan steamed straight for the two nearest vessels, the *Congress* and the *Cumberland*, both of which opened fire, as did Union army batteries stationed on shore. The well-aimed shells just bounced off the iron plating, like hailstones on a tin shed roof. Then the *Virginia* laid a broadside into the *Congress*, and rammed the *Cumberland*, which caved in like an apple basket. She began sinking so fast that she almost took the *Virginia* down with her, and might have, had the weld on the ram been stronger. Instead it snapped off, freeing the *Virginia* to turn and lay more fire into the *Congress*, which had run aground. Helpless to move, her decks awash in blood, she ran up the white flag. (As a blow-by-blow account was telegraphed to Washington, Commodore Joseph Smith followed the battle. When the report came in that the *Congress* had surrendered, he dropped his head and said, "Then Joe is dead." He was correct; his son, Lieutenant Joseph Smith, commander of the *Congress*, had been struck by a shell and killed.)

As was the custom, the *Virginia* halted firing, and sent two officers to the ship to take prisoners. The army batteries on shore, however, continued to fire, and their shells killed the emissaries from the *Virginia*. "I know the damn ship surrendered," Union general Joseph Mansfield later explained, "but we hadn't." Furious that the truce had been violated, Captain Buchanan shouted, "Sink that damn ship!" and had red-hot cannonballs fired into the *Congress*, setting it ablaze. He did this even though he knew that his brother McKean was paymaster on the vessel. Then, grabbing a rifle, the feisty Franklin Buchanan began firing at Yankee soldiers on the shore. This lasted but a moment, until he was then shot in the leg. His second in command, Lieutenant Catesby ap Roger Jones, took the bridge.

While this was happening, the frigates *Minnesota*, *Roanoke*, and *St. Lawrence* made efforts to join the battle, but in the tricky currents and shallows of Hampton Roads, each ran aground. After finishing with the *Congress*, Jones turned the *Virginia* and began to fire on the *Minnesota*. His shells smashed her decks and splintered her sides, but his ship's deep draft prevented him from getting any closer than two hundred yards, and now the light was fading. His men were exhausted and hungry, and some were wounded; he was low on coal; his ship had sustained ninety-eight hits, leaving three guns damaged and the funnel riddled with holes. Jones elected to return and to refit. Those wooden ships would be there in the morning, he reasoned. He left victorious: two ships destroyed, three frigates aground, four hundred Yankee sailors dead against two of his own. The United States Navy would not suffer another defeat on such a scale until Pearl Harbor, seventy-nine years later.

Cushing spent most of the historic dawn of the ironclads as a spectator, albeit one with a reasonably privileged seat. Early in the day, the *Cambridge* had been ordered to sit alongside the *St. Lawrence,* an 1848 sailing frigate, nearly obsolete, except for its fifty-two guns. The thinking was that the *Cambridge* would tow the larger ship into position where it could deliver a broadside. It was late afternoon before the *Cambridge*, acting as a tug, could nudge the *St. Lawrence* into position. By that time, the *Virginia* was preparing to depart the field, and the *St. Lawrence* ran aground. As the *Cambridge* took the *St. Lawrence* back in tow, the *Virginia* fired one final shell. That last shot of the day removed a chunk of Will Cushing.

"We have just come out of action with the rebel fleet," Cushing later wrote his mother.

Two of our frigates are destroyed, and the Minnesota *is terribly cut up. We did some good fighting—were struck a number of times. I am the only man on this vessel that was wounded. A hundred pound Armstrong shell from the* Merrimac *burst over my head, and a splinter has taken out an inch of flesh; it is slight, but bled considerably. I am all right for tomorrow's fight. I was highly complimented by the Captain and Commodore. The Captain said, "You are highly honored in being the only officer wounded." I do feel so. My hand is very stiff and I can't write more. The rebels took us by surprise and we were much cut up. Some of the frigates must have lost a great deal of life. Two were destroyed. You can imagine how hot the fire was. I shot the rebel flag staff away, on the Sewall's Point battery with my rifle gun, and I will try to do as well tomorrow.*

As the day ended, the *Cambridge* received orders to weigh anchor and head for Beaufort, North Carolina, causing Will to miss the battle's conclusion. He did get a chance to observe the newly arrived *Monitor*: "something far from prepossessing in appearance and calculated to excite laughter," he wrote. Its fighting abilities were another matter entirely.

CHAPTER 14

The *Monitor*

I N THE WAKE OF SATURDAY'S THRASHING, President Lincoln summoned his cabinet for a rare Sunday morning meeting. The awful report of ships sunk and run aground brought out the worst in some of the officials. A frantic secretary of war, Edwin Stanton, paced about, envisioning catastrophes to come. The *Merrimack* could destroy every ship in the navy! Take Fort Monroe! Hold every city on the coast under ransom! "It's likely she'll come up the Potomac, disperse the Congress, and destroy the Capitol! Or she may go to Philadelphia! Or New York! Or Boston! It's not unlikely that we shall have a shell or a cannonball from one of her guns in the White House before we leave this room!"

Only one man was entirely calm: Gideon Welles, usually as excitable as a rooster, waited until Stanton raved himself out. First, he replied, a deep-draft vessel like the *Merrimack*, with her heavy armor, wouldn't make it up the Potomac past Kettle Bottom Shoals, which was fifty miles away, making it unlikely that anybody in the cabinet would be ducking cannonballs this morning. "Besides," he added archly, "if she did attack Washington, she couldn't also be attacking Philadelphia, New York and Boston, too."

He then shared with his colleagues a reassuring piece of information. "We have an ironclad, too," he said. "It left New York for the Chesapeake on Thursday. It should be there any time."

This news relieved the cabinet's anxieties immediately. "How many guns does it have?" Stanton asked eagerly.

"Two," Welles replied, "but of large caliber."

INDEED, THEY WERE of large caliber, and even as Welles talked, they were being fired. The *Virginia* had come downriver early on Sunday morning to resume its destruction of the Yankees. By 7:30 a.m. she was opposite the *Minnesota*. As the *Virginia* was preparing for action, out of the shadows of the Union frigate came a short, squat, alien machine that placed itself between the enfeebled *Minnesota* and the *Virginia*. Aboard the Confederate ironclad, a few of the men thought it was just a raft taking away one of the *Minnesota*'s boilers or its magazines; another famously likened its appearance to "a cheesebox on a raft." Yet there was little levity. As one of the *Monitor*'s mates put it, "You can see surprise in a ship just as you can see it in a man, and there was surprise all over the *Merrimack*."

There ought to have been surprise on the *Virginia*; there ought to have been surprise everywhere. Before them was one of the most revolutionary vessels in history, and it was the product of a shunned designer and a procurement system that until recently had shown no interest in ironclads. Not until word leaked out of Gosport—the place was a sieve—that the *Merrimack* was being converted did anyone in Washington start to think that maybe the navy ought to reconsider the ironclad idea. Quickly, a three-man naval board was convened to examine proposals (Commodore Joseph Smith was a member) and to select a winner.

One of the designs selected for testing had been submitted by Cornelius Bushnell, a Connecticut shipbuilder. His idea was to attach rails to the hull of a ship, and then affix iron plates to the rails, similar to the way builders put siding on a house. The board liked Bushnell's idea, called the *Galena*, but had concerns about the subsequent stability of the vessel. Bushnell knew boats, not iron, so he came to New York to consult with Cornelius Delamater, the owner of an iron foundry on West Street, between Hubert and Vestry. I know nothing about ships, Delamater said. You need to go over to Brooklyn, to the Continental Shipyards, and talk to John Ericsson.

Prickly, difficult, egotistical, Ericsson, the inventor of the screw propeller, was one of America's greatest inventors, a true genius of the industrial revolution, and he knew it. He also had a score to settle with the navy. In 1844 he had designed most of the machinery for the *Princeton*, the navy's first vessel with a screw propeller, as well as two spectacular guns for the ship, both ten-ton giants that could fire a 250-pound ball five miles. Ericsson personally oversaw the casting of one of the guns, the Oregon. The other, called the Peacemaker, was supervised by a navy captain named Robert Stockton, who deviated from Ericsson's design. He was also the vessel's supervisor of construction and its first commanding officer.

So proud of the ship was the navy that much of official Washington turned out for the *Princeton*'s launch in February 1844. President Tyler, the entire cabinet, and two hundred guests took an excursion on the Potomac. The first test firings of the guns went well, and the party went belowdecks for lunch. Afterward, the guns were fired again, and this time the Peacemaker blew up, killing the secretary of state, the secretary of the navy, two congressmen, key naval officials, the father of the president's fiancée, and the president's manservant, a slave named Armistead. In the subsequent hearings, the politically connected Stockton made sure the blameless Ericsson took the fall. In the end, no charges were filed, but the navy stiffed Ericsson out of $15,000 he had earned while working on the *Princeton*.

Expecting little cooperation, Bushnell called upon Ericsson at his workshop in Brooklyn and was received very graciously. Ericsson examined Bushnell's plans and designs and said, yes, with some modifications, the ship will be stable. Then, as a grateful Bushnell was about to leave, Ericsson modestly asked if he would like to see *his* design for an ironclad. Naturally, Bushnell assented.

Ericsson went off and returned in a moment, carrying a dusty nine-inch box that contained a cardboard model of the most revolutionary warship of the nineteenth century—a raft-like structure, topped with a rotating cupola, mounting a single gun. It was light yet fully protected, and highly navigable. Ericsson had developed it for Napoleon III, but when the Crimean War ended, France lost interest, and Ericsson put the model on a shelf. Bushnell immediately recognized its advantages and urged Ericsson to take the design to Washington. Ericsson didn't want anything to do with the navy, but he allowed Bushnell to take the model to Gideon Welles. The secretary often said he didn't know anything about design, but he was a Connecticut man and he knew Bushnell. On the basis of Bushnell's enthusiasm and support, Welles promised to fight for the Ericsson machine before the ironclad board.

He wasn't alone. Through Secretary of State William Seward, Bushnell arranged to see President Lincoln, who was also intrigued. When the ironclad board next met, interested observers included supporters Lincoln and Welles. Nonetheless, the board resisted, highly skeptical about the design's seagoing survivability. The thing was so unconventional, and it came from John Ericsson. The session lasted three hours. When Lincoln finally had to go, he blessed the project with one of his homey aphorisms. "All I have to say is what the girl said when she put her foot in the stocking—it strikes me there's something in it."

The board adjourned without a decision; days passed without a word. Bushnell sensed that the opportunity was slipping away. He contacted Ericsson and told him, if this is going to work, you're going to have to come down and answer their questions.

And that's what Ericsson did. Containing his considerable ego, he went to Washington, and spent two hours with the board explaining his design. In the end, his arguments carried the day. (Construction on the *Galena* was approved as well.)

Ericsson built the ship in his shop in Greenpoint, Brooklyn, with parts made in dozens of foundries from Buffalo to Baltimore. In the end, it was 172 feet long, 41 feet wide, and had a 10-foot draft (the *Merrimack* was nearly 100 feet longer, 10 feet wider, and had a draft of more than 20 feet). An overhanging iron deck, 5 feet tall, was nearly awash, and a timber hull below held all the magazines, berths, and engines.

It had a revolving turret, 20 feet in diameter and 9 feet tall, constructed of eight layers of 1-inch plate. It sat in a brass ring and revolved on four gear wheels. Inside were now two powerful, 11-inch Dahlgren guns. Aft the turret was a pilot house, just 12 feet square and rising only 4 feet above the deck where the pilot, the helmsman, and the commanding officer worked during battle. It was connected by a speaking tube to the turret.

Construction of Ericsson's ship went more smoothly than the conversion of the *Merrimack*. Ericsson signed a contract on October 5 and launched the vessel in mid-January. "This is a celerity which has never been equaled in this country or in England," praised *Harper's Weekly*. And after Ericsson declared, "This ironclad will prove a severe monitor to the confederate leaders," the vessel had a name. Still, there was a great urgency about finishing its trials, getting its guns sighted, and taking it south. The reports were flowing in—the *Merrimack* was nearly done.

In February, around the same time that Buchanan was being given the *Virginia*, the *Monitor* received its commander, Lieutenant John Worden, at forty-four a twenty-seven-year veteran of the navy, and by one account its toughest and saltiest officer. In April 1861 he had been sent on a mission to deliver orders to the command at Fort Pickens in Pensacola, Florida; on the way back he was captured and held as a prisoner of war for nine months. In giving him his orders, Gideon Welles said, "I believe you have the right sort of qualities for the job." Perhaps that meant he was a man with something to prove, willing even to take command of an untested and entirely preposterous-looking ship.

Worden met some setbacks. The *Monitor* spent a day drifting from one side of the East River to the other before finally washing ashore by the New York Gas Works. Ericsson had to remove her rudder and replace it. Finally, on March 6, the same day Buchanan first tried to take the *Virginia* down the Elizabeth, the *Monitor* left Brooklyn, headed for Chesapeake Bay. She made fine time in the Atlantic, answering for the while the doubts about her seaworthiness that had been brought up by skeptics on the navy board. But as night began to fall on the seventh, the same storm that had caused a delay in the launch of the *Virginia* began to trouble the *Monitor*, now off the coast of Maryland. There, gale-force winds pounded the ship as high waves washed her deck and, unexpectedly, leaked into her hold. Ericsson had specified that the turret be lowered in the event of a storm, contending that it would seal itself against its brass ring. But the navy felt otherwise, and specified that the turret be raised to its highest position, and that the bottom be wrapped in oakum, tar-infused hemp used to prevent leakage. But the oakum washed away in no time, and water poured belowdecks, soaking the fan belts of the blower pipes and preventing them from working. Soon the entire area was filled with gas, steam, and smoke, and choking, gasping men were fleeing. The chief engineer led below a gang of men who struggled with the blowers until they lapsed into unconsciousness.

Then, with the *Monitor* on the verge of foundering, the storm blew itself out. A doughty tug traveling with the *Monitor* towed her to shallow water, where repairs could be made and the toxic air belowdecks could clear. After a perilous night, the crew worked through the morning of March 8; the ship got under way by midday, and by late afternoon reached Cape Henry, about twenty miles from Fort Monroe. They could hear cannon fire from up the bay. Overnight, the *Monitor* made her way to Hampton Roads, and anchored in the shadow of the *Minnesota*.

The meeting between the *Monitor* and the *Virginia* on March 9 would go down in history as the world's first battle between ironclad ships, but the battle didn't start until the crippled, pugnacious *Minnesota* fired a broadside at the *Virginia*, which scornfully responded. On the *Monitor*, Lieutenant Worden, hearing the gunfire above his iron-hooded head, saw two of his men manhandling a 166-pound cannonball into the muzzle of one of his eleven-foot guns. "Send them that with our compliments, my lads," Worden said, and ordered the ship to open fire, a surprise pop in the jaw from an undersized opponent. The *Virginia* replied with a broadside that shook the smaller vessel, which then closed on its fearsome opponent. The fight was on.

The battle lasted about four hours. The ships steamed in circles, the *Virginia* in its large, ungainly arcs, the *Monitor* in sharper, tighter turns. As a result, the ships closed on each other and then pulled apart; sometimes they shot at each other at a distance of a hundred yards, and sometimes at fifteen feet. Once Jones aimed to ram the *Monitor*, but the best he could manage was a glancing blow that shook the teeth of everyone on both ships but did no harm. Worden tried to fire into the *Virginia's* lightly clad stern, but couldn't manage an accurate shot. Jones aimed to pull up to the *Monitor* and board her with crew members armed with cutlasses, a maneuver from the days of Francis Drake or Horatio Nelson; at the last moment, the *Monitor* veered away.

The *Virginia* ran aground, but freed herself before the *Monitor* could react; Worden thought he had the *Virginia* lined up for a damaging shot, but his cannon jammed. Despite hit after hit, neither ship pierced the other's armor, though the *Monitor* had split and chipped the *Virginia's* plate. Had the *Monitor* been able to aim better—the revolving turret allowed the ship to maintain a high rate of fire, but it couldn't be stopped precisely in its spin—she might have stripped away some of the *Virginia's* iron plating and exposed a vulnerable underside. In time, the gunners grew frustrated. When one on board the *Virginia* stopped, his commander asked him why. "Our powder is precious," he replied, "and I find I can do as much damage by snapping my thumb at her every two minutes."

After more than three hours of this, neither side had gained an advantage, although there were so many holes in the *Virginia's* smokestack that she could hardly get any draft for her boilers, which meant that the speed of the already sluggish southern ironclad was halved. Jones maneuvered his ship opposite the *Monitor*, and from a distance of ten yards, delivered a nine-inch shell against the *Monitor*'s pilothouse. It exploded directly against a narrow slit though which Worden was at that moment peering. Blinded, eyes full of powder, ears ringing, his beard smoldering, Worden collapsed on the floor. "Sheer off!" he shouted. And his helmsman turned away.

The *Monitor* headed for the shoals to take stock. Worden was taken to his cabin, though not before ordering his subordinates to turn back and save the *Minnesota*. But the *Virginia*, having waited what she took to be a suitable period, assessed her wheezy boilers and leaky seams and decided that the best course of action would be to declare victory and head home.

That night, the officers and crews of both ships were celebrated for their efforts. Both sides claimed victory, though any fair-minded person would have called the fight a draw. The real winner was the ironclad, whose story was just beginning to be written.

CHAPTER 15

Rising

WILL'S SHIP, THE *CAMBRIDGE*, had missed the historic battle in order to go to Beaufort to help capture the Confederate blockade runner *Nashville*, a 1,221-ton side-wheel steamer, which was bottled up in the straits. Originally a passenger steamer that ran a Charleston to New York circuit, she was seized by the rebels, equipped with two guns, and converted to a cruiser. Crossing the Atlantic under the command of Lieutenant Robert Pegram, the *Nashville* became the first vessel flying a Confederate flag to travel in British waters. On November 19, 1861, she captured and burned the sailing merchantman *Harvey Birch* in the English Channel. Returning to American waters three months later, she captured and burned the schooner *Robert Gilfillan*. Together the prizes were worth $66,000. Two days later, she ran the blockade into Beaufort, carrying a load of Enfield rifles. In Beaufort, private interests bought her; they expected that she would earn them substantial profits running the blockade.

When the *Cambridge* arrived, she learned that the *Nashville* was anchored in a small harbor behind a screen of barrier islands. The *Cambridge*'s Captain Parker proposed to prevent the *Nashville* from escaping by blocking the channels. Cushing thought this tactic flawed. After all, she had several channels to choose among, and she was much faster than the *Cambridge*, which had only a small sailing vessel, the *Gems-*

bok, for support. Cushing proposed that he lead a cutting-out party—a small group of raiders—into the harbor to capture or destroy the ship. Parker rejected the idea out of hand—maybe he didn't trust Will's judgment, or maybe he disqualified Will because the midshipman's wound had become infected. Whatever the reason, he didn't act, and therefore suffered the embarrassment of learning that on March 17, the *Nashville* had snuck past the two Yankee ships and made her way to Charleston unimpeded. "[Parker] should have worn petticoats instead of the blue and gold of a dashing service," Cushing sneered, and the navy's high command did not disagree. "This is not blockade," fulminated Assistant Secretary Gus Fox, adding, with some exaggeration, "It is a Bull Run to the Navy." Parker was ordered to report to Hampton Roads to explain himself, but before he left, he sent Will home to Fredonia on sick leave.

WHILE WILL AVAILED himself of his mother's care, two of her other sons were marching directly into harm's way. Howard, the second of the four Cushing boys and four years Will's elder, was the most independent. He left home at sixteen to take a job as a printer's apprentice in Boston, and was working as a typesetter at *The Farmer's Advocate*, a Chicago newspaper, when the South fired on Fort Sumter. Despite having been diagnosed with tuberculosis, Howard quit his job and enlisted as a private in Captain Ezra Taylor's Battery B, First Illinois Light Infantry. The unit participated in operations in Missouri and Kentucky in 1861 and at Fort Henry in February 1862, then joined a movement of Union forces to Pittsburg Landing, Tennessee. On the morning of April 6, Battery B was among the units on the right of the federal line under General William Tecumseh Sherman when the rebels under General Albert Sidney Johnston came howling out of the trees. Sherman's regiments bore the brunt, and though they fought stubbornly, they eventually fell back and regrouped at Pittsburg Landing, where they awaited the next charge. It never came; General Beauregard, thinking the Yankees could be finished up in the morning, held up the assault overnight. But during that time, the Yankees reorganized and were reinforced; in the morning, they won back the ground they had lost. Total casualties were 23,746, a number that shocked both sides. Among the 1,754 Union soldiers who were killed was Private Theodore Tupper, son of Edward and Rachel Cushing Tupper of Putnam, Ohio. Theodore was first cousin to the brothers Cushing, and the second of their kin, following the navy's Joseph Smith, to die in battle within a month. Howard was unharmed.

ALONZO, MEANWHILE, was in the thick of George McClellan's Peninsular Campaign, the boldly conceived, haltingly executed attempt to capture Richmond from the south. The campaign began in late March, and culminated with McClellan's evacuation in June after a series of fierce and bloody battles neatly summarized as the Seven Days. Alonzo spent these weeks as an adjutant on the staff of General Edwin V. "Bull" Sumner of the Second Corps, riding back and forth along the lines, conveying messages and reporting on the status of the troops and the state of the conflict in front of them. It was a position in which a young officer could learn a lot about the ebb and flow of battle, and Alonzo sharpened his combat skills. Often he was right in the thick of the action, particularly in the Battle of Fair Oaks on May 31, where Lon had his horse shot out from under him, his second mount lost in two days. Lon was also struck in the chest by a bullet, but blocked by a thick dispatch case and the butt of a revolver, it never reached his body.

Like Will, Alonzo found combat thrilling—"the grandest sight I ever witnessed." Describing the scene at dusk, he wrote, "there were two long parallel sheets of flame from the opposing lines and I can conceive of nothing more grand than the spectacle presented, nor nothing so exhilarating as that splendid bayonet charge. It was enough to almost lift one out of his boots." In recognition of his extraordinary heroism, Sumner twice recommended Alonzo for brevets; had they

gone into effect after the battles of the Seven Days, he would have had
the temporary rank of major, but the recommendations for some reason
were never acted upon.

AFTER FOUR WEEKS of convalescence in Fredonia, Will fully recovered from his infected wound and reported for duty. To his surprise,
he found that he had been returned to the repaired *Minnesota*, where
he had achieved a mixed record under Silas Stringham, now several
months gone. The new flag officer was the three-hundred-pound Louis
M. Goldsborough, who had been described by one officer as "a huge
mass of inert matter known throughout the fleet as 'Old Guts.'" Yet
another naval officer with a half century of service, Goldsborough's
résumé listed much combat experience but also years of exploration and
scientific innovation, as well as a stint as superintendent of the Naval
Academy, where, in one legendary incident, his outdoor privy had been
set on fire by a group of middies. "I'll hang them!" the big bear roared.
"Yes, I'll hang them. So help me God, I will!"

Described as "coarse, rough, vulgar and profane in speech, fawning
and obsequious to his superiors, supercilious, tyrannical and brutal to
his inferiors," Goldsborough was not destined for a long or successful
run as commander of the North Atlantic Blockade Squadron. Gripped
by fear of what might happen if the *Virginia* should slip out of Gosport
again, he rejected any operations that proposed to use the *Monitor* as an
offensive weapon, and held it in reserve in case her mighty metal coun-
terpart emerged. He made a poor impression in May when President
Lincoln came to Hampton Roads looking for an opportunity to prod
McClellan into action. McClellan wasn't available, so Lincoln spent
his time prodding Goldsborough, who at Lincoln's instigation shelled
rebel batteries on Drewry's Bluff, and then launched an operation that
recaptured Norfolk. This denied the *Virginia* her port, and with no
escape route available, her captain chose to scuttle the fearsome beast
in the James River rather than allow her to fall into Yankee hands.

Instead of issuing congratulations, Lincoln asked Goldsborough what had taken him so long. On July 6, Welles assigned a third of Goldsborough's ships to another commander, who would report to Welles alone. Clearly, Goldsborough would soon be replaced.

But Goldsborough must have liked William Cushing. Although he was being phased out, Goldsborough was summoned to a July 8 summit meeting with Lincoln and McClellan at Harrison's Landing on the James River, and he asked Will to accompany him.

As a group, the Cushing brothers had an astonishing ability to show up at the Civil War's most important moments. But unlike Bull Run, Hampton Roads, Shiloh, Antietam, Gettysburg (the battle and Lincoln's Gettysburg Address), and Fort Fisher—all events where one brother or another was present—this moment is not widely known. In some ways, however, it is among the most vital. It was here that George McClellan, on the heels of a defeat in which he squandered enormous advantages in men and matériel, gave Lincoln a letter essentially repudiating all of the president's war aims. He told Lincoln that he should acknowledge that the South had the right to secede, that there should be no more efforts to abolish slavery, and that Lincoln should appoint a single commander in chief of the army—presumably McClellan. Lincoln accepted the letter quietly, then responded forcefully. He did appoint a commander in chief—only it was General Henry Halleck who got the nod; Lincoln instructed Halleck to bring McClellan into line or replace him. And rather than acknowledge the right to secession or discuss a right to own slaves, Lincoln began working on a draft of the Emancipation Proclamation.

With little to actually discuss at the summit, McClellan suggested a review, and Will was chosen to be among those riding behind the president. Sitting on his horse straight and erect, Will defined military bearing. The soldiers he was reviewing did not look like a beaten army, and the president he was following did not look at all daunted. Despite setbacks, the war could yet be won.

Alonzo was also present at the summit, and he introduced Will to his boss, General Sumner, who in turn introduced Will to generals John Sedgwick, Joseph Hooker, and Darius N. Couch and to other members of the brass. Will still hoped to transfer to the army and fight with Alonzo, but he received no encouragement. Instead Will abandoned Goldsborough and left the conference to join Alonzo in camp. When he returned to Norfolk, Will was suspended, only to learn that Goldsborough "was a typical seaman of the old school, imposing in person, loud in voice, genial in temperament, and very much inclined to let the youngsters have their own way up to a certain limit." Although it led to a nominal punishment, the incident was soon forgotten. "As a midshipman is hardly considered a responsible being," Will wrote, "I was soon released."

And with good timing. On July 16, 1862, Congress authorized an increase in the number of personnel the Department of the Navy could employ, opening many new opportunities for promotion. Will Cushing had not favorably impressed most of his immediate superiors, or everyone he had met in the service, but Gideon Welles and Gus Fox never lost confidence in their first impression. When Will first heard about the bill, he was reasonably sure that he would be promoted one grade to master, and possibly even two grades, to ensign. But Welles bet heavily on the young man's future, and raised him three grades, all the way to lieutenant. "I can glory in being the only man who has reached my rank at anywhere near my age," he crowed in a letter to his mother. "Just think! A lieutenant in the most exclusive branch of the service! I rank with a captain in the regular army, and get nearly $2000 a year!" Like a good son, he promised to send a chunk of his salary home every week. "No more work for you, dear Mother."

CHAPTER 16

Reenter Flusser

A S AN ADDED FILLIP TO HIS PROMOTION, Cushing got to
request his next assignment. Whether this was a courtesy
extended to all new promotions, or whether Sumner, Welles,
or Gus Fox were trying to insure their deepening investment in Cushing, Will finally was handed the opportunity to work with someone
who appreciated his creativity and spirit. Shrewdly, Cushing chose his
friend and mentor Lieutenant Commander Charles Flusser, another
highflier who earned the navy's trust while serving in the Carolinas.
Will responded to Flusser as he did to no one else, even Alonzo; Will
certainly loved Alonzo, but he looked up to Flusser. Somehow, Flusser
inspired Will, and brought out his best.

Both men were fierce fighters. After the joint army-navy operation
to seize Fort Hatteras, there were further joint expeditions in North
Carolina that captured Roanoke Island, Elizabeth City, New Bern,
Morehead City, and Beaufort. Flusser—"a cool and daring officer,
always to be found where the fighting was going on," wrote Admiral
David Dixon Porter in his memoirs—had been in the heat of the action,
particularly at Elizabeth City, where fourteen Union ships destroyed
the Mosquito fleet, a motley group of vessels pulled together to defend
the Carolina coast. Flusser commanded the *Commodore Perry*, a con-

verted ferry, which ran down and sank the rebel flagship *Sea Bird*. "He is the fighting man of the North Carolina Sounds," Will wrote to his mother, delighted that he had been chosen to serve under Charlie as executive officer of the *Commodore Perry*. "He is daring to the death and chuck full of fight."

Working on a small, squatty, smelly ship—the *Commodore Perry*, a side-wheel steamer that had a crew of twenty-nine and just four guns—was hardly every sailor's dream, and neither was slowly patrolling the swamps and bogs of the shallow sounds and the slow-moving rivers of the lowlands. Will, however, relished his post; it offered much more opportunity for action than boring blockade duty.

In September, during Cushing's second month on the ship, the *Commodore Perry* saw some real fighting. Major General John A. Dix, commander of the Seventh Corps at Fort Monroe, had received intelligence that about 7,000 rebels were massing in Franklin, Virginia, preparing to attack a Union base in Suffolk, Virginia. Dix had the idea to trap the rebels in Franklin by leading a force of 12,000 men against the Confederates. When the rebels fell back on Franklin, which was located on the Blackwater River, they would find themselves facing Union army gunboats from the Albemarle Sound, which would have come up through North Carolina on the Chowan River, then through Virginia to Franklin on the Blackwater, a tributary of the Chowan. After consulting with an army officer about the likely pace of Dix's troops, Flusser contacted Dix and told him that he would be at Franklin by six in the morning of October 3.

General Dix, however, wanted more time, and asked Flusser to delay his departure. But the message never reached Flusser, who had headed up the Chowan on the *Commodore Perry* in the company of two other gunboats, *Hunchback* and *Whitehead*, long before Dix's missive arrived. Upon learning that his messenger had literally missed the boat, Dix did the only thing he could, which was to contact Colonel Samuel Spear, who was located nearer to Franklin, and ask him to send some troops to Franklin. Spear sent 1,300 men, a pathetic number given that

7,000 rebels were suspected of being in Franklin. Spear's men, moreover, were going to arrive late.

Fortunately, there were nowhere near 7,000 Confederates in Franklin, but there were still a lot more than the 200 Union sailors who were aboard the three gunboats and who, even before the rebels discovered them, were having a difficult time.

The Blackwater, sluggish and clotted with branches and debris, was a terrible river to travel. In 1856, a writer and illustrator named David Strother, using the pen name Porte Crayon, described the river as a "narrow, black ditch, embanked with mangled bushes and cypress knees, and overarched completely with trees clothed in vines and hanging moss. The stream being barely wide enough to float the boat, she is obliged to crab her way . . . [backwards] for a considerable distance, her . . . sides butting the cypress knees, and her wheelhouses raking the overhanging boughs."

Flusser's sailors labored to get their ships upriver. On the night of October 2 they stopped just three miles south of Franklin, and after breakfast on the third, embarked again at 5:45 a.m. At that point their task was considerably complicated by the presence of rebel troops on the bank, who opened fire on the Yankees stranded in the river. The three ships managed to muddle along with little damage, using ropes tied to trees to pull themselves around the sharpest turns. As they cleared one hairpin turn, they found the river blocked by fallen trees—an ambush. "At once every stream and bush and log sent forth a stream of lead, and a yell burst out that seemed to come from all directions," wrote Cushing in his memoirs. "We were in an ambush." Flusser ordered all hands to take cover from the withering gunfire. As the sailors hid, the rebels prepared to board the ships.

ASSIGNED TO TRAP the Confederates withdrawing from Suffolk, the navy had also been ordered to bring supplies for the arriving soldiers. Roped and netted to the decks were sacks of flour and boxes of ammunition and barrels of powder—and, Cushing realized, a field gun, a howitzer. Will quickly called for volunteers, and six men jumped to his side. They cut loose the gun, mounted it, wheeled it to the side where the rebels were massing, and loaded it with canister, which does enormous damage when fired against troops at close range. "By that time I was alone again," Will later wrote, "all the volunteers being dead or wounded at my feet." Will sighted the gun and fired, wreaking havoc among the Confederates. Wounding or killing most and panicking the rest, Will's shot cleared the scene before him, "excepting the leader, a splendid looking fellow with long curly hair, who came on, waving his sword, seemingly unconscious that he was alone. He met his death ten feet from our side."

With the incoming fire momentarily smothered, the sailors were able to mount their guns, and waged a ragged shoot-out, ebbing and flowing in intensity for the next three hours. Flusser was determined to hold on and wait for the army, but he soon suspected that Dix's troops weren't coming. At about ten fifteen, he ordered the gunboats to go back the way they came, and although the rebels had felled trees in the river to entrap them, the ships got up a full head of steam and plowed through the obstacles. Spear's men showed up sometime after lunch, only to discover that the Battle of Crumpler's Bluff, as the engagement came to be known, was over.

For such an intense engagement, casualties were light, at least on the Union side: four dead, thirteen wounded. Cushing said he counted more than a thousand bullet holes in the *Commodore Perry*. To the degree that the battle meant anything, it marked Will Cushing's debut, the moment he first displayed the quickness of thought and improvisation that would be his hallmark. In his report, Flusser wrote, "I desire to mention as worthy of praise for great gallantry Lieutenant William B. Cushing, who ran the fieldpiece out amid a storm of bullets, took a sure and deliberate aim at the rebels, and sent a charge of canister among them that completely silenced their fire at that point." In a private letter, Flusser elaborated: "Cushing behaved like a gallant boy. I had frequently to oblige him to seek shelter from the enemy's fire."

Cushing was the only officer Flusser mentioned in his report. Even better than a mention, Will's conspicuous bravery earned him his first command, the *Ellis*.

On October 26, Admiral Samuel P. Lee, who had replaced Goldsborough as commander of the North Atlantic Blockade Squadron, sent a note to Gideon Welles. "Lieutenant W. B. Cushing has been put in command of the gunboat *Ellis*, and is increasing his reputation by active operations."

CHAPTER 17

Adventures of the *Ellis*

USHING HAD SPENT ONLY three months with Flusser, but during that time, he matured. Before, he was a puppy, falling over himself with eagerness to be part of the action. After his two months with Flusser, he was steady, straightforward, in command. Gone and seldom to be seen again was Fun Will, the skylarker who so annoyed Silas Stringham. More and more he emerged as Lieutenant Cushing, a young man who aspired to be the best damn officer in the navy. Surely some of this change could be ascribed to Flusser's influence, and some to a change in circumstances: the navy had finally put Will in a position where his talents could blossom, and where the people around him were more interested in helping him succeed than in fitting him into their idea of what he ought to be.

Cushing was the first Union commander of the *Ellis*, a pugnacious former tugboat that had been captured from the rebels in the lopsided battle of Elizabeth City in February. Her appearance and condition meant little to Cushing; this was his first command, and he saw her through the gauze of love. "She was of iron," as Cushing described her (which is not to say that the converted tugboat was an ironclad), with an eight-pound rifle forward and a twelve-pound rifle howitzer aft. She drew about six feet of water, a shallow draft perfect for duty in the sounds, where she had been serving since her capture. Cushing took command of her at New Bern, finding a crew of twenty-eight, all but six of whom were older than he. Such a group may have tested their young commander, but Will struck the right tone with his crew from the outset. He was a strict disciplinarian who did not incite resentment, and his insistence on being the first to experience any danger or hardship earned respect. Men always wanted to serve with him.

While Will loved the *Ellis* and was appropriately grateful to have been given a ship at nineteen ("a thing before unheard of in the service," he wrote to cousin Mary on October 18), he did not take long to grow discontented with the narrowness of his orders. He was told to patrol Bogue Inlet, a sleepy place where most days his men saw no action beyond foraging for a cow or sheep for dinner. Before very long, Cushing began to cast a covetous eye on nearby communities like Swansborough, a rebel stronghold, or the busy New Topsail Inlet. Will had leave to make his own decisions in Bogue Inlet; with no one around to discourage him, he simply enlarged orders.

On the nineteenth, Cushing took the *Ellis* down the coast to New Topsail Inlet and spotted a Confederate schooner at anchor, alone and unprotected. The *Adelaide,* from Halifax, contained six hundred barrels of turpentine, along with thirty-six bales of cotton and some tobacco, estimated to be worth $100,000 if it could get to Nassau in the Bahamas. Cushing took the *Ellis* directly at the blockade runner, whose captain promptly set her on fire and fled with his crew. Cushing's men quickly boarded the ship and extinguished the fire, but that was a temporary victory; lacking a pilot who knew which channels in the Inlet were too shallow and needed to be avoided, Cushing kept running her aground; after umpteen failures, Cushing put the ship to the torch.

In his report to his superior, Commander H. K. Davenport, Will slipped into his account of this bold strike a conscientious admission that he had somewhat exceeded orders. Just as Will hoped, Davenport was more impressed with results than punctilio, and told him "to continue to act in accordance with the dictates of your best judgment."

Will did not have to be told twice. On October 29, the *Ellis* returned to New Topsail, where Cushing spotted on the shore smoke from a fully operational saltworks "capable of supplying the whole city of Wilmington." This plant was one of many saltworks that had sprung up throughout the South, an early indication of how deeply the blockade was disrupting ordinary life. Depriving people of salt not only hurt at the dinner table, but affected meat curing and leather tanning. The impromptu factories attempted to fill the gap by evaporating brine, and the navy's strategy was to destroy them in order to maximize the pain of the blockade.

A raiding party from the *Ellis* quickly seized the plant, demolishing the brickwork, kettles, pans, flatboats, cisterns, and waterworks, burning the buildings, and dumping the salt that was on hand. As the *Ellis* was getting ready to depart, Confederates showed up with two pieces of artillery and supporting infantry. Cushing opened fire, silencing the rebels and making his escape with no injuries.

Almost a full month passed before the *Ellis*'s next raid, on November 23, 1862. This time Cushing took his ship to the New River Inlet, aiming for Jacksonville, home of the Onslow County Courthouse. This was a fairly daring mission, since Jacksonville stood about thirty-five miles up the New River, and Cushing had no idea how many rebel troops might be stationed in the area.

Approximately five miles up the river, the *Ellis* met a schooner, which, like the vessel she had encountered the month before, was filled with cotton and turpentine, and just like that vessel, was set on fire by her crew. The *Ellis* reached Jacksonville at around one p.m. and in the next ninety minutes captured two more schooners and twenty-five stands of arms, seized the mail (a valuable source of intelligence), and took the postmaster's slaves. Cushing did not make a clean getaway, however, and on his way back downriver he swapped fire with some rebels on the shore. They were tracking Will and, by nightfall, when Will was forced to anchor about five miles short of the mouth of the river (he would never be able to get over the bar in the dark), he could mark how his pursuers were progressing by the signal fires lighting both banks.

Cushing got the *Ellis* going at first light, and with a head of steam, a flood tide, and two schooners in tow, he might have begun to look ahead to leaving the river and a celebratory return to port. But the *Ellis* did not get far; her pilots misread the channel, and the ship, usually maneuverable in shallow water, ran hard aground. The rest of the day evaporated amid fruitless efforts to refloat her.

Sitting on his immobile tug that night, Cushing could see and hear the rebels taking positions on the shore. At that point, the teenage lieutenant began making life-and-death decisions. "I felt confident that the Confederates would come at me in overwhelming force," he wrote in his memoirs, "and now it became my duty to save my men." He ordered the crew to load most everything that was on the *Ellis* onto one of the captured schooners, leaving only the pivot gun, some muskets, and some coal. He then asked for six volunteers to stay with him on the *Ellis*, hoping that in the morning the *Ellis* would refloat and they would break away downriver. Failing that, he and the volunteers would hold the *Ellis* as long as possible, enabling the schooner to escape. As it happened, not six men but the entire company stepped forward; Cushing chose the most experienced men.

During the night, Cushing's schooner moved down the channel out of range of the guns and waited to see if the *Ellis* would refloat on the tide. The tug never got the chance. Just after first light, the rebels opened up with four heavy guns, and soon the *Ellis* was in shambles. "The only alternatives left were surrender," Cushing later wrote, "or a pull of one and a half miles, under their fire, in my small boat. The first of these was not, of course, to be thought of, the second I resolved to attempt." He torched the *Ellis* in five places, made sure the battle flag was raised, and loaded the pivot gun and trained it on the enemy with a slow match "so that the vessel might fight herself after we left her." Then he led his volunteers into a rowboat and began to pull for the schooner.

The men rowed through the splashes of misaimed shells; with the current behind them, they swiftly moved downriver, and after about ten minutes they cleared the range of the guns and completed their row to the schooner in safety. There was still trouble, however. Overloaded and heavy in the water, the schooner had to battle heavy seas as she made her way through the mouth of the inlet, just ahead of several companies of rebel cavalry who had chased her down the banks in hopes of foiling a breakout. Arriving just moments too late, the rebels watched, Cushing wrote, as "we hoisted our flag, gave three cheers, and were off." Four hours later, they were back in Beaufort.

Apart from a certain exhilaration he must have felt at not being dead, Cushing had mixed feelings about his adventure. He was certainly pleased with the fight he and his men had made, with the information gathered and the property destroyed. At the same time, the proud nineteen-year-old who had been given the responsibility of commanding a ship was now the lad who had within five weeks lost that ship, in part because of his restlessness for action.

Perhaps to head off accusations of irresponsibility, he concluded his report on the loss of the *Ellis* with a request that a court of inquiry be convened in order to examine his conduct "to see if the honor of the flag has suffered at my hands." Commander Davenport scoffed. "I think the courage of this young officer should meet the commendation of his superiors," he reported to Samuel Lee, the new commander of the North Atlantic Blockading Squadron. Not only did the admiral agree, but Gus Fox of the Navy Department put his imprimatur on Cushing's conduct. "We don't care for the loss of a vessel," he said, "when fought as gallantly as that."

Even rebels were impressed. "Young Cushing had been a pupil of mine at the Naval Academy in 1861," wrote Captain William H. Parker of the Confederate navy, who had happened "to get hold of his report of the loss of the U.S. Steamer *Ellis*. . . . I was impressed with this part of his official report (the italics are mine): and the only alternatives left were surrender or a pull of one and a half miles under their fire in my small boat. The first of these was not, *of course,* to be thought of. Knowing him to be at that time but 19 years old, I comprehended his heroic qualities and was not at all surprised to hear more of him."

Will also received a letter from Alonzo, who got caught up on Will's exploits while on leave in Washington. "Accept my hearty congratulations on your success and your promotion," Lon wrote. "You have undergone more transformations since we met than myself, and finally you being up in command of U.S. gunboat. . . . In another year you will command a squadron."

Alonzo was nearly right. While resting on leave in New Bern, Will received one of the more sincere compliments a naval officer can receive: he was recruited by the army. Major General John G. Foster, commander of the Department of North Carolina, invited Cushing to command a squadron of five army steam gunboats. Though flattered, Will declined. "I did not wish to relinquish actual naval service," he said, "and desired one vessel of the navy more than a fleet of army boats." Perhaps this, too, can be seen as evidence of Flusser's stabilizing influence. Five months before, Will was in Harrison's Landing introducing himself to the Union brass, examining the possibility of a transfer to the army. Now all he wanted was another command.

Cushing would get one soon, and it would take him away from the Carolinas, if only temporarily. Before he left, however, he would have one more adventure.

CHAPTER 18

Pilot Hunting

B ACK ON DUTY, Cushing learned that Admiral Lee was contemplating launching an attack on Wilmington. The biggest impediment was that Wilmington sat twenty-five miles up the Cape Fear River, protected by shoals and channels and gun batteries and numerous other obstacles natural and man-made. With pilots who knew how to navigate the shape-shifting river, the attack might succeed; if not, many a navy vessel would end up a rotting hulk on the Carolina coast.

Cushing quickly came up with a plan, which he presented to Commander H. K. Davenport. He proposed disguising the schooner he had captured as an English blockade runner. He would then ask navy ships to chase him into New Inlet. Seeing the chase, the rebels on the shore would jump to the conclusion that he was a friendly vessel in need of help, and they would send out a boat to pilot him to Wilmington. Union sailors would then capture that vessel, and the Union fleet would have its pilot.

Brilliant, imaginative, audacious—the idea was too risky for any one man to approve. Davenport studied it, then punted it up to Admiral Lee. Like his third cousin Robert E. Lee, the fifty-year-old admiral was a Virginian, the scion of patriots, and impeccably groomed. Unlike the grizzled Stringham or the obese Goldsborough, Lee had the posture and bearing of someone raised to lead. Unlike Robert, he was a solid Union man. When asked about his loyalty, Samuel replied, "When I find the word Virginia in my commission I will join the Confederacy."

Lee mulled over Cushing's plan, then brought the young officer in for discussions. Lee could see the possibilities of this bold stroke, but sent a tepid recommendation. "Cushing's account of his past action impresses me very favorably. [His plan] may succeed if the idea has not leaked out," was how he referred the question to Gus Fox, whose position at the Department of the Navy was due almost entirely to his own ingenuity and initiative. Fox was intrigued and brought Will to Washington to discuss the plan. He then deferred the decision to Lee. "I told him he might go at any scheme you consented to," Fox said, appending a line that Lee could use for cover if necessary: "Rashness in a young officer is rather commendable." With that subtle nod, Lee approved the plan, but with caveats. "Young Cushing's scheme ventures more than it promises," he wrote to Fox, "but liking the morale of the thing I would not stop the project."

The decision-making process lasted much longer than Cushing's charade. After the schooner was disguised, Cushing took it into the ocean outside New Inlet and made a show of racing past the Yankee guns for the rebel safety of the Cape Fear River. Three times he tried it; three times he sped in with earnestly chugging naval vessels making a show of pursuit, and three times, on both the eastern and western ends of the harbor, he was suddenly becalmed, left to sit nakedly in the middle of the water in plain sight of the Union navy and rebel artillerymen. Perhaps no one on the shore could have figured out what the crazy sailboat was up to, but no one would have suspected that she was anything but a friend of the United States Navy.

Will didn't dwell on his failure. Fortune may have forced him to abandon his idea, but he still had a plan. He had heard that there was a pilot station at Little River, some thirty miles below Fort Caswell, south of Cape Fear, close to the North Carolina–South Carolina border. Will headed south, reaching the Little River on January 5, 1863.

CUSHING PLANNED TO find the pilothouse and capture all who were inside. With twenty-five men in three cutters, he headed up the narrow river. After traveling about a mile in darkness, they came under a smattering of musket fire from the shore. Concluding that he had reached the pilothouse, Cushing turned his boats toward the bank. "I sprang up in my boat and sang out, 'Follow me in!'" he recalled in his memoirs. In the dark, the sailors then charged across two hundred yards of sand to a position that was dimly lit and otherwise incomprehensible; nonetheless, "at the enemy we went, yelling like demons." At the double-quick they crossed a ditch and scaled a parapet, only to find themselves "sole possessors of a fort and parapet from which the frightened garrison five times our number had run away." In Admiral David Dixon Porter's memoirs, written years later, you can hear his undiminished amazement as he described this event: "The fearless fellow never stopped to consider whether he was charging fifty men or a thousand. It seemed immaterial to him, when his blood was up, how many of the enemy faced him; and his men, inspired by his intrepid example, followed him without hesitation."

However many soldiers had once been there, the entire company was now gone. The sailors looted the abandoned fort, wolfed down the dinner of pork and greens left on the cook stove, and hustled back to the ship. On their way out, they exchanged shots with some of the rebels who had returned to investigate what sort of invasion force had run them out of their fortifications with little more than yelling.

The expedition had turned into a comedy. The becalmed schooner that sat in the channel and fooled no one was Act One; the pilotless pilothouse with the runaway rebels was Act Two. Act Three, however, was anything but amusing.

Cushing anchored overnight at the mouth of the river tucked into the soft underbelly of the Carolinas coast that runs almost east–west for a short time before dropping on a southward diagonal toward Florida. At the eastern end of that brief stretch is Cape Fear, where the river flows into the sea. Extending like a lance in a southeast direction toward Africa are the Frying Pan Shoals, thirty miles of sandbars built of silt washed out of the Cape Fear River; they have been the site of countless shipwrecks. Cushing was west of those shoals, and needed to pass them.

By morning, a heavy swell was rolling in; a storm was close, a big one. The ship carried only one anchor and just fifteen fathoms of chain, not enough to hold the vessel still while the storm blew itself out. Will couldn't stay where he was; the wind would carry him onto the shoals and wreck him. Now, just as on the day in November when the *Ellis* sat stuck on a sandbar, Cushing had to choose between two perilous alternatives. "I might bear up for the beach and go ashore at Fort Caswell, as a prisoner of war . . . or I might run the thirty miles that separated us from the shoal." In other words, sail through the storm. To do that would require him not only to find the narrow gap between the shore and the start of the shoals but also stay in it, through near-gale-force winds and slapping waves, until they reached the other side.

Naturally, our man Cushing chose to risk death rather than sit in prison.

Indifferent to this bold choice, the storm worsened. "Time wore slowly by and the moment drew near when our fate would be decided," Cushing later wrote.

All at once, I saw the old quartermaster at the lead turn deathly pale as he sang out, "Breakers ahead! For God's sake, sir, go about!" In an instant the cry was, "Breakers on the lee bow!" then "Breakers on the weather bow!" and we were into them. All seemed over now; but we stood at the helm, determined to control our boat to the last. A shock—she had struck. But it was only for a second, and she fairly flew through the great white breakers. Again and again she struck, but never hard. She had found the channel, and in twenty minutes we were safe, and scudding for Beaufort.

The expedition that began in embarrassment and frustration ended with a white-knuckled trip through the heart of a mid-Atlantic storm, to be topped with compliments from Admiral Lee applauding "the gallantry of this promising young officer." It also concluded an astonishing period in Will Cushing's career. In the six months since he had been promoted to lieutenant—really, in the four months since the Battle of Crumpler's Bluff—Will had demonstrated steadiness, resolve, coolness, courage, originality, imagination, audacity, and excellent helmsmanship. Now it was off to Hampton Roads, and a new command.

CHAPTER 19

Alonzo at Antietam

FTER MEETING WILL AT HARRISON'S LANDING, Alonzo spent a good chunk of the summer of 1862 camped in Virginia with the rest of the Army of the Potomac. Idling there, theoretically posing a threat to Richmond, McClellan sulked like Achilles, watching unsympathetically as his putative successor, General John Pope and his Army of Virginia, took a pasting at the hands of General Stonewall Jackson and General James Longstreet at the Second Battle of Bull Run. McClellan was confident that Lincoln would come back and reassign to him the forces he had given to Pope, and reinvest in McClellan the authority he had begun diluting at Harrison's Landing earlier in the summer.

McClellan was right. With Lee's army just a day's march away from Washington, Lincoln had no better choice than to hand McClellan a mighty force of close to seven corps and call upon him to protect the capital. But Washington wasn't the rebels' destination, at least not immediately. As part of a coordinated strategic campaign, three rebel armies moved north—generals Kirby Smith and Braxton Bragg into Kentucky, and Lee into Maryland. Alonzo, back with the First Artillery, harnessed his guns and, with the rest of the Army of the Potomac, went after Lee.

On September 17, 1862, Alonzo stood outside Sharpsburg, Maryland, stationed near the center of a federal line opposite rebel positions on the other side of Antietam Creek. At dawn the battle commenced to Lon's right, with Union attacks against Confederate brigades east of the Dunker Church. For hours, in cornfields and on open ground, the two sides slaughtered one another, General Alexander Lawton's ruined Georgia regiment reinforced by General John Hood's soon-to-be-destroyed Texans, the smashed federal corps of General George Meade and General James Ricketts replaced by General Abner Doubleday's similarly fated bluecoats, men by the hundreds racing to replace the newly dead lying in the nearly ripe croplands of western Maryland. By ten o'clock, the vicious fighting had shifted south, toward Alonzo's position east of the Hagerstown Turnpike, on the farmlands of Samuel Mumma, whose home had caught fire and was burning to Alonzo's rear. In front of him, a murderous struggle covered what just days before had been a gentle, haystack-dotted swale that drifted toward the Dunker Church. The rebels there had been attacked by the regiments of Sedgwick and Sumner, but the assaults were broken and became confused, and now Sedgwick was down and Sumner was lost and hundreds of Yankees were dead on the ground; out from the church and through the smoke came thousands of General Jubal Early's men and General Richard Anderson's butternut-clad troops, in a full-throated advance.

They were marching through dense smoke into the jaws of eighteen federal cannon—a dozen ten-pound Parrotts from New York and Pennsylvania units, and six twelve-pound brass Napoleons of the United States Artillery, two of which were commanded by Alonzo. The Union gunners poured on the fire mercilessly, blasting the rebels with canister even when it meant firing on the stragglers and the wounded of their own army. Soon the attack stalled; like a boxer who has taken a wallop in the head, the troops faltered, then collapsed. Union infantry came running up to bolster the artillery line, and then pushed the rebels off Mumma's property back to the safety of the woods behind the Dunker Church. If it weren't for all the dead and wounded, the proceedings on this part of the field would have ended with the two armies as they had begun. The heart of the battle then moved south, toward the Sunken Lane and then to the stone bridge, like a ferocious typhoon that dumped its rain and stove in roofs, and then moved on.

The battle was a draw. The federal army thwarted the South's entire war strategy, but although it had the men and the matériel and the opportunity to destroy Lee's army and end the war, it allowed the opportunity to get away.

McClellan returned to reorganizing the army. Some of his plans involved Alonzo, whose future, it seemed to McClellan and others, belonged in the Corps of Topographical Engineers; McClellan went so far as to order Alonzo to draw up plans for a topographical engineering command at army headquarters. Alonzo still wanted an artillery command, but acquiesced. As a topographical engineer, he would join the army's leadership, advising them on terrain, the placement of troops, the conduct of battle, and other subtle, crucial matters.

On the rainy evening of November 5, however, McClellan's plans were interrupted. A fifty-four-year-old general of volunteers named Catharinus Putnam Buckingham took a train up from Washington to the army's headquarters in Rectortown, Virginia, and presented Little Mac with a letter from the president. The note informed McClellan that he was out, to be replaced by General Ambrose Burnside. General Buckingham, who had been a trusted friend of Secretary of War Edwin Stanton ever since they were classmates at Kenyon College, was also the cousin of Milton Buckingham Cushing, the father of Alonzo and Will. Probably Buckingham had no idea that while he was delivering McClellan's much-deserved decapitation, his first cousin once removed was sleeping in a tent nearby.

McClellan may have been relieved of command, but his reorganization plan continued. Burnside divided his army into three "grand divisions" under the commands of generals William Franklin, Hooker, and Sumner; Sumner requested that Alonzo be assigned to his staff to perform topographical work. Just a month later, in December, during the four-day-long battle of Fredericksburg, Alonzo served under Sumner as an aide to the commander of one of his corps, General Darius Couch. During the battle, Lee induced the anxious Burnside to order his men to attack the protected rebels uphill, across an open field, resulting in a slaughter. Couch and Cushing moved about the battlefield, often under heavy fire, assessing the conflict; the general often required Alonzo to ride into the shooting to deliver orders to forward-placed officers without regard for his own safety. "Lieutenant Cushing," wrote Couch in his official report, "was with me throughout the battle, and acted with his well-known gallantry." Accepting Couch's recommendation, Lincoln brevetted Alonzo captain "for gallant and meritorious services."

In January 1863, Burnside and Sumner were relieved of command. As part of the shake-up, Alonzo would be reassigned, but first he was given an extended leave that allowed him to go home to Fredonia. First he stopped and spent several happy days visiting Sumner at his home in Syracuse. "On the first night, I was hustled off on a big sleigh ride. . . . I was between a couple of feminines, both of whom were as 'pretty as spotted purps' [sic]. We had an elegant ride and supper and dance and returned to Syracuse on Sunday morning." He proceeded to Fredonia for a week, found it exceedingly dull, then accompanied his mother to Chelsea, Massachusetts, where they visited her five cousins. After one more visit with brother Milton in Washington, Alonzo was back with the army on February 22 and learned that his much-desired assignment had come through. Captain Alonzo Cushing was now the commander of the two officers and 147 enlisted men of Battery A, Fourth US Artillery.

CHAPTER 20

In Old Virginia

MIDWINTER IN WASHINGTON: "Mud and contractors," wrote Will waggishly, "were thick in the street." During a twelve-day leave spent mostly with his brother Milton— now in the navy, working at the yard for Cousin Joe—Will frequented the theater, caught up with a newlywed cousin and her spouse at their hotel, and embarked on a misbegotten journey to Falmouth, Virginia, with the aim of visiting Alonzo in camp. Instead, hauling a heavy carpetbag full of sherry and cigars through driving rain, he reached the Sixth Street dock in time to see the ferry bound for Aquia Creek pulling away. With a shrug, Will headed the three miles back to Milton's, his cargo destined for consumers unknown.

The merry leave did admit one piece of business: a visit with the secretary of the navy. Gideon Welles had decided to offer Cushing his choice of two ships: the *Violet* or the *Commodore Barney*. With the *Violet*, small and fast, Cushing's orders would be to return to Cape Fear and chase to ground blockade runners gunning for Wilmington. At 512 tons, the *Commodore Barney* was larger, heavier, slower, and, with seven big guns, more lethal than the *Violet*; she carried a crew of thirteen officers and 125 men. The *Barney* would patrol Hampton Roads, which suited Cushing just fine. "There was a good appearance of coming war about Norfolk," Cushing later wrote. He had heard that General Longstreet, one of Robert E. Lee's most capable corps commanders, was coming to Suffolk. This almost guaranteed action, he reasoned. Welles elliptically confirmed Cushing's thinking, intimating that before long there was apt to be fighting south of Norfolk.

The *Barney* possessed another attraction. "The command of her belongs to some officer of higher grade than myself," Cushing wrote cousin Mary. "But they (the powers that be) are pleased to think that I have earned the distinction—of course I am proud as a peacock at being the only Lieut. in the regular Navy who has a [separate] command." No wonder Cushing chose the *Barney*.

In late February, Longstreet headed for southern Virginia, in part for the opportunity to prove himself with independent command. Along with Jackson, Longstreet was a key contributor to Lee's success, but he chafed in the knowledge that inferior men like Braxton Bragg commanded independent armies in Tennessee and Georgia, and were using those positions to squander the South's chances of victory. Longstreet wanted to lead; to get that chance, he would have to produce a victory.

In exchange for this opportunity, however, Longstreet had to serve three masters: First, President Davis wanted Longstreet to defend Richmond above all else. Second, General Lee wanted Longstreet to simultaneously provide him with supplies from the farmlands of southeastern Virginia by securing supply routes from North Carolina, and be available to return to the Rappahannock should General Hooker decide to march south. Third, the Confederate secretary of war John Seddon wanted Longstreet to move against the Union army of General John Peck, which would also serve the purposes of both Davis and Lee.

Peck and his 15,000 men held Suffolk, a fourteen-mile salient jutting west from Hampton Roads to the head of the Nansemond River, a tributary of the James, nearly twenty miles long, and on the average a mile wide. Though Suffolk had been in Union hands for about a year, the strategic value of maintaining a force there was mostly theoretical; Washington had no intention of sending Peck's army into Richmond, but as long as those troops sat in Suffolk, the possibility existed. As a result, the undermanned Confederacy had to waste troops on garrison duty outside Richmond.

Longstreet examined the possibility of attacking Peck. His only chance, he concluded, was to mount a joint army-navy effort; Longstreet's men could cross the river if the ironclad CSS *Richmond* would come down the James River and seal off the mouth of the Nansemond, preventing Union gunboats from getting into the river and supporting Peck. For the *Richmond* to participate, however, the navy would have to remove many of the obstacles they had planted in the James to stop Yankee gunboats from coming upriver and shelling the capital. That decision was left in the hands of President Davis, and he couldn't have his cake and eat it too. If the ironclad was going to be free to come down the river, the gunboats were going to be free to go up. After lengthy consideration, Davis declined.

At that point, Longstreet decided to lay siege. On April 11, 1863, he stretched his 30,000 men between the James and the Nansemond rivers opposite Peck and began a bombardment that he hoped would dislodge the federals from their position. Just as he predicted, Union gunboats moved into the Nansemond. "Who do you suppose was selected," Cushing wrote his mother, "to perform the dangerous task of guarding the rear and preventing the crossing of ten thousand of the flower of the Southern army? Who but your son! That ex-midshipman, ex-master's mate, hair-brained, scapegrace, Will Cushing! Yes, it is even so."

Cushing's first two months on the *Commodore Barney* had been pretty boring; little illicit traffic tested his force. Will had banked on Longstreet's reputation as a fighter, but the burly Georgian had been busy foraging. Finally, to Will's delight, Longstreet decided to engage. Peck was more than happy to let the navy lead the response.

Admiral Lee ordered Cushing to take the *Barney* to the Suffolk area to assist Peck's forces. Four other vessels were sent: the *Mount Washington*, a river steamer; the *Stepping Stones*, a converted ferry; and two tugs, the *Cohasset* and the *Alert*. Lee named Cushing overall commander of the flotilla, but he specifically ordered Cushing to remain in the lower part of the Nansemond, and never to cross the bar into the upper river. Operations there were to be conducted by the commander of the *Mount Washington*, the tall, black-bearded Lieutenant Roswell Lamson. Although several years older than Will, he was a year behind on service, finishing second in his class at Annapolis after taking his finals while serving on a warship at sea. The two became close friends; each frequently praised the other in his reports.

For an entire week, the battle was fought between the Union gunboats and Confederate artillery and sharpshooters. For the gunboats, the twisty Nansemond was as much a threat as the rebel gunners; the ships had to contend with artillery fire as well as the tides and the riverbanks, and all the ships at one time or another ran aground and had to be towed. On the fourteenth, the *Mount Washington* ran aground and sustained damage by artillery fire, and when she tried to leave the river, she got stuck on the bar and was shot up again. The *Barney* managed to free the *Mount Washington*, but not before Lamson's ship was damaged beyond immediate repair; Lamson was forced to transfer his command to the *Stepping Stones*. The next day, the shoe was placed on the other foot. The two federal ships were shelling a rebel position, and this time the *Barney* ran aground, and was towed off by the *Stepping Stones*.

"Well, it was a hard fight," Will wrote his mother during the week.

Their infantry riddled the two vessels with bullets. Crash! go the bulkheads—a rifle shell was exploded on our deck, tearing flesh and woodwork. A crash like thunder is our reply—and our heavy shell makes music in the air, and explodes among our traitor neighbors with a dull sullen roar of defiance. Up goes the battle flag, and at once the air is filled with the smoke of furious battle, and the ear thrills with the unceasing shriek and whistle of all the shell and rifled bolts that sinful man has devised to murder his fellow-creatures. Crash! Crash! Splinters are flying in the air; great pools of blood are on the deck, and the first sharp cry of wounded men in agony rises upon the soft spring air. The dead cannot speak—but there they lie motionless, lifeless, and mangled, who a moment ago smiled on the old flag that floated over them, and fought for its glory and honor. Sprinkle ashes over the slippery deck—the work must still go on.

Once again, one has to pity Mrs. Cushing, who surely looked forward to receiving Will's letters, but could not feel so happy about their bullet-riddled contents. Perhaps she learned to take them less literally after she heard that Will had made a deal with the editor of the Fredonia *Censor* to run his letters as war correspondence.

In reality the sides were frequently engaged, but the battles varied in intensity and length. "I had a great fight or small fight nearly every day," Will later told a cousin. Once the possibility of naval cooperation was closed, Longstreet seemed to lose interest in prosecuting this battle. Without boats and naval protection, he wasn't about to try to cross the Nansemond, and with Davis fretting about invasion, he wasn't about to leave the area. Instead, he focused on foraging. Some of his better troops were put to work by the quartermaster, gathering food and packing wagons.

On April 19, one of the sharpest engagements on this front took place, when Lamson managed to land 270 Union soldiers under General George W. Getty at Hill's Point, where the five guns of the Fauquier Battery had been a nemesis to the gunboats all week. The rebels had been caught napping—"a most remarkable and discreditable instance of an entire absence of vigilance," read the official report by Longstreet's aide—and after a short, sharp skirmish, all five guns and 130 prisoners were in Union hands. But neither Admiral Lee nor General Peck was interested in pressing this advantage, and the position was abandoned. Lee ordered Lamson to cease his patrols of the upper Nansemond.

However, the intermittent floating gunfight continued, and men remained in harm's way. On April 21, the *Stepping Stones* spotted a man on the rebels' side of the river who seemed to be waving a white flag. A group of sailors in a small boat were sent to investigate, but as they neared the shore, gunfire erupted from behind the tree line. One sailor was killed and four others taken prisoner.

Cushing was livid. This was a violation of the rules of war, and he intended to make someone pay. Throughout the engagement, Cushing and his comrades had noticed civilians giving direct aid to Confederate forces, and Cushing made it clear that if he caught civilians in the act of helping the rebels, there would be reprisals. The next morning he called together four of the ships he commanded in the Nansemond, and from them assembled a ninety-man landing party. Bringing with them a twelve-pound howitzer, they rowed to the rebel riverbank. Quickly they located the boat that the sailors had used, abandoned on the shore, along with the body of the Union sailor who had been killed.

Leaving a small group with the body, Cushing pushed on, bound for the village of Chuckatuck, burning buildings along the way. They encountered rebel pickets a mile and a half outside the village. The pickets fled, leaving a mule-drawn cart to which the sailors tethered the howitzer.

By the time the sailors reached Chuckatuck, it was late afternoon, and the streets were empty. Suddenly, a group of forty rebel cavalrymen turned a corner two hundred yards ahead. They drew their swords, and charged. Cushing set up the howitzer and fired it at the same time that the sailors emptied their muskets. A couple of rebels were unsaddled but, more consequentially, the loud noise frightened the captured mules, who galloped straight at the Confederates, dragging all the extra ammunition in the cart to which they were still tethered. Perhaps inspired by the mules, Cushing ordered his sailors to attack, and with a shout they sprinted toward the rebels, who immediately turned their horses about and fled.

In some respects, it was a repeat of the incident on the Little River. Cushing was learning the lesson of boldness, seeing that a straightforward attack loudly and confidently performed can unnerve even a superior force. In this case, it's not even clear that the Confederates were the superior force. If they were low on ammunition and relying on their sabers, Cushing's men would soon have the advantage in fire-power. And while it's true that the rebels fled, no one really knows what the cavalry was doing there or what their orders were. If, as was often the case, they had been assigned the duty of protecting wagons full of supplies that the rebel foragers had collected for Robert E. Lee's troops in northern Virginia, an officer who risked losing those wagons in order to engage an enemy unit of unknown size or origin would probably lose his command as well.

The sailors' charge was nevertheless as audacious as the cavalry's retreat had been inglorious, and another story was added to the Cushing legend. Will thought something more practical had come out of the encounter: intelligence. Why had he seen so few rebels? He and his men had hiked all the way to Chuckatuck and back and encountered almost no one. Longstreet was clearly pulling out, he reported to his superiors; he had left only a scrim of skirmishers to cover his maneuvers. Now was the time to attack, he urged Lee and Peck. His superiors, however, were too cautious.

Cushing was right: the Confederates were slowly withdrawing. There were still small battles; indeed, in one engagement, when the *Barney* came within twenty yards of the rebel shore, musket fire broke out, and Will had a very close call. "Three buckshot penetrated my clothing to the skin, and my hair at the crown of my head was cut off close to the scalp," he recalled in his memoirs. Within a few days, however, all was quiet on the Nansemond. On April 28, General Joseph Hooker had launched an invasion across the Rappahannock River with 130,000 men, Alonzo Cushing among them. Robert E. Lee, facing Hooker with about 65,000 men, telegraphed Longstreet and told him to come "with the least practicable delay." The Suffolk adventure was over. "We are now going to inflict such punishment on the Confederate army as they have never received before," Alonzo wrote his brother. "I shall write to you immediately after the Reb Army is annihilated."

That letter was written on April 27. On May 7, after Union troops suffered an upset thrashing by the Confederates at a place called Chancellorsville, Alonzo wrote again. "The fighting has been terrific but as usual void of results. Jo [Joseph Hooker] is not the man. He did not fight the army as it ought to have been fought. I will write again in a day or two. I am tired now." For the fifth time in a year, a Union army that had enjoyed advantages in manpower, firepower, and resources had seen them fumbled away, leaving a gallant rebel army to continue the bloodletting long after its practical hope for success ought to have been smashed.

The record of Alonzo's Battery A during the battle of Chancellorsville is thin. Part of General Winfield Hancock's division of Couch's Second Corps, it took a strong position on May 1 on the right wing of Hooker's forces; twenty-four hours later, the corps was inexplicably withdrawn. The battery then stood in reserve around Hooker's headquarters, even during most of the celebrated surprise attack of Jackson's men into the unprotected flank of the Union army on May 2. Released for combat operations late in the day, the men saw only light fighting. There are several reasons for thinking that Alonzo spent little time with his battery, but he was once again, as at Fredericksburg, pulled into staff duty by Couch. First, Couch had lost several members of his staff to wounds. Second, Alonzo filed no report on his battery's actions during the battle, suggesting that he hadn't been involved. Third, Alonzo was again brevetted, to the rank of major, "for gallant and meritorious services at the battle of Chancellorsville." The incomplete account suggests that in the chaos of the evening of May 2, during and after Jackson's blitz, Couch grabbed the cool and competent Alonzo and sent him into the maelstrom to help restore order. Fighting persisted for two more days; on the sixth, Hooker ordered the Army of the Potomac to cross back over the Rappahannock in a driving rainstorm, down 17,000 men from the week before.

WHILE ALONZO EARNED citations for his service at Chancellorsville, Will was receiving praise for his efforts on the Nansemond River. General Peck, whose slow and irresolute leadership had so often made him the butt of Will's disdain, nonetheless praised Lamson and Cushing as "gallant spirits," and cited "their untiring energy, unfailing resources, and excellent judgment." Admiral Lee also offered praise in his report to the secretary of the navy that Lamson and Cushing had "exhibited remarkable zeal, courage, and discretion." Welles in turn wrote a letter of commendation to Cushing in which he praised his "gallantry and meritorious services."

"I am in high favor with the department," wrote Will to his cousin, with uncustomary modesty.

AFTER LONGSTREET LEFT for Chancellorsville, the navy also withdrew from the Suffolk area. Will deposited the badly damaged *Commodore Barney* in Baltimore for repairs, then went to Washington and stayed with brother Milton; once again, according to their letters, they spent many evenings at the theater. The highlight of Will's leave was a private audience with President Lincoln, arranged by Gideon Welles. The president and the lieutenant talked for nearly an hour, although the topics of their conversation are not known.* One wonders if Alonzo's name

---

* In *A Chautauqua Boy in '61 and Afterward*, David Parker mentions one possible topic. He and Cushing met up during this leave, and Will discussed his recent experiences on the Nansemond. According to Parker, Cushing suggested to General Peck that he land troops on the Confederate side of the river with some artillery and take the fight to the rebels, but Peck declined. In this telling, Cushing took some men and a howitzer and did some reconnaisance, finding that the Confederates had departed. Cushing told Parker that he filed an official report in which he called Peck "an old granny." Secretary of War Stanton then demanded that Will be called to account, and that Will go see Lincoln. "Let me explain it to you fully," Will supposedly said to the president, "and I can prove that he is an old granny." Lincoln said, "You go back and tend to your business," and the matter ended without court-martial. Could the story be true? Many details are wrong: Parker has Cushing on the James instead of the Nansemond, facing Beauregard, instead of Longstreet. What's probably true is that Will was laying it on thick for his old pal, making himself seem a bit braver, badder, bolder, and better connected than he already was. What is no doubt true is that Will did meet with Lincoln, and did think Peck an old granny.

came up; Lincoln had been signing brevets for Alonzo for months; did he make no connection with the Cushing sitting in front of him? If so, there is no record of Will relaying the story to Alonzo. "The President was pleased to compliment me on my success," was all Will had to say. "He seemed rather subdued and sad—and did not talk about the war. It is said that Chancellorsville was a blow to everyone here, and that the President was very depressed by it."

CHAPTER 21

At Gettysburg

REPAIRS ON THE *BARNEY* PROCEEDED SLOWLY; Will's three-week leave was doubled. He used some of the extra time to visit his mother in Boston. "I must say that I never have enjoyed myself before as I did there," he wrote. "I had a dozen different engagements a day, laughed, talked, smoked, enjoyed the society of the ladies, and had some grand rides, good fishing, and some splendid dinners on the sea beach."

While Will and Alonzo recovered from their recent engagements, a third Cushing brother, Howard, was engaged in active combat a half continent away. Still an artilleryman in the Illinois regiment in which he had begun the war, Howard and the rest of General Ulysses S. Grant's Army of the Tennessee were at Vicksburg facing General John Pemberton's defenses. On May 19, and again on May 22, Union troops attacked the city, but the fortifications were too strong. After the second repulse, Grant decided to lay siege. That night, federal batteries began a bombardment that would last forty-seven days. Howard fired his share of shells; there is no indication whether or not he was aware that among those residing inside the city was his cousin Lawrence Houghton, along with his pregnant wife Jane and their eight children.

Will once again hoped to use some of his leave to get over to Falmouth and visit Alonzo, but they couldn't work it out. Not only were there too many newcomers in Battery A after Chancellorsville, but there was also the sour taste of defeat, and Alonzo threw himself into training his unit, sharpening its performance and its combative spirit. He was hoping to find time to see Will, but in June word got around that the rebels were on the march. Lee wanted to take the fight north—to forage in the Pennsylvania pastures, to seize Philadelphia or Harrisburg, or to capture Lincoln and hold him ransom to impress the European powers and win the war outright. On June 10 came reports that General Richard S. Ewell, who had replaced Stonewall Jackson after his death at Chancellorsville, had begun moving northward from Culpeper to Cedarville, where he met up with cavalry. A few days later Longstreet's men were seen crossing the Bull Run mountains, headed into the thin panhandle of Maryland that separates Virginia and Pennsylvania. This was no ordinary maneuver.

On June 14, Alonzo received orders from General Hancock, who had replaced Couch, to begin moving north, on a path that paralleled the march of the Confederates. Hancock specified that one section of the battery accompany him; he didn't say so, but he meant Alonzo. Like Couch, Hancock admired Alonzo's skills as a staff officer and wanted him nearby.

By the end of the month Will was back on duty, assigned to bring the *Barney* to Washington to protect the city should Robert E. Lee's new invasion target the nation's capital. "My vessel is in good repair, and my crew is replenished, my battery is heavier than before," he wrote. "It is not going to be a dull summer."

FOR TWO WEEKS, the Army of the Potomac, massed east of the Blue Ridge Mountains, trailed Lee's forces west of the hills in their long, hot, dusty march through the Shenandoah Valley and into the Cumberland Valley and Pennsylvania. On June 30, Lee's troops were spread out, with Ewell in Carlisle, General A. P. Hill in Cashtown, and Longstreet's corps still marching through Maryland. Lee didn't know where the Union army was—General Jeb Stuart's cavalry, famously, was cut off—but he ordered Hill and Ewell to concentrate north of Gettysburg, the seat of Adams County. Sitting at the hub of ten roads, Gettysburg almost invited battle.

General George Meade, who had just replaced Hooker as the commander of the federal forces, wouldn't have picked the place. Like Lee, Meade was ignorant of his adversary's position, but he intended to create a defensive line at Mine Run, in Maryland. But on the morning of July 1, rebel soldiers under General Hill encountered Yankee cavalry forces. Against Lee's orders, a fight broke out; against Meade's orders, General John Reynolds's corps moved to Gettysburg to reinforce the Union troops. With that, the battle was on.

Camped in Taneytown, Maryland, Meade was slow to receive information about what was happening ten miles to the northwest. Although he could hear cannon fire all morning, not until about one p.m. did he learn from a messenger that General Reynolds had committed First Corps to a battle against Hill's men, a decision that cost Reynolds his life. Meade immediately rode to Hancock's headquarters and ordered Hancock to relinquish command of his regiments to another officer, go directly to Gettysburg, and take charge of the battle. Hancock for a moment demurred, pointing out that he was junior to two other corps commanders already on the scene. Meade cut him off, and showed him written authorization from the secretary of war to change whatever he saw fit.

Grabbing Alonzo, Hancock rode to Gettysburg. The roads were jammed; they did not arrive until 3:30. Standing in the Edgewood Cemetery on a hill just south of town—then and forever after called Cemetery Hill—they surveyed a spectacle of chaos: men from two corps of the Union army, the First and the Eleventh, fleeing through the little town, pursued by rebels.

Steadying the panicked troops, putting an end to flight, deploying the arriving regiments on Cemetery Hill and on Culp's Hill to the east, Hancock and his staff over the next hours managed to staunch the Union defeat. By drawing a line at Cemetery Hill, Hancock defined the remaining course of the battle. All night, troops continued to arrive. The Union troops, coming up from Maryland, filled in a line stretching south along a crest known as Cemetery Ridge. The Confederates, using the town as a base, filled a line in the woods on Seminary Ridge, about a mile opposite the Yankees. In his report to Meade the following morning, along with the news that the retreat had been stopped, and that a Union line was now established on high ground, Hancock took time to praise Alonzo Cushing for his fearlessness under fire. "He is the bravest man I ever saw," Hancock said, and Meade brevetted Alonzo a lieutenant colonel on the spot.

Alonzo found his battery on the Taneytown Road on the night of the first and guided them into the federal line on Cemetery Ridge near a group of chestnut oak trees overlooking the Emmitsburg Road.

Fighting on July 2 did not begin until almost four p.m., when Lee attempted to flank the left of the Union line. Furious fighting took place in the Peach Orchard, the Wheat Field, Devil's Den, and Little Round Top, and by the time night fell, the rebels had driven the Yankees off some of these positions without successfully breaking the front. Stationed at the center of the Union line, Alonzo and his men could feel the fighting getting closer to them. At dusk a brigade of Georgians led by General Ambrose Wright overran a position held by a Rhode Island regiment. The Georgians turned their newly seized guns toward Alonzo's position, but before they could even load the cannon, Alonzo coolly ordered his six ordnance rifles, each loaded with canister, to open fire. The volley abruptly stopped the assault, and a regiment of Pennsylvanians chased the survivors back to Emmitsburg Road.

Had Lee's army failed? Lee preferred to think that they had almost grabbed victory—total victory, the type of victory that would have left Lee's army free to march on Washington, and demoralized and frustrated northerners to sue for a peaceful settlement. Lee was sure Meade had weakened his center to protect his flanks; if only Lee had coordinated his attack a bit better, the gaps that had momentarily flashed open in the federal line might have been breached. The line would have been broken, and the whole position would have begun to collapse. Victory was still possible, especially since Lee now had fresh troops, who had arrived overnight.

CHAPTER 22

Alonzo's Glory

L EE WAS CERTAIN THAT Meade's center would be weak. If the rebels could strike there, Meade's line would evaporate. Lee had seen his men break a strong Yankee line at Fair Oaks, had seen his outnumbered forces rout the bluecoats at Chancellorsville, had seen the Union army in panicked flight just two days before. He did not doubt that it would happen again.

Lee determined to send nearly 11,000 men against the Union line, including nearly 5,000 fresh men under the command of General George Pickett. This time, their attack would be preceded by a massive artillery bombardment that would shred their defenses and shake their will even before his men stepped off. Studying the federal position on Cemetery Ridge, Lee looked for a landmark at which to point his troops. There was a small group of chestnut oaks, a copse of trees. He would tell his officers to direct all their men to shatter the line at that point.

Under those trees stood Alonzo Cushing, and Battery A of the First US Artillery.

Throughout the hot, hazy morning of Friday, July 3, Colonel Porter Alexander arranged the Confederate cannon in front of Seminary Ridge. General William Pendleton was officially the chief of artillery for the Army of Northern Virginia, but after Pendleton botched rear-guard operations after Antietam—he panicked during an engagement, and in the middle of the night woke Lee up to confess that he had lost all his men and guns, which was not nearly true—Pendleton was left to handle administrative matters while Alexander handled the guns. He collected almost everything the rebels had—some 150 cannon—and emptied the ammunition trains, then arranged the guns in one long line. Studying Alexander's cannon choreography through his binoculars, General Henry Hunt, the chief of the Union's artillery, knew in a glance what was happening. "Never before had such a sight been witnessed on this continent," he later wrote. "It most probably meant an assault on our center, to be preceded by a cannonade in order to crush our batteries and shake our infantry; at best to cause us to exhaust our ammunition in reply, so that the assaulting troops might pass in good condition over the half mile of open ground which was beyond our effective musketry fire."

It would be, Hunt said, "a magnificent display," and at about one p.m. it roared to life with a thunderous shriek that was heard in Pittsburgh, almost two hundred miles away. "The earth shook beneath our very feet and the hills and woods seemed to reel like a drunken man," reported the correspondent of the *Richmond Enquirer*. "The very air seemed as if about to take fire," said Colonel Hilary Hebert of the Eighth Alabama; "as if all the demons in hell were let loose and were howling through the air," recalled Sergeant Benjamin Hirst of the Fourteenth Connecticut. "There was an incessant discordant flight of shells, seemingly in and from all directions—howling, shrieking, striking, exploding, tearing, smashing and destroying—producing a scene that words cannot present and was well nigh unbearable. The ground was torn up; fences and trees knocked to splinters; rocks and small stones were flying in the air; ammunition boxes and caissons were exploded . . . guns were dismounted; and men and horses were torn in pieces," wrote Sergeant James Wright of the First Minnesota. "When the heavens are rolled together as a scroll in the last days I doubt whether it will present a more awe-inspiring spectacle than that historic field presented on that fatal day," wrote M. B. Houghton of the Fifteenth Alabama.

It was a picture, said Alonzo's sergeant, Frederick Fuger, "terribly grand and sublime."

And effective. Alonzo was enormously proud of his men. It must have been excruciating to stand waiting on the crest of that hill, while rebel fire remorselessly subtracted his battery's capability, this shot taking a horse, that one a gun, this one an artilleryman. At the outset, two caissons were hit and exploded; then gun number six, then gun number five. A shell hit a horse, mangling the driver, who assessed his situation and shot himself. Murphy at gun number four was killed, then Sergeant Au, then the bugler Keyser. Gun number three lost a wheel and its cannoneers began to run. "I'll shoot anyone who tries to leave this field," Alonzo shouted, and directed them to fix it, as they had so often trained to do.

Then Alonzo was hit—a piece of shrapnel in the shoulder. Just seconds later he was hit again, in the genitals and both thighs. According to Fuger, he suffered terrible pain and nausea and lost a lot of blood, but then went into shock and continued to function. Fuger demanded that Alonzo go to the rear. "No," replied Alonzo. "I will stay here and fight it out, or die in the attempt."

Around two thirty, the Confederate cannonade slackened, and from behind the trees on Seminary Ridge there emerged nearly 11,000 rebels. It was, according to Captain Azariah Stratton of the Twelfth New Jersey, "the grandest sight I ever witnessed . . . [t]he different lines came marching toward us, their bayonets glistening in the sun, from left to right, as far as the eye could reach." When the sun struck their sabers and bayonets, Captain Winfield Scott of the 126th New York likened the sight to "a river of silver."

Using Fuger as a crutch, Alonzo hobbled over to General Alexander Webb, the twenty-eight-year-old New Yorker who was commanding the regiment right behind Cushing. Webb could see that Alonzo was in terrible shape. Most of Alonzo's men were dead or scattered. He told Webb he could still work his two remaining guns if some of Webb's men would serve as cannoneers. They repositioned Alonzo's guns forward, right behind the stone wall that ran across the crest of Cemetery Ridge.

Emmitsburg Road ran about halfway between Seminary and Cemetery ridges, but long before the great Confederate parade reached that point, the rebels were being smashed by federal shells. Though Cushing and the other battery commanders had done considerable damage to the Confederate infantrymen waiting for the signal to attack, Porter Alexander's barrage had not been matched. But now the secessionists were out of ammunition, and the Union batteries pasted the Confederates advancing in the open field. With each loss the Confederates closed up their columns, trying to maintain in their assault the power of a closed fist. At the same time, however, they were also tightening the Yankees' target. Everything the bluecoats fired struck somebody.

As the rebels reached Emmitsburg Road, they were slowed by rail fences they had to scale. Cushing blasted away. The ones who survived lowered their heads and advanced. "Here they come! Here they come!" officers shouted, as though their men could not see. As the rebels closed, Alonzo opened up with canister. The vicious mix of shot and shrapnel stripped away lines of men. On came the survivors. Cushing switched to double canister, and continued to deal death.

The remaining rebels closed to within a hundred yards of Alonzo. They were massing, with many of their flags right in his face. The whine of bullets was everywhere. Lieutenant Milne, commanding the guns next to Alonzo's, was shot and killed. Alonzo was failing now, the blood loss draining the life out of him. "Double canister, both guns," he said to Fuger, who barked the command. "Fire!" the twenty-two-year-old ordered, and as Fuger repeated the order and the cannons exploded and their lethal stew killed and maimed that rapidly shrinking force of attackers, a bullet hit Alonzo below the nose and ripped across the base of his brain. He died at his guns.

Fuger laid down the body and continued to fight. The last of the canister, a triple load, was rammed home. "Now?" asked a gunner as the rebels closed to within point-blank range.

"Wait . . . ," replied the deliberate Fuger, "wait . . ." When he finally said, "Fire," he blew a hole in the line that the Confederacy never restored.

From all over the field, Union regiments poured into the gap that Cushing and his fellow artillerists had held. General Lewis Armistead, who had indelibly placed his hat on his sword and gallantly led his brigade of Virginians into the maw of the Union army, arrived at the distant copse of trees that General Lee had targeted and advanced so far as to place his hand on Alonzo Cushing's smoking gun and to roar "Turn the guns!" before a Union bullet pierced his breast. The last of the Confederates who had reached the hilltop now died, ran, or surrendered. The great charge had melted into nothingness, except for a narrowing wake of wounded and dead that ended at Alonzo's guns.

It rained that night in Gettysburg. Sergeant Fuger secured Alonzo's body, wrapped it in a tarpaulin, and took it to where the battery had bivouacked on the Baltimore Pike. Later that night, he stopped to eat, fell asleep with the food in his hands, and spent the night on the ground next to Alonzo's body.

WORKING IN THE navy yard, Milton Cushing not only heard the results of the battle on Friday afternoon, but learned that Alonzo had been killed. He took a train to Gettysburg, arrived the next morning, and found Fuger. After managing to obtain a casket, he carried the body by train to West Point, where Alonzo had said that he wanted to be buried. The following week, on the twelfth, his wish was granted.

CHAPTER 23

Grieving

T HE FIRST WEEKS AFTER Alonzo's death were spent in grief and sadness; as Will wrote to his mother, "There is suffering greater than the dying know, the prolonged anguish of those left behind to mourn them." No doubt he wanted to do something to alleviate his feelings, but even that opportunity was denied him when the *Commodore Barney* was withdrawn from service and he had to wait for a new ship. In August, Cushing was offered the *Shokoken*, a speedy ferry boat with a shallow draft, potentially useful in the rivers and along the coasts of Carolina. Although there were considerable doubts that the *Shokoken* could withstand the region's heavy storms, Cushing agreed to give the ship a try.

For a while he managed to get good service from her. The *Shokoken* joined the blockade off New Inlet, and helped the USS *Niphon* run aground a blockade runner, the *Hebe*, that was trying to reach Wilmington. Efforts by Union sailors to take the ship as a prize or at least salvage her valuable cargo of coffee, medicines, clothing, and silk were thwarted by high seas and shore fire from rebel guns, so a frustrated Will finally elected to shell the ship until it caught fire.

During the action, reconnaissance informed Cushing that another schooner was moored at a wharf about six miles into New Topsail Inlet. He proposed to his immediate superior, Captain Ludlow, that he go into the inlet and cut the schooner out. Ludlow, for whatever reason, declined, but Will went ahead anyway.

Positioning the *Shokoken* at the mouth of the inlet where every Confederate eye could see it but no Confederate gun could touch it, Cushing then sent seven men in a dinghy to proceed along the shore until they were close to the ship.

Once the landing party ascertained that the schooner was lightly held, they rushed it and captured the ship, a dozen prisoners, and a saltworks that was on the shore. Although the landing party had planned to sail out on the schooner, other rebels in the area had begun to respond, so they torched the ship and the saltworks, took three prisoners, and retreated in the dinghy. It was a nifty little operation, which Cushing capped off by returning to the place where the *Hebe* was beached and burned. He took twenty men and pounced on the guns, scattering the crew. Once again, this was a venture that Cushing had proposed and had been denied permission to undertake, but nobody said anything once he had spiked the guns and put them out of commission.

Cushing's time with the *Shokoken* shortly came to an end at the hands of a gale that almost splintered the erstwhile ferry. He managed to bring her back into position in the blockade line, but he recommended that the ship be deemed unfit for blockade service, and Admiral Lee did not disagree.

The *Shokoken* was ordered to Hampton Roads for repairs, and Will went to Washington with dispatches from Lee. In one of them Lee praised Cushing as a "zealous and able young officer," and requested that he be reassigned to the blockading squadron.

Which he was. As reward for "distinguished services rendered," he was given command of the *Monticello*, a handsome screw steamer that had already seen considerable action during the war. It was one of the fleet's very best ships for one of its very best young officers. With this assignment, Will would have been the envy of nearly every man of his rank in the service, and many above him besides.

He spent the fall and part of the winter in Philadelphia, overseeing the repairs to the *Monticello*. He was able to get home for a time and visit his mother, and grieve with her for Alonzo. In November he visited Gettysburg at the time of the dedication of the national cemetery. He had difficulty making out the great oration by Edward Everett, and he could hear none of Lincoln's brief remarks.

Later in the month, Will's brother Howard's long silence was broken with a letter. He had fought in the battle at Chattanooga and was safe; he was also going to be promoted to second lieutenant, and assigned to the Fourth US, Alonzo's old unit.

Almost certainly the most dramatic event of those boring, restless, melancholy months in Philadelphia came in early November, on the eve of the gubernatorial elections. The Republican incumbent, a stalwart pro-Lincoln man named Andrew Curtin, was running neck and neck with the Democratic challenger, George Washington Woodward. Cushing was returning from one of his trips, and had gone to the Continental Hotel, then at the corner of Ninth and Chestnut streets, to take a room.

Philadelphia was a Democratic town, and the partisan newspapers were wearing themselves out stumping for Woodward and trashing Lincoln and Curtin. As David Parker recalls in *A Chautauqua Boy in '61 and Afterward,*

> *Cushing was writing his name on the register when a man at his elbow said "Here's another one of Lincoln's hirelings come to intimidate us at the election." Cushing completed his negotiations for a room, and then turned and used a small cane he carried on the man who made the remarks, cutting his face quite severely. The people in the rotunda separated, as if about to engage in a row, when the police entered and quelled the disturbance and arrested Cushing. . . . As many as fifteen or twenty wealthy citizens went along to the station house and gave bail for Cushing. He appeared in court the next morning and paid a fine. The second day after that, Cushing's*

ship departed without him. Cushing planned to join it at Norfolk, and after timing the ride to the Southern station and having his belongings in a cab ready, he ran to the drugstore kept by the man who had insulted him, pulled him from behind the counter, and thrashed him severely. Then Cushing jumped into the cab, went to the station,* and boarded the train as it was about to move.

---

* The station was almost certainly the terminal of the Philadelphia, Wilmington and Baltimore Railroad, located at Broad and Prime streets, now demolished.

CHAPTER 24

The Essence of Impudence

I N CIVIL WAR LORE, two events consistently stand out for dash and panache. Both were performed by Confederate cavalrymen acting behind Union lines. In one of them, thirty men led by Lieutenant John Singleton Mosby, the famous Gray Ghost, snuck behind Union lines on March 9, 1863, and headed for Fairfax Court House, a town in northern Virginia. There they found a private home where a brigadier general, Edwin Stoughton, was staying. Creeping up the stairs in the early morning hours, Mosby delicately opened a bedroom door. "On the bed we saw the general sleeping," wrote Mosby in his memoir. "There was no time for ceremony, so I drew up the bedclothes, pulled up the general's shirt, and gave him a spank on his bare back, and told him to get up." Stoughton shot straight up.

"General, did you ever hear of Mosby?"

"Yes," replied Stoughton, "have you caught him?"

"I am Mosby. Stuart's cavalry has possession of the courthouse; be quick and dress."*

The other great feat took place eight months earlier, when General

---

* Over the years, some talented writers improved the conversation, so that Stoughton's reply to Mosby's question is "Have you caught the devil?" To which Mosby reponds, "No, he has caught you." Alas, the more prosaic language appears to be the more accurate.

Jeb Stuart undertook a brazen bit of information gathering in which, though detected and pursued, he led 1,200 cavalrymen on a four-day reconnaissance mission that encircled the whole of the Union army. The adventure, during which only a single trooper lost his life, did much to justify the cape and ostrich plume Stuart sported as a sign of his élan.

Within three months of Will Cushing's arrival at the mouth of the Cape Fear River on the *Monticello* in late February 1864, he came close to matching those legendary deeds. He returned to the Albemarle Sound as part of an increasing federal effort being trained on the coast of the Carolinas. Winfield Scott's Anaconda strategy had progressively diminished the Confederacy's access to the world: Cape Hatteras went first; in 1862, Roanoke Island, Norfolk, Pensacola, Fort Pulaski, Biloxi, and New Orleans fell. In 1863 Charleston was all but closed by a siege. Now, in 1864, the navy aimed to strangle commerce on the last stretches of the Carolina coast that were still open to blockade runners.

Although the navy spent considerable energy catching blockade runners, the blockade's success can't be measured by how many ships were caught or the amount of goods that got through. In fact, most blockade runs were successful. As James P. McPherson points out in his book *War on the Waters*, about 1,000 out of 1,300 trips in or out of southern ports of ships bound for an international port were successful. Perhaps as much as a million bales of cotton got out, and about 400,000 rifles, three million pounds of lead, two million pounds of saltpeter, and other supplies came in. Nonetheless, the South suffered terrible shortages of all sorts of goods. The point is not what got through, but what was not attempted. The million bales of cotton (if it was indeed that much; some estimates place the total closer to 500,000 bales) represented a tenth of the total exported in the three years before the war. No matter how much came in, the schooners that ran the blockades were too small to even contemplate carrying material like railroad iron or machinery.

Ultimately, ships and men made the blockade work: enough ships to form wooden walls that could be penetrated only with great diffi-culty and effort and luck; and enough men to impose higher and higher costs on those who would try to run the blockade.

By late 1863, the preferred port for blockade runners was the town of Wilmington, North Carolina, twenty-eight miles above the mouth of the Cape Fear River. Well served by railroads, and close to the Bahamas and to Caribbean ports where much of the exported cotton was traded for goods, Wilmington was exceptionally well protected. In the Atlan-tic, the northern approaches to the river were guarded by the formidable Fort Fisher, and the southern approaches by Fort Caswell. Natural fea-tures also made the place conducive to furtive transport: the mouth of the river was split by Smith Island, creating two connections to the sea, New Inlet and Western Bar Channel. With the shifting currents, the changing depths, the shoals and marshes and hidden inlets and covered docks and the batteries dotting the whole way up to Wilmington, block-ade runners loved this haven as pirates did in earlier centuries.

Cushing arrived at the mouth of the Cape Fear River on February 17, and began scouting the vicinity for a point of weakness that he could exploit. Within two weeks, he brought his superiors a customarily bold proposal: he wanted to take two hundred men to seize Smith Island and hold it until the army could occupy it in force. Taking the island would change the balance of power dramatically, enabling the navy to close off the Western Bar Channel to all Confederate traffic, and tightening the path through New Inlet as well. But Cushing's superior, Captain Sands, doubted the feasibility of the plan and denied permission with a curt, "Can't take the responsibility." As Will wrote later, "This, I confess, provoked me, and I told the Senior Officer that I could not only do that, but if he wanted the Confederate general off to breakfast, I would bring him."

Cushing shrugged off his superior's disapproval. Shortly after sun-down on February 29, he took twenty men in two small boats and rowed several miles, past the guns of Fort Caswell and Fort Johnston, past the town of Smithville. There, on the southern side of the river,

General Louis Hébert, the commander in charge of the region, made his headquarters.

Having snuck past Smithville, Cushing's raiders turned and approached Smithville from the opposite direction, as though they were coming downriver and therefore couldn't possibly be the enemy. Quietly, they beached their boats. Splitting his forces, Cushing led about half his men into a typical small, one-street town. Its layout wasn't hard to discern: the store, the livery stable, the hotel. Down at the end of the street, the building with the narrow windows would be the fort. General Hébert would be staying in a house. Which one?

Ahead Cushing could see a dark building where a large fire was burning—a saltworks. Two black men were sitting by the fire, no doubt slaves. Cushing took them into custody; they offered no resistance. "Where's the general?" Cushing asked. One of the slaves led him and two of his officers, Ensign J. E. Jones and Master's Mate W. L. Howorth, to a house with a large veranda.

Cushing crept onto the porch and quietly opened the door. Easing his way along, he gradually deduced that he was in a dining room, then a hallway. Starting to climb a flight of stairs in the still-quiet house, suddenly he heard a crashing noise from downstairs and Howorth calling, "Captain! Captain!" Cushing hurried down the stairs and back into the dining room, where he was confronted by a large man in a nightcap who brandished a chair above his head. Cushing punched him in the face. "I had him on his back in an instant with the muzzle of a revolver at his temple and my hand on his throat."

Up to this point, Cushing has it all over Mosby, who found his champagne-soggy prey sleeping in an isolated house, not a town; Cushing's quarry wielded some heavy furniture in his defense, while Mosby's man yielded to a slap on the bum. But after lighting a match, Cushing received a blow of his own: the man on the floor wasn't Hébert, but Captain Patrick Kelly, the chief engineer of the installation. Hébert was hours gone, on his way to Wilmington. The crash Cushing had heard was the sound of his adjutant general, W. D. Hardman, clumsily escaping through a window. Cushing tossed Kelly his pants and waved him to the door; the three Yankee officers, the rebel captain who should have been a general, and the two men who were a boat ride from freedom all headed for the river. Behind him, Will could hear the shouts of alarm as rebels filled the street, "but like the old gent with the spectacles on his forehead, [they were] looking everywhere but in the right place." Cushing's party was halfway home before the rebels at Smithville ignited signal fires alerting other bases on the river that Yankees were about. "At one [o'clock]," wrote Cushing, "I was in my cabin, had given my rebel dry socks and a glass of sherry, laughed at him, and put him to bed."

Kelly didn't sleep long; Cushing roused him for breakfast on the commanding officer's ship. Mosby got a general; Will got a self-satisfying gloat in front of his commanding officer (and before long, a letter from Gideon Welles complimenting him on his gallantry). That afternoon, Cushing sent Ensign Jones to Smithville under a flag of truce to get some clothes and money to make Kelly's stay in a northern prison more comfortable. Jones was taken to the commander of the fort, a colonel also named Jones. After an awkward beginning, Colonel Jones showed his sporting side. "That was a damned splendid affair, sir!" he said. That broke the ice, and the two went on to have an amiable chat, at the end of which Ensign Jones produced a letter from Cushing to General Hébert:

My Dear General:
    I deeply regret that you were not at home when I called.

Very respectfully,
W. B. Cushing.

Adjutant Hardman, whose pride was hurt along with his arm, thought the letter "the essence of impudence," but Colonel Jones laughed. He said that he'd like to meet Cushing, but didn't think it would be likely, since no Union officer would ever tease the river's defenders as Cushing had done.

A week later, the roll of Cushing's exploits unfortunately slowed when the *Monticello* collided with another member of the blockade fleet, the *Feterhoff*, a converted blockade runner. A court of inquiry put all the blame on the officer of the watch, Acting Ensign Joseph Hadfield, who failed to notice that the *Feterhoff* was at anchor, and took the *Monticello* right into the smaller ship, and sank her. *Monticello* had to return to Norfolk for repairs, and it was April before the ship, and Will, were back in action.

During this break, Cushing appeared in correspondence between Admiral Lee, the commanding officer of the North Atlantic Blockading Squadron, and Gus Fox, the assistant secretary of the navy.

In a letter written on April 4, 1864, Lee wrote, "You say what a pity that Cushing's undaunted bravery and good luck cannot be put to a useful purpose in a manner to tell upon the enemy. Please explain this. I have always encouraged his dash, and am ever ready to do so. What can he do now? He is urging me to let him cruise off for prizes. He went into Cape Fear River to get prizes. I am rejoiced that he returned with such éclat to the *Monticello*. Pity he did not get a prize then."

Lee then asked Fox about Cushing's proposal to seize Smith Island. "Will you in any manner . . . justify the attempt? The idea is taking and the thing is possible, though Nelson failed in such an effort. But I like enterprises, and have always encouraged them. Is this what you hint at? I have a good idea of, and a good feeling for this youngster."

Fox replied on the eighth. "What I meant about Cushing was that it was a pity [that] so much luck and dash had not brought fruits equal to the risk. You notice the Department never finds fault with these exploits. I believe they ought to be encouraged. To be sure, the people will say, when he is captured, 'Damned fool!' The Department will not." Fox emphasized his position: "Going into the river to destroy a blockade runner about to sail is a most happy idea, and most serious to the enemy, because cotton and dispatches would be burned. The first officer who destroys one in this way I think I can promise will go up several numbers of the [promotions] list . . . and if it is Cushing we can add his former exploits and give him thirty numbers up."

Fortified by Fox's support, Lee acceded to Cushing's wish and gave him a roving commission. Cushing spent most of April hovering outside the navy's blockade line, waiting to catch a blockade runner who had broken through or was waiting to dash in. He had no luck. His greatest success came when he found the British schooner *James Douglass* abandoned, carrying a cargo of decaying coconuts and bananas. The most active officer in the navy had been presented with its most enterprising command, and it turned out to involve waiting, waiting, more waiting, and rotten fruit. Will was rusting.

On the night of May 6, however, some relief from this failing experiment suddenly floated out of the mouth of the Cape Fear River and attacked the blockaders in New Inlet. It was the CSS *Raleigh*, an ironclad that had been built in Wilmington. Intended for the defense of Wilmington harbor and the Cape Fear River, the *Raleigh* was never designed to engage an enemy in open waters. However, when inspectors found another ironclad based in the river, the *North Carolina*, riddled with shipworms, they declared it structurally unsound, even though it was just six months old and had never engaged the enemy. The *Raleigh*'s commander didn't want to risk having such shame fall on his shoulders, and he took his ship into battle.

It turned out to be a farcical exercise. The *Raleigh*, intended for calm waters, lurched about on the waves without being able to close on the federal ships, and she steamed haphazardly about the blockading squadron, firing occasionally without finding a target, and scattering a few of the smaller, more vulnerable vessels. During the confusion, a blockade runner steamed through the federal lines, but otherwise no damage was done. At dawn, the *Raleigh* returned to New Inlet and disappeared over the bar back into the river.

Will was appalled—or at least made himself appear so. A year had now passed since he had been in action on the Nansemond River; since then, he had done nearly as much fighting with a Philadelphia pharmacist as he had with any Confederate, and he desperately wanted a shot at the *Raleigh*. "I feel very badly over the affair, sir," wrote Cushing to Admiral Lee in a melodramatic letter on May 9, "and would have given my life freely to have had the power of showing my high regard for you and the honor of the service by engaging the enemy's vessels. If they are there when I arrive, I shall use the *Monticello* as a ram, and will go over her or to the bottom. . . . I enclose a copy of application and plan of operations." In other words, *Can I please go chase this ironclad?*

Several days passed, and Cushing heard nothing from Lee. Itching to move, he then asked the senior officer present, the careful Captain Sands, for permission to enter the harbor and board the *Raleigh*. Sands refused.

Impatiently going over the heads of both Sands and Lee, Cushing then wrote to Welles and Fox, letters full of details about how he planned to board the *Raleigh* and overpower her men. "One shell down each hatch would be likely to bring all hands to terms," he confidently asserted.

Before they could reply, Will heard from Lee, who "heartily" approved of the plan and authorized Cushing "to apply to the senior officer"—that is, himself—whenever he needed authorization to take extra men on a mission. Then Cushing heard from the Navy Department. "Lieutenant William B. Cushing has proposed a scheme with regard to . . . [the *Raleigh*] which it would be well to encourage," Welles said in a letter to Lee. "Risks to accomplish an important object ought to be taken without hesitation, and never will be disapproved by the Department if well arranged and intrusted to good officers."

Will now had permission to sink the *Raleigh*. But first, he wanted to get a closer look at the lay of the land.

CHAPTER 25

Marsh Grass and Cattails

At 8:40 P.M. on June 23, Cushing, his officers Jones and Howorth, and fifteen volunteers armed with small arms and cutlasses took off in a cutter to find the *Raleigh*. Rowing through Old Inlet with muffled oars, they passed Fort Caswell and the other outer batteries without catching a whiff of the ironclad. Cushing had hoped that the ship would be waiting, but it really didn't matter; he was determined to row to Wilmington if he had to.

They traveled the first twelve miles, close to half of the thirty that spread between the port city and their point of embarkation, half hidden by shadows. When they passed Fort Anderson, however, they found themselves in full moonlight, spotted by sentries who lit signal fires and took potshots with their muskets. Cushing turned the boat around and rowed obliquely, feigning retreat. As soon as a cloud slipped in front of the moon, however, he changed direction and resumed his northward passage. Behind them the hubbub continued, the rebels searching in the wrong direction for something in the water that was no longer there.

By dawn the men were seven miles south of Wilmington. They pulled ashore and hid amid the thick marsh grass and cattails. They spent the day resting and observing; Cushing counted nine steamers cruising past, three of them blockade runners. Later they saw the *Yad-*

kin, the flagship of Flag Officer William Lynch, the commander of all
Confederate naval vessels in the Wilmington area ("a wooden propeller
steamer of about 300 tons; no mast, one smokestack, clear deck. English build, with awning spread fore and aft, and mounting only two
guns. Did not seem to have many men").

Cushing figured that once night fell, he would take the men up to
Wilmington and check out its defenses. As they were about to go, two
small boats came into view, hugging the shore. Cushing first thought
they had been discovered, that this was a Confederate attack. Not so,
just a fishing party, seeking no trouble; Cushing detained them nonetheless. They carried news: the *Raleigh* was gone, done. Days ago—the
day after her wild ride, in fact—she had run aground at high water. As
the tide fell, her bottom had split open, and now she was a toothless
wreck. If Cushing was disappointed that he wasn't going to get the
chance to battle with an ironclad, he didn't show it. Making mischief
in the enemy's backyard, Cushing might have figured, was the next
best thing.

With the fishermen as guides, the Yankees headed farther north
toward Wilmington. Cushing was able to catalog its defenses—earthworks, guns, iron-tipped spikes, three rings of obstructions in total,
backed by a battery of ten naval guns. At Cypress Swamp they located
Mott's Creek, and poled up this shallow stream to a point where it was
crossed by a log road. They followed this rough path for about two miles
until it intersected a turnpike, which one of the fishermen identified as
the main connection between Fort Fisher and Wilmington. The telegraph line above their heads seemed to confirm that.

Inevitably, Cushing figured, someone or something of interest
would come down this path.

CHAPTER 26

High Time We Went

USHING'S MEN, AND HIS CAPTIVES, lay in the high grass, waiting for something, hoping it would show up soon. They were hungry. The sailors had brought two days' worth of rations, confident that some other source of provisions would appear. Now the rations were nearly gone, and nothing appetizing had emerged. And still they waited.

Shortly before midday, a hunter sauntered by. The sailors jumped him, and quickly learned that he was in fact the owner of a general store located about a mile away. Before they could question him further, a horseman clopped into view—a soldier, toting a mailbag. In the face of eight or nine muskets and pistols, he dismounted and surrendered it; it turned out to contain hundreds of letters full of morsels of information about the size of the garrison at Fort Fisher, the state of supplies, and the deployment of the guns.

Next, thoughts turned to food. Howorth suggested a daring plan. He would take the courier's coat, hat, and horse and go to the hunter's general store that, they had learned, was just a mile away. Flush with Confederate money found in the mailbag, he would stock up.

While Howorth went shopping—he eventually returned with chicken, milk, and blueberries, the makings of a tasty picnic that, according to Cushing, "could not be improved in Seceshia"—Cushing and his men continued to detain passersby, questioning them about matters both military and civilian, soaking up any information that could conceivably prove useful. Eventually they were holding twenty-six people. Cushing figured that they would sit there until the afternoon mail carrier bound for Fort Fisher came by, since it was likely that he would be carrying the afternoon newspapers from Wilmington. Just as he at long last appeared, however, he apparently caught a glimpse of a blue jacket, and went racing back to Wilmington. Cushing pursued him for two miles, but never caught up.

Some of Cushing's captives had reported that they heard there were Yankees in the river the night before, but that musket fire from the forts had turned them back. Once the mailman got back to Wilmington, however, they would know that that story, at least the second part of it, wasn't true. There would be signal fires, patrols, extra guards. Rebels up and down the river would be on high alert. It was time to get going.

Cushing ordered the telegraph wire cut, and the whole group began marching out of the swamp. Once they reached the river, he loaded the prisoners in some canoes his men had collected and tied the canoes to the back of the cutter. Setting sail around seven, Cushing led his fleet to an island in the river on which a lighthouse stood. He intended to discharge his captives there, confident that they would be rescued soon, but not too soon. Just as they reached the island, however, a steamer appeared on the horizon; it seemed to be heading right at them. Everyone hid behind the boats, and the ship passed, close enough to hail, seeing nothing in the gloaming. For some reason, Cushing changed his mind about the prisoners, and cut them loose in the canoes without sails or paddles; by the time they were rescued, their news about Yankee raiders would be quite out of date.

Cushing kept a couple of the more notable persons, one of them a pilot from the fishing party, who guided the group to the place where the *Raleigh* had gone down. Cushing then saw with his own eyes that it was true. On a buoy, he affixed a note addressed to Colonel Jones, the

Confederate officer who vowed after Cushing's visit to Smithville in February that no Yankee would ever buzz about the river again.

Morning had not yet broken by the time Cushing's cutter neared the forts above New Inlet, but word of the sailors' presence had been communicated up and down the river. Cushing's expedition to Wilmington was coming down to the final maneuvers, with three outcomes possible: escape, capture, or death.

CHAPTER 27

Zigzag

As Cushing's cutter now drove for the mouth of the river, it overtook a small boat making for shore. It contained four sailors and two women, whom Cushing took into his already overloaded boat. The new prisoners, as though unable to stop themselves, ragged on Cushing: *There are guard boats looking for you. You'll never get past Federal Point. There are seventy-five soldiers in a boat waiting for you.* As though on cue, the moon appeared. Sunrise was still an hour off, but the midday sun could have scarcely lit the little boat in the wide river any more clearly.

Cushing had the tide in his favor. "I concluded to pull boldly for the bar," he reported later, "run foul of the guard-boat, use cutlasses and revolvers and drift by the batteries in that way since they would not fire on their own men." But just five minutes after starting for the channel, the plan failed; a large boat, certainly large enough to hold seventy-five soldiers, loomed ahead. Surrender was out of the question. "We determined to outwit the enemy, or fight it out."

Fight it out, most likely. Twenty yards from the ship, Cushing was planning to stick his cutter's nose into its side when he saw three more boats pull out from the bar on the left, then five more from the right. Too many, Cushing realized; a score of sailors used to the brawling style of shipboard fighting might have overpowered seventy-five soldiers who would be getting in their own way. But nine boats of musketeers?

Quickly he steered the boat to the right, toward the Western Bar Channel. His men pulled hard and in perfect sync, opening precious space between themselves and their pursuers. The rebels were surprised, fumbled with their oars, lost time turning. Had they thought for a moment, they might have realized what Will had already figured out: there would be no escaping that morning through the Western Bar. There was a strong southwest wind, which would be filling the passage with breakers too strong to surmount; he'd be left there, his men straining, his overloaded little boat a perfect, bobbing target for the guns of Fort Caswell. But the rebels didn't think, they reacted, and chased the Yankee cutter, becoming all the more confused when he vanished. "Dashing off with the tide in the direction of Smithville," he reported, "I passed the sailboat, and by my trick of sheering the cutter so as to avoid reflecting the moon's rays, caused the main line of enemy boats to lose sight of her in the swell."

The Confederates were now chasing something in the blue predawn light they could no longer really see. Then Cushing pulled his next maneuver. So furiously were his pursuers chasing him that they neglected to assign someone to protect their rear. The other side of the river had been left entirely undefended. Feeling the pull of the tide and the current under him, Cushing also realized that he was at the point in the channel where the tide split: one channel led back to Fort Caswell, close to where his trip began, and one channel past Fort Fisher to the Atlantic. Cushing called for one more quick turn, and the cutter caught the channel to Fort Fisher; his men then rowed as though they had shifted into some higher gear. Before the Confederates could even grasp what was happening, the cutter was heading in the opposite direction. "That was my time," Cushing remarked later. Leaving the small boats struggling to turn around, the cutter shot ahead and, borne by the current, began opening up distance from the rebel flotilla—thirty yards, fifty yards, a hundred yards—all but vanishing against the horizon. There was a final plunge into the breakers off Caroline Shoals to thwart the gunners at Fort Fisher, and the expedition was over. Cushing hailed the steamer *Cherokee,* which towed the small boat back to the *Monticello.* By mid-afternoon the raiders were in their bunks. Cushing had gone sixty-eight hours without sleep.

Cushing's raid on Smithville was audacious, but bringing home a captain instead of a general still leaves bragging rights with Mosby. Does Cushing's ride around the Cape Fear River rank with Stuart's ride around McClellan? Probably not—1,200 cavaliers galloping on horseback must have been a fairly awesome sight. But the drama of Cushing's escape in a little cutter from a closed area where all eyes are watching, and dozens are gunning for you may offer more in sheer excitement.

CHAPTER 28

Letters from Welles

N O ONE WAS MORE PLEASED with the outcome of Cushing's reconnaissance mission than Gideon Welles. "The boldness exhibited by you in this reconnaissance," he wrote to Cushing on July 14, "and the success attending it are most gratifying to the Department." He offered Cushing an uncommon official benediction, the Thanks of the Navy.

Six weeks later, Welles wrote to Cushing again. This time he was in a very different frame of mind.

One day in July, while on patrol off Wilmington, Cushing in his cabin, the *Monticello* sighted a small brig. Although the ship, the *Hound*, was flying the British flag, the *Monticello* called for her to stop and produce her papers. When the *Hound* kept going, the *Monticello* fired several musket shots across her bow, which brought the ship to a halt and her cursing captain to her deck. Ensign Hadfield of the *Monticello* then boarded the brig; as he checked her papers, he continued to get an earful of profanity from the furious captain, who was angry that his ship, quite obviously not a blockade runner, would receive musket fire, not blanks, and would have its freedom so impinged. Discovering no irregularities, the well-scolded Hadfield let the *Hound* go.

Back on the *Monticello*, Cushing became furious at Hadfield's treatment. That "unnecessarily insolent" captain needed to be stopped again, Will declared, since the insolence might just be a ruse to distract attention from some greater subterfuge.

So they stopped the *Hound* again. This time its profanity-prone captain was brought aboard the *Monticello*. "I took his papers," Will wrote in his report, "telling him I would look them over at my leisure, and he could remain or go aboard his ship as he pleased. He informed me he would remain, with my permission. I inquired what his conduct had been, and he answered by lame excuses and final retraction. I told him that he should see the propriety of apologizing to the boarding officer, and he expressed his willingness to do so. I then examined his papers, and finding them correct, told the captain to proceed." Cushing capped his defense by saying, "A national ship must be treated with respect."

Do tell. The British captain protested strongly to his government, which instructed its minister in Washington to protest to the American secretary of state, who alerted Welles, who contacted Cushing. Will's conduct had clearly been high-handed and insolent and entirely deserving of an apology if not more serious action. What made it worse for his superiors was that it came during a period of tension between the United States and Great Britain. The United States had worked hard and so far successfully to prevent Westminster from recognizing the Confederacy, at the same time raising objections to British firms building Confederate raiders. The *Hound* incident echoed the 1861 *Trent* affair, the previous time the US Navy ignored international rules at the expense of a British ship. The interception of the *Trent* had caused great diplomatic tension. Cushing would have to pay for his insolence.

Gideon Welles's letter this time was a stern and strongly worded rebuke. "The Department fails to find in your explanation any excuse for your disregard of international law and courtesy," Welles wrote. "Something more than the verification of the vessel's papers is apparent in your procedure; a disposition was exhibited . . . to punish the master of the brig for an offense against courtesy." Welles drove to an emphatic conclusion. "I must enjoin upon you to be more cautious in the future. Such proceedings repeated cannot fail to bring upon you the serious displeasure of your Government and result to your regret and injury."*

Cushing never received a letter like that again.

---

* In a letter to Secretary Seward about the event, Welles was rather less severe. "Lieutenant Cushing is quite young, which fact may be pleaded in extenuation of his improper conduct," he wrote. "The Department regrets the occurrence and hopes it may not find cause again to censure one of its officers for failing to observe international law and courtesy."

CHAPTER 29

The Coming

ONTHS BEFORE THE *Virginia* had her great day of glory rampaging through the wooden ships of Hampton Roads, the rebel secretary of the navy Stephen Mallory was dreaming ironclad dreams. The way to nullify the North's advantage in ships, he maintained, could be expressed with three words: Get More Ironclads. Mallory planned to build or convert larger ironclads in the shipyards near the ocean; to build smaller, more maneuverable ironclad ships in river ports; and to buy ironclads abroad.

The vision of an ironclad fleet never worked out. The South lacked industrial capacity. Prior to the start of the war, it produced only a tenth of America's industrial goods; it had only a tenth of the country's industrial workers. It did not have sufficient deposits of iron ore, or the capacity to mine what it had. Foundries were few, and the railroad system far more limited. Often when travelers moved between states, they had to change trains at the border because the track gauges changed, requiring everyone and everything to unload and reboard.

But the North had everything. Once the US Navy lost its ironclad skepticism, it built dozens of monitors and deployed them in harbors and rivers throughout the South. Forced to react to a changing dynamic, the Confederacy rushed its response. The result was a hodgepodge of bad outcomes: unfinished ships, poorly built ships, behind-schedule

Midshipman William Barker Cushing, ca. 1860. "His restless, active mind was filled with zeal to accomplish something," observed Secretary of the Navy Gideon Welles. *(Nimitz Library, United States Naval Academy)*

Lieutenant Alonzo Cushing (standing, center), Will's brother, with fellow artillery officers at Antietam, Maryland, 1862. *(Library of Congress)*

Cushing's teacher, confidant, and mentor, Lieutenant Commander Charles Flusser set an example that helped Will mature into a leader. Flusser's death in battle against the *Albemarle* added a personal element to Cushing's exploit. "I shall never rest," said Cushing, "until I have avenged his death." *(Naval History and Heritage Command)*

Lieutenant William Barker Cushing, USN, in a photo for a carte de visite attributed to Mathew Brady. Neither the photo's date nor which of Brady's studios (New York or Washington) produced the image is available, but the three stripes on Cushing's sleeve are the insignia of a lieutenant, the rank he held from July 1862 to October 1864, when he would not yet have turned twenty-two. His lean and weathered appearance suggests that this picture was taken while he was on leave after a period of active duty. *(National Archives and Records Administration)*

Lieutenant Commander James Cooke of the Confederate navy not only made important contributions to the construction of the *Albemarle,* but captained the ship in two battles with federal ships, and during the battle of Plymouth. More than anyone, he recognized the ship's vulnerabilities, and resigned his post. *(Naval History and Heritage Command)*

This drawing, *Wood Versus Iron*, depicts the battle that took place on May 6, 1864, in which the *Albemarle* engaged seven US warships and fought them to a draw. The artist, Acting Second Engineer Alexander C. Stuart, USN, was present at the scene. "She is too strong for us," said one navy officer after the engagement. *(Naval History and Heritage Command)*

"Cushing's Daring and Successful Exploit," an illustration credited to Bacon for the 1907 book *Deeds of Valor*, does a good job of showing the relative sizes of *Picket Boat No. 1* and the *Albemarle*. *(Naval History and Heritage Command)*

"Lt. Cushing's Torpedo Boat Sinking the Albemarle," an engraving credited to A. Stachic, was published in Edward Shippen's 1898 book *Naval Battles of America*. The artist took the unusual approach of imagining Cushing and his crew abandoning ship after detonating the torpedo. *(Naval History and Heritage Command)*

The naval assault on Fort Fisher. "Board the fort in a seaman-like way," Admiral Porter ordered his ill-prepared sailors. Print by L. Prang and Co., 1887. *(United States Naval Academy)*

Admiral David Dixon Porter and his staff aboard his flagship, the *Malvern*, in December 1864. The thickly bearded Porter stands near center; Cushing, fresh from his triumph over the *Albemarle*, is at far left. *(Library of Congress)*

Katherine Forbes Cushing, in a photograph that may have been taken for her wedding. "Oh Kate, dear darling Kate!" Will wrote during their long engagement. "All my hopes are bound upon you." *(Naval History and Heritage Command)*

The Sinking of the Albemarle, illustration by C. E. Monroe Jr., for *Life* magazine, which published it in the January 6, 1961, issue. Along with the drama of the event, Monroe brilliantly captures Cushing's conspicuous heroism. *(Courtesy C. E. Monroe III)*

projects. Of the thirty-five ironclads that the Confederacy produced, only a third actually engaged in combat with Union ships; others were underemployed as floating batteries or mine layers, an acknowledgment that they were unusable as warships and that the huge investment made in building them had to be amortized, if only a little, with other uses. The poorly built *North Carolina* never fought, and broke up in the Cape Fear River. The *Raleigh* had her single foray in 1864, and sank. The *Neuse* ran aground, shelled some Yankee troops, and then was destroyed to prevent capture. The *Columbia* ran aground on the day she was commissioned, and was lost. The well-built *Atlanta* fought one engagement with federal ships in Wassaw Sound, Georgia, and was damaged, run aground, and finally captured. Others—the *Tennessee*, the *Arkansas*, the *Palmetto State*, the *Chicora*, and, of course, the *Virginia*—lasted longer or did more damage in abbreviated careers. None was more successful than the *Albemarle*; none had to overcome more challenges in its path to existence.

In the latter half of 1861, the Confederate navy began casting about for regional shipyards where vessels could be built, especially in North Carolina. The swamps and dense forests between the state's twisty rivers would make it difficult for the Union army to move about the interior with ease; if the Yankees hoped to establish a blockade and sever the supply lines to Virginia, they would have to hold the rivers. And therefore on the rivers they would have to be stopped.

William Martin was a lawyer and the owner of a shipbuilding company on the Pasquotank River town of Elizabeth City, North Carolina. In 1851, on his thirty-eighth birthday, a man named Gilbert Elliott died, leaving behind a wife and five children. William's relationship to Gilbert is not known, but he took an interest in the future of Gilbert's very bright seven-year-old son, his third and youngest child, also named Gilbert. By the time young Gilbert turned eighteen, he was not only a clerk in William's law office, but he was helping to run the shipbuilding business as well.

When the war broke out, William became a colonel in the Seventeenth Regiment of North Carolina Troops, and he left young Gilbert in charge of all his affairs. Soon William was taken as a prisoner of war, but before that happened, he arranged for Gilbert to meet Stephen Mallory. The Confederate naval secretary wanted to build ships at Martin's yard. Gilbert tried to explain how small and inexperienced they were, but Mallory and his aides were insistent, mostly because they had few alternatives. In January 1862 they gave him a contract to build three gunboats.

The following month, however, the federals captured Roanoke Island and, soon after, Elizabeth City as well. That put a stop to shipbuilding at that site; Elliott relocated to a spot near the shipbuilding center of Norfolk, where he could continue work on his naval contracts, but in May Norfolk fell. Out of options, Elliott enlisted in the infantry.

Stephen Mallory wouldn't hear of it. He believed that young Elliott had special talents. He persuaded Gilbert to go back to North Carolina and build an ironclad in Tarboro, on the Tar River. Elliott then made a counteroffer: *I'll build a ram on the Tar, but why don't I build another one somewhere along the Roanoke River?* Mallory not only agreed, but sent Elliott help, a naval officer, Lieutenant Commander James W. Cooke. A thirty-three-year veteran of the US Navy, Lieutenant Cooke resigned when the war began and took command of the CSS *Ellis*, a small ship that was part of the so-called Mosquito fleet. In a hard fight near Elizabeth City in February 1862, Cooke defended the *Ellis* with cutlass drawn, until he was wounded and captured. He was later paroled and returned to the fight; so was the *Ellis*, in a way. She was turned over to Lieutenant William Cushing, who fought her gallantly until she ran aground in the New River Inlet in November 1862.

Cooke soon put his stamp on the project, finally securing a long-delayed iron shipment. He then dedicated himself to the zealous collection of scrap, earning himself the nickname "The Ironmonger Captain."

In March, Elliott secured a place to build the ship: a cornfield near Halifax, in a place called Edwards Ferry. Conditions were primitive: no pulleys or derricks or machine tools. Little by little, however, what once seemed ridiculous began to seem real. First a sawmill was built, then a toolshed. Trees were felled, beams were cut, then a hull began to rise from the ground. By June, the developing hull was attracting the attention of the neighbors and other curious parties. At least one loose-lipped worker, Michael Cohen, a onetime plumber and gas fitter, shared what he'd been doing with Union sympathizers.

Based on this information, Charlie Flusser was able to send his superiors a sketch of the vessel's cross section, along with the information that she was built on the plan of the *Merrimack*. By early fall Admiral Lee updated the report, emphasizing that Flusser thought that the ship under construction was "a formidable affair."

The navy was concerned. Had the Roanoke been deep enough, the navy would have sent gunboats up the river and torched Edwards Ferry. Instead, they asked for the army's help. Only a small detachment would be necessary, Flusser argued, no more than a hundred cavalry. The army said it didn't have the troops. The argument went to the cabinet heads; Gideon Welles warned Edwin Stanton that the construction of an ironclad suggested that the rebels were planning to attack Plymouth, in which case the navy would be facing the ironclad only with wooden ships. In the meantime, the Ironmonger Captain collected 450 tons of scrap and arranged to have it shipped to the Tredegar Iron Works in Richmond and the Clarendon Foundry at Wilmington to be rolled into plates.

But as the summer of 1863 gave way to autumn and autumn to winter, the urgency ebbed. In the midst of a quiet winter, General Benjamin Butler, who parlayed his successful collaboration with Silas Stringham against forts Hatteras and Clark in 1861 into command of all army forces in the Carolinas, wrote to Admiral Lee: "I do not much believe in the ram."

CHAPTER 30

Rampage

BUTLER'S FATUOUS DISBELIEF NOTWITHSTANDING, the ram took shape in the Halifax cornfield. As the winter came to an end, the Confederacy began envisioning how to use her. Though no one in the Richmond government would officially admit it, the possibility of outright victory over the Union ended with Gettysburg. Now the South's best hope was to outlast the North, to prolong the war with the idea that northern voters, frustrated with a standoff, would turn Lincoln out in the fall presidential election and choose a candidate who would negotiate peace. To that end, rebel armies stepped up operations outside Virginia, believing that successes in other theaters would force Washington to reassign some of its troops, reducing pressure on General Lee.

North Carolina assumed a prime focus of interest; short-term successes there would relieve Lee in Virginia; larger successes might disrupt the blockade, with material benefits to strengthen the rebel armies and rejuvenate southern morale. Moreover, success might be obtained without a large number of troops. Sliced by so many rivers, North Carolina was a place where relatively small combined army-navy operations might deliver outsized successes.

At the suggestion of General Lee, the first effort was made on February 1, 1864, against New Bern, which had been in Union hands since

General Butler occupied it in March 1862. After almost two years, the town was lightly defended: just two federal regiments, along with three or four Union gunboats, were based there. Lee's idea was to send General George Pickett and his division down from Virginia to lead one phase of the attack. Pickett's soldiers would distract the Union garrison and enable approximately 250 Confederate sailors and marines under Captain John Taylor Wood to row down the Neuse River in a dozen small boats and attack the federal gunboats. Grandson of President Zachary Taylor and nephew of Jefferson Davis, Wood, thirty-three, was a Cushing-like character. He had fought on the *Virginia* at Hampton Roads, seized seven Yankee ships in raids, and held the rank of colonel in the cavalry.

The attack did not go well. Pickett split his forces into three groups, each assigned to seize a Union position. Although each group enjoyed a manpower advantage, two of the commanders called off the attacks as soon as they were met by artillery fire. Wood's assault achieved total surprise, including that of Wood himself, who found only one federal gunboat in port. After a fierce fight, the rebels took the ship, but Wood's hope of seizing it faded when he learned that the ship's fires had been banked; it would take an hour to build up enough steam to sail away. When he discovered that the ship was also chained to a buoy, he gave up and torched it. Wood desperately wanted to return and take another crack at the base, but Pickett felt that they had lost the advantage of surprise.

The raid on New Bern failed, but went well enough to tease Richmond's imagination about other actions in North Carolina, notably Plymouth, on the Roanoke River. Ousting the Yankees wouldn't be easy; the Union army had held the town for two years, and had improved its fortifications. But if the *Albemarle* was ready, she could sit imperviously in the middle of the river and with her big guns smash what the Yankees had spent two years constructing. And the *Albemarle* was nearly ready.

Around the first of April, Cooke brought her down twenty miles from Edwards Ferry to the town of Hamilton. Soon after, General Robert Hoke, commander of the Confederate land forces in the area, paid Cooke a visit. Only twenty-six, Hoke commanded a regiment in the Army of Northern Virginia, and had fought with distinction at nearly every major battle between Big Bethel and Chancellorsville. He admired what he saw: the ship was 158 feet long, 35 feet in the beam, and 8 feet deep, built of solid yellow pine, and covered in two layers of two-inch iron plate. She had two engines of 200 horsepower each, a pair of 6.4-inch Brooke rifles, and a sharpened, iron-plated prow to be used as a ram.

Though highly impressed, Hoke knew of the Confederacy's disappointing record with ironclads. He had been ordered to attack Plymouth on April 18, and he was going to be betting the lives of his men that this untested ship and its untested crew would be able to clear the river of Yankee gunboats and offer supporting fire. "We will attack whether you are there or not," Hoke said. Cooke assured him that the ship would be ready, "in fifteen days, with ten additional mechanics." After they broke up, Hoke helped Cooke round up the needed workers.

On April 17, Cooke launched the *Albemarle*. She still wasn't ready, not completely. Even as the ship began her trip down the Roanoke, her deck was crowded with armor plates, portable forges, and carpenters and blacksmiths, who continued their labors almost all the way to Plymouth. The workers could do nothing for the steering, however. The river was full of twists and turns and the spring current was strong, but the ship's handling was often unresponsive and Cooke had to be careful. At one point he concluded that he needed to slow things down, so he turned the ship around, steered it stern-first, and dragged a heavy chain behind to increase his control. Six hours were lost when the main driveshaft came loose and had to be repaired; almost immediately thereafter the rudder head broke, costing four hours more.

Three miles above Plymouth, near Thoroughfare Gap, the *Albemarle* came to anchor; there were reports that the Union navy had blocked the way with mines, sunken hulks, and other obstructions. The ship's builder, Gilbert Elliott—the man who had nurtured her through many obstacles—had tagged along on this maiden voyage, and he volunteered to examine the apparent impasse. Venturing forward with three other men in a small boat, he determined that there were still ten feet of water above the obstacles, enough for the ship to get through.

Slowly, Cooke proceeded. He was now more than ten hours behind schedule, and he was concerned that he had missed Hoke's attack; from reports Cooke was hearing from the shore, he pieced together that Hoke had launched his assault on Plymouth, but called it off when he came under fire from four federal warships, the *Miami*, the *Southfield*, the *Bombshell*, and the *Whitehead*. The *Bombshell* suffered damage during the battle and pulled away, Cooke learned, but the others were still patrolling the river.

After the *Albemarle* passed the obstacles, she received fire from two Union outposts, which she ignored, intent as she was on finding the federal ships. Shortly after four a.m. on April 19, they found each other. The *Albemarle* was spotted by the *Whitehead*, which was serving picket duty. Easy prey for the *Albemarle*, she turned and sped downriver for all she was worth. The *Albemarle* chased, firing as she went.

Suddenly, there were the Yankee ships *Miami* and *Southfield*, two big, double-ended side-wheel steamers, lashed together "with long spars, and with chains festooned between them." The aim of the chains was to trap the beast and nullify its ram, and then, with the *Albemarle* wrapped up, either blast her apart with close-range bombardments or board the ship and fight it out. It was a good strategy, but after thirty years, few tricks were unfamiliar to Cooke; besides, he had confidence in his armor. He steamed on, hugging the south shore, then veered into the middle of the channel. "All ahead full!" Cooke ordered, aiming his 376-ton vessel for the chains that were supposed to hold him. He didn't make a perfectly clean job of it and glanced off the *Miami*, then banged into the *Southfield*, delivering a lethal blow with his ram, which ripped a ten-foot gash in her hull that ran all the way to her fireroom. It was a powerful strike—too powerful. Although Cooke reversed engines immediately, the ship was stuck, and as the *Southfield* began going under, she held the beak in her innards. The *Albemarle's* bow sank so low that water poured into her portholes. Victor and victim seemed equally doomed, but just then the *Southfield* touched bottom and rolled over, freeing the ram. The *Albemarle* bobbed back to the surface.

The collision snapped most of the fastenings between the *Miami* and the *Southfield*, which freed the *Miami* to maneuver alongside the *Southfield* and start taking on its surviving crew. At the same time, she maintained a furious bombardment, as though the sheer will of the Union gunners could push the shells through the iron plating. Shot after shot struck its target, only to fall harmlessly away, leaving mocking half-moon dents in the plate. When the *Miami* could get no closer, her commander took charge of one of the nine-inch Dahlgrens and, personally pulling the lanyard, pumped three explosive shells point-blank into the behemoth, now not twenty feet away. The first two shattered futilely against the armor, but the third bounced straight back and landed at the feet of the captain, lanyard still in hand. Then it exploded, blowing him to pieces.

The captain of the *Miami* was Charlie Flusser.

The ships briefly were positioned so closely that the Union sailors stood at the rails, poised to board the *Albemarle* and settle the contest hand-to-hand, but Cooke maneuvered his cumbersome craft, not only thwarting that threat, but positioning her to begin shelling the *Miami* again. With boarding no longer a possibility, Lieutenant Charles French, the commander of the *Southfield* who was now in charge of the *Miami*, pulled back, perhaps deciding that he didn't want to lose two ships in one morning. Gilbert Elliott's cornfield ironclad owned the day.

After quick repairs, Cooke coordinated with Hoke, and the two began a joint bombardment of the Union positions in Plymouth. "This terrible fire had to be endured without reply," wrote the Union commander, Colonel Henry Wessells, "as no man could live at the guns." He surrendered the next day, leaving the Confederates at least 1,600 prisoners, twenty-five pieces of artillery, and two hundred tons of valuable anthracite coal. On the naval front, the loss of the *Southfield* and the numerous casualties on the two Union ships were incurred at the cost of a single rebel sailor, whose mother apparently never told him not to stick his head out of a porthole during a battle lest he get shot.

Will Cushing took the news about Flusser's death hard. "I shall never rest," he said, "until I have avenged his death."

CHAPTER 31

Too Strong

T HERE WAS A NEW BULLY on THE ROANOKE. The *Albemarle* strutted around what was once again a Confederate river, barges or tenders tagging along after her like hero-wor-/ shipping schoolboys. Occasionally she would round a bend and there, within her line of sight, would be a federal gunboat that would quickly slink away.

The *Albemarle*'s victory changed the balance of power in North Carolina. Despite warnings from Flusser and others about the *Albemarle*'s progress, Washington never made developing the capability to stop an ironclad in Carolina waters a priority. The navy had failed on numerous occasions to bring a monitor over the bar into the sound, and now it was too late to build one on-site. The distraught federals had no answers. "The ram has possession of the river," Commander H. K. Davenport wrote to Admiral Lee, begging for reinforcements. "The ram will probably come down to Roanoke Island, Washington and New Bern," reported the district commander, General John Peck, whom Will Cushing had called "granny," here at his timorous best. "Unless we are immediately and heavily reinforced, by both the army and the navy, North Carolina is inevitably lost."

Although the rebels did not match Peck's panic with commensurate arrogance, they, too, began thinking again of taking New Bern. General Beauregard, now the commander of all troops in North Carolina, developed a plan similar to the one Hoke used so successfully in Plymouth—bring the *Neuse*, an ironclad moored upriver in Kinston, and use it in a two-pronged assault against New Bern. The *Neuse* had run aground in her maiden voyage and could not be refloated, forcing Beauregard to cancel his plan. But now the *Albemarle* was on hand, just sixty miles away. Beauregard's mind whirred. Could Cooke and Hoke repeat their success at New Bern?

Though reluctant, Cooke agreed. Although the *Albemarle* had proven to be a better vessel than he had expected, Beauregard's plan required him to take the ship across Albemarle Sound, through Croatan Sound off Roanoke Island, across Pamlico Sound to the mouth of the Neuse River, a route much longer than sixty miles, and one larded with federal torpedoes, batteries, and ships. But he would try.

Bereft of ideas, Admiral Lee did the leaderly thing and brought in an expert, Captain Melancton Smith, a fifty-four-year-old veteran with thirty-eight years of naval service. He commanded one of the ships that brought the ram *Manassas* to heel in 1862, though the lesson of that experience was that the most effective strategy was to get your opponent to run aground. Still, Smith collected the best advice the navy had accumulated during its short experience battling ironclads, and passed it along to the captains in the sound: fight from close quarters; load your guns with extra-heavy charges; put fire onto the ram's ports, stern, and roof; and try to drop a shell down its smokestack. He might as well have added, try to go into battle in a state of grace, so that when the ram kills you, you can go straight to heaven.

In the afternoon of May 5, the *Albemarle* began her trip to New Bern, accompanied by two smaller ships, the *Bombshell*, which had been captured at Plymouth, carrying provisions and coal, and the *Cotton Plant*, which would carry troops for the assault on New Bern. The voyage was taking place about a week earlier than originally planned;

Confederate spies got word that Union spies had learned of the launch date, so Cooke concluded that his best chance to achieve surprise was to leave immediately.

Leaving the mouth of the Roanoke, the Confederates spotted about ten Union ships, including a trio of gunboats, the *Ceres*, the *Commodore Hull*, and the *Whitehead*, laying torpedoes (or what we would call mines). Once they saw the *Albemarle*, the ships scattered like birds, the gunboats all making a run for the sound, a federal stronghold. Cooke decided to give chase to the eminently sinkable gunboats and had nearly caught them when, much to his surprise, they turned about and faced him. Quickly they were joined by four other ships: the repaired *Miami* and three large, formidable cruisers, the *Sassacus*, the *Wyalusing*, and ironclad expert Melancton Smith's flagship, the *Mattabesett*. Smartly, the ships formed parallel lines about a half mile apart, and moved toward the *Albemarle*. In the battle of the spies, it would appear the Union agent got the last word.

Seven to one seemed like fair odds to Cooke. He ordered the vulnerable *Bombshell* and the *Cotton Plant* back to Plymouth, and around 4:40 p.m. ordered his Brooke rifles to fire on the *Mattabesett*'s pivot gun.

Smith's plan soon made itself known. The three cruisers were to come down on either side of the *Albemarle*, lay broadside into her, and then swing around and repeat as necessary. The *Commodore Hull* had a skein that it would try to place under the *Albemarle* in hopes of befouling its propeller, and the *Miami* had a spar torpedo that it would try to place under the *Albemarle*'s hull and detonate. The smaller ships were to engage any support ships accompanying the ironclad.

The *Wyalusing*, *Sassacus*, and *Mattabesett* were big, rugged steamers carrying fourteen, ten, and nine guns respectively. They circled the ironclad, letting go at a distance of about a hundred yards with the very best shells the vaunted Yankee munitions industry could produce. The shells scored direct hits. And they had no effect.

From atop the second deck of the *Sassacus*, Edgar Holden, a navy surgeon, had a privileged view. "The guns may as well have fired blank cartridges, for the shot skimmed off into the air," Holden later wrote. "The feeling of helplessness that comes from the failure of heavy guns to make any mark on an advancing ironclad can never be described. One is like a man with a bodkin before a Gorgon or a Dragon, a man with straws before the wheels of Juggernaut." And yet the Union sailors fought through their frustration. Their task was challenging: the ships had to get close but not too close lest they fall victim to the ram, had to lay down heavy fire but not so heavy as to endanger Union vessels facing the opposite side of the *Albemarle*.

Cooke knew he couldn't sit there and endure the shelling in perpetuity. Holes were appearing in his smokestack, which would eventually limit his ability to draw air for his engines. Some of the armored plates were chipping away; eventually this could create a fatal opening. A well-aimed shell chopped about twenty inches off one of the ironclad's guns, although the men kept using it. Sooner or later, something would yield.

The break came when the *Sassacus* went after the *Bombshell*, which somehow had missed the order to retreat. Suddenly the *Sassacus* found herself about four hundred yards away from the *Albemarle*. Forgetting the *Bombshell*, the captain of the *Sassacus*, Lieutenant Commander Francis Roe, a forty-one-year-old graduate of the Naval Academy who had already distinguished himself fighting with Farragut at New Orleans, suddenly realized that his ship was ideally positioned to ram the *Albemarle*, which at the moment was broadside to him and engaged with the *Mattabesett*. Roe seized the opportunity. "Give her all the steam she can carry!" Roe ordered the engineer, then told the master's mate to aim the ship for the point where the *Albemarle*'s casemate met its hull. The crew was ordered to lie down, the better to absorb the coming impact. "Straight as an arrow we shot forward and struck full and square on the iron hull, careening it over and tearing away our own bows, ripping and straining our timbers at the water-line," wrote Dr. Holden.

The crash was stupendous. Gilbert Elliott recalled that the impact caused "every timber within the vicinity to groan, though none gave way." Still, the effect was less than Roe had hoped; the *Sassacus* just missed the casemate, and now the federal steamer was lying atop the *Albemarle*'s hull, while her side wheel continued to grind the ship forward, pushing on the ironclad's afterdeck and forcing it several feet below water. Water poured in through the *Albermarle*'s open starboard port, creating confusion among the Confederate sailors, who couldn't tell if the ship had been compromised. "Stand to your guns," Cooke ordered. "If we must sink, let us go down like brave men."

As soon as the Confederates realized that the *Sassacus* was stuck, the *Albemarle*'s gun crews acted swiftly to remove her. Firing into the Yankee ship from a distance of ten feet, they rocketed a shell that went into the ship on one side and out the other. The Union sailors responded with grenades, but met no success. Confederate gunners then put a second hundred-pound shot right into the *Sassacus*'s starboard boiler, sending scalding steam through the ship. Moments later, with dozens of men blistered and burned, the *Sassacus* floated free and drifted away. An Ensign Meyer, who fired the pivot gun "incessantly" during the battle, sometimes muzzle-to-muzzle with the ram's, kept shooting until the ship was finally out of range.

Once the *Sassacus* disengaged, all the other Union ships attacked, and a kind of free-for-all pertained. ("[The ships] appeared to be ignorant of all signals," Smith said in his report, "as they answered without obeying.") The *Miami* tried to detonate her torpedo, but she handled poorly, and the men couldn't plant the thing. The *Commodore Hull*'s skein failed. The *Wyalusing* unloosed yet another futile broadside.

This might have continued indefinitely, but the ironclad's Achilles' heel proved to be her unarmored smokestack, which had become so badly shot up that it was impossible to keep up pressure in the boiler. Reaching New Bern now was not feasible; Cooke wasn't sure that he would have enough draw to get back to Plymouth, and he didn't want to run out of power entirely and sit helplessly as the Yankees rammed the *Albemarle* to pieces. He pulled his ship away; before he got back home, the rebels would be throwing bacon, lard, and butter into the boiler to generate steam. But though she was leaving the field, the *Albemarle* had won the day. She had taken on seven Union ships and fought them to a draw. She had received nearly six hundred shots, had been rammed, and continued to fight.

"She is too strong for us," said Lieutenant Commander Roe.

CHAPTER 32

Proceed to New York

THROUGH THE MONTH OF JUNE, the goal of destroying the *Albemarle* became topic A among the officers and men of the North Atlantic Blockading Squadron, and within the Navy Department in Washington. Everybody had a plan, and nobody had a plan. Commander Davenport called for more ships; Admiral Lee refused, citing the pointlessness of sacrificing more wooden ships. Gus Fox asked John Ericsson to reexamine the chances of getting a monitor over the bar into the sound; Ericsson replied that they all drew too much water. After a coal heaver named Baldwin and four mates from the *Wyalusing* went upriver in a dinghy and almost set torpedoes under the *Albemarle* before being spotted, Melancton Smith proposed sending a tug to torpedo the beast, but he had no idea how to get the tug close enough to plant the bomb. Only one plan seemed feasible: some kind of small boat attack, like the one the dashing John Taylor Wood pulled off that had been the only successful part of Pickett's attack on New Bern. But who would be the Union's John Taylor Wood? Welles and Fox favored Commander Stephen Clegg Rowan. The fifty-six-year-old native Dubliner had served courageously throughout the war, and seemed just the man. They offered him command of the expedition. "With the conviction begotten of long experience," he declined.

Thus did the triumphant spring of the *Albemarle* pass into summer, and still the navy had no answer to the metal monster that had thwarted all comers. One day at the beginning of July, Admiral Lee sat in his cabin on the *Minnesota* catching up on paperwork. After reading Cushing's report of his resourceful reconnaissance of the Cape Fear River, an idea came to him. "Bring me Lieutenant Cushing," Lee said to his adjutant. "I've got some work for him."

Meanwhile, the Confederates sidelined the weapon the Union feared the most, and for which it had no response.

Many months had passed since the South tasted victory, and an even longer time since it felt that momentum was swinging its way. The *Albemarle*'s victory in the Roanoke lifted spirits throughout the South, and encouraged demoralized southerners: if they could build an ironclad in a cornfield that could stand toe-to-toe with seven Yankee ships, then independence was still possible.

Perhaps the only man in the South whom the *Albemarle* didn't inspire was its captain, James Cooke. Make that outgoing captain; Cooke's health had been tested by the two desperate and prolonged battles he had waged, and he felt that his time of usefulness had reached an end. In the same way that the battles had forced Cooke to recognize his own shortcomings, he also saw the *Albemarle*'s. "[She] draws too much water to navigate the sounds well, and has not sufficient buoyancy," he wrote to Mallory. "She is very slow and not easily managed." He explained the *Sassacus* problem—the *Albemarle*'s low decks allowed other vessels to come onto her and push her underwater. It was a perceptive analysis; his recommended remedy—build a new and better ironclad along the Roanoke—was a practical impossibility.

The Confederate government then moved in opposite directions at once. It replaced Cooke with Commander John Maffitt, who as captain of the commerce raider CSS *Florida* had captured twenty-three Yankee prizes. Maffitt was an energetic and even heroic figure, and his new command was a powerful and awesome ship—and they were not going to be allowed to fight. "The loss of the gunboat which you command would be irreparable and productive of ruin to the interests of the Government, particularly in this State and district, and indeed would be a heavy blow to the whole country," wrote General Laurence Baker. And so they patrolled the Roanoke River, the enterprising officer and the beast of a ship, symbolizing the South's defiance while doing little more aggressive than swatting flies. One day in August, Maffitt took his ship out and, to his surprise, encountered the Union gunboat *Chicopee* and some smaller vessels. The *Chicopee* offered battle, but as a crowd of spectators lined the banks, the *Albemarle* pulled away. A month later, the ironclad captured and burned the *Fawn*, a federal mail boat. Such small prey seemed almost beneath its dignity. Maffitt soon left the *Albemarle* to command the blockade runner *Owl*. The *Albemarle*'s new captain, Alexander Warley, had commanded the CSS *Manassas*, a humpbacked ram that was run aground and destroyed in the battle of forts Jackson and Philip in the Mississippi in April 1862.

BY LATE SUMMER Will had met with Admiral Lee and proposed two plans. One would be a classic cutting-out expedition: take eighty men up through the swamps and attack the ship with pistols and grenades, overpower the crew, loose the ship, and bring the beast back to the Union fleet. The other would be a torpedo attack, using some small vessel—a tug or an India-rubber boat or a swift steam barge—fitted with a torpedo, accompanied by another vessel or two for support. Lee sent Will to Washington to present the plans to Gus Fox.

Fox hated the idea of a raid. He didn't think it would work, and he thought it would get everybody killed. He kept turning the proposal around in his head, but those two opinions remained the same: the odds of success were long, the odds of calamity short. But two other facts also remained unchanged. First, something needed to be done about that damn ship. And second, nothing he had said about the danger of the mission or the likelihood of success had reduced young Mr. Cushing's enthusiasm and determination one whit.

On July 28, 1864, Will received a note from Gideon Welles. "Proceed to New York and report to Rear-Admiral Gregory, who will assist you in the purchase of a suitable tug and India rubber boat."

CHAPTER 33

No One Else

S ITTING IN HIS OFFICE at the headquarters of the Brooklyn
Navy Yard, forty-six-year-old engineer William W. Wood was
surprised to find knocking at his door a young lieutenant—"a
mere youth"—who was seeking Wood's advice. "He stated to me, in
strict confidence, that he was North on a secret mission, under the
sanction of the Honorable Secretary of the Navy," Wood recalled, "the
object being to cut out or destroy the rebel ironclad *Albemarle*." Wood,
then in the nineteenth year of a distinguished career that would see
him become the navy's engineer in chief, had been spending nearly
all of his time working on ironclads—how to build better ones for the
navy, how to destroy the ones built for the rebels. He agreed to help
out the youth.

Under Wood's guidance, Will abandoned the idea of a tug or an
India-rubber boat in favor of some cutters Wood knew were being built
for picket duty. These open launches were about thirty feet long, with
small engines, and propelled by a screw. Capable of carrying the men
Will required, they also had a twelve-pound howitzer affixed to the
bow. Wood also introduced Will to Assistant Engineer George W.
Melville, who demonstrated a torpedo and spar device that had been
the invention of Engineer John L. Lay.

Torpedoes (mines) had been used in other wars, but came into widespread use during the Civil War. Part of the Confederate effort to wage asymmetrical warfare, torpedoes were wooden or metal containers filled with gunpowder that exploded on contact or were detonated by a human operative. The Confederates deployed thousands of them, enjoying limited success, although the sinking of the *Tecumseh* in Mobile Bay via a torpedo in August 1864 inspired Admiral Farragut's famous line, "Damn the torpedoes! Full speed ahead!"

Though floating torpedoes were dangerous, they were poor offensive weapons because they could not be directed. Using a spar, or pole, to help place the thing where it could do most damage was considered a great leap forward, even though using a spar was dangerous and unreliable. Successful deployment and detonation required a lot of practice—and luck. Two lines were connected to the torpedo. One detached the torpedo from the spar, the other detonated it once it was placed under or floated under the target. The lines had to be handled delicately and pulled at precisely the correct moment. If they were pulled too early or too tightly, the charge would explode prematurely.

Will took a ship onto the Hudson River and blew up several torpedoes; he pronounced the device acceptable. Later he would say that it "had many defects and I would not again attempt its use," but at the time he thought it was fine, perhaps because he never figured he would use the thing. His plan was to cut the *Albemarle* out.

Will purchased two of the picket boats and sent them to North Carolina on September 22 in the hands of his ensigns, William Howorth and Andrew Stockholm. Meanwhile, with Gus Fox's implicit permission, Will went home for a visit.

For a young man who had often professed how much he loathed the town where he grew up, Will returned to Fredonia in tremendous spirits. Visiting a cousin's house, he directed his horse up the porch steps and into the kitchen, grandiosely announcing "I've come to call" above the shrieks and laughter of the children. But soon it became clear that his gregariousness was a thin veneer. Will Cushing was quieter now than anyone could remember. His manner may have seemed strange, but it wasn't incomprehensible: he had seen a lot of war, and his fighting wasn't done.

He visited, he caught up, he accepted condolences for Alonzo. One night friends threw him a party. At the end of the evening, Will surprised everyone by taking the forward step of asking a young lady for a personal keepsake. Explaining that "It's a custom of the old navy," he kissed the hand of young Mary Colman and, as the room watched in silence, he reached behind her neck and unclasped a gold chain and pendant, which he then fastened around his own. He liked the girl—they'd seen each other a few times during the visit—but he barely knew her.

The next morning, cold and bright in the western New York autumn, he harnessed the family carriage and took his mother for a ride. Pausing at a vantage point overlooking the rolling red- and gold-leafed Arkwright hills, he told Elizabeth of the terrible Confederate ironclad called the *Albemarle* that had seized control of the Roanoke River. It had sunk two federal warships in one encounter and smashed up seven others in another, and now threatened to wreck the Union blockade of the Carolina coast. But he had a plan, Cushing said, and despite the many warnings he had received about the extreme hazards of such a mission, he intended to take two small boats up the river to where the *Albemarle* was berthed at Plymouth and capture the vessel, or failing that, sink her.

"I don't understand all of this," Elizabeth Cushing angrily replied. Almost fifteen years a widow, she had one son dead on the field at Gettysburg, and three others in uniform serving at one place or another. Now the youngest of them, the one who had already done more than his share of fighting, was telling her that with a handful of men in two light wooden boats he expected to take on a murderous metal Goliath and succeed where nine ships and a thousand men had already failed.

"I will succeed, Mama," he said, "or you will have no Will Cushing."

If the last phrase was meant to convey a confident insouciance, it failed miserably. "I still don't see why it has to be you," she said harshly.

"Because there's no one else," Cushing replied. Then he asked his mother to join him in prayer.

CHAPTER 34

In Case of Failure

U SING CANALS AND INLAND WATERWAYS, ensigns Howorth
and Stockholm headed south—New Brunswick, the Delaware and Raritan Canal, the Chesapeake and Delaware
Canal, the Chesapeake Bay. At Point Lookout, at the southern tip of
Maryland, Stockholm experienced engine trouble. Howorth pushed on
for Fort Monroe, while Stockholm, in the face of a harsh wind, held up
for the night at Reason Creek, in the Great Wicomico Bay. There he
was spotted by a unit of the home guard, a group of pro-Confederacy
irregulars. Stockholm tried to escape, but he and his crew were captured, and his boat burned. Years later, Cushing was still angry about
the loss. "This was a great misfortune and I never understood how so
stupid a thing occurred," he wrote. "I forget the name of the volunteer
ensign to whose care it was entrusted, but I am pleased to know he was
taken prisoner. I trust that his bed was not of down, nor his food that
of princes while in rebel hands."*

Cushing arrived in Hampton Roads on October 10 to find that he
was missing one cutter and had a new boss, Admiral David Dixon Porter, who had scored great victories at New Orleans and Vicksburg. For

---

* Stockholm said he thought he was in the Patuxent River in Maryland, where he would
have been quite safe.

many months Admiral Lee had been urging a joint army-navy attack on Fort Fisher, the Confederate stronghold that protected the Cape Fear River. Now that the plans were coming to fruition, Gideon Welles concluded that Samuel Lee was not the man to lead it. "Lee is true and loyal, careful, and circumspect almost to a fault," wrote Welles in his diary, "but while fearless he has not dash and impetuous daring." Welles then chose Admiral Farragut, but Farragut's poor health caused him to beg off, and Welles named Porter to the position.

In the transition, Will lost a steady backer, and received instead a man who thought Will a gambler more lucky than good. When Cushing and Porter first met, Cushing had just arrived from bringing *Picket Boat No. 1* down from New York to Hatteras. "His condition at this time was pitiable," Porter later recalled, noting that Will had lost all of his spare clothing and had eaten poorly. "He had been subjected to terrible exposure for more than a week," Porter said, but this did not ameliorate his displeasure that Will had allowed a lowly ensign to get lost with a cutter. He made Cushing search for a few days before granting him permission to proceed with only one boat. "I have no great confidence in his success," he wrote to W. H. Macomb, commanding the squadron in the North Carolina sounds, "but you will afford him all the assistance in your power, and keep boats ready to pick him up in case of failure." Porter also told Macomb that if the *Albemarle* should again show up around Plymouth, Macomb should attack it boldly. "Make a dash at her, even if half your vessels are sunk."

Porter wasn't the only person unhappy with Cushing over the lost cutter. Gideon Welles sent Will a sharp, angry note:

Have you given your personal attention to getting those vessels to Hampton Roads? A full report of your proceedings from the time you left New York is required. The Department has been in almost total ignorance of your movements and action since you have been on special duty, and what has been learned of the progress of your boats to their destination has been learned from others. You have not replied

to the Department's letter of September 14th, in relation to allega-
tions that you improperly disposed of certain articles belonging to the
schooner James Douglas, *and inflicted illegal punishments while on*
board the Monticello, *nor has the Department been able to pick up*
a report from you of the picking up of the schooner just mentioned.

Porter said that Will was upset by Welles's note—"He dreaded a court-martial more than the enemy," wrote Porter. He also said he looked into Welles's issues, found them meritless, and convinced Welles to drop the matter. But even if Welles had continued to seek answers, it's unlikely that Will would have been distracted. He had his mind elsewhere. As he put it to his cousin George White when he passed through New York, "Cousin George, I am going to have a vote of thanks from Congress, or six feet of pine box by the time you hear from me again."

CHAPTER 35

Dead Ahead

CUSHING LEFT NORFOLK via the Chesapeake and Albemarle Canal, and arrived on Roanoke Island. There he received information that led him to think his mission might not be the surprise he had hoped it would be. First, he learned of the failed attempt by the men of the *Wyalusing*. Second, he was presented with a copy of a newspaper in which the plan for attacking the ironclad was revealed. The report was inaccurate—lots of details were wrong—but it almost certainly meant that the rebels would now be on high alert.

Cushing asked Macomb to help him recruit a few more men. His crew presently consisted of ensign Howorth, engineer William Stotesbury, fireman Samuel Higgins, and landsmen Lorenzo Deming, Henry Wilkes, and Robert King. Macomb discreetly contacted commanders of the other ships and, without offering details, asked for volunteers for an extremely hazardous undertaking. By the afternoon, the group collected on the *Shamrock*: acting master's mate John Woodman of the *Commodore Hull*, engineer Charles L. Steever of the *Otsego*, coal heaver Richard Hamilton of the *Shamrock*, and ordinary seamen William Smith, Barnard Harley, and Edward J. Houghton of the *Chicopee*.

While Howorth briefed the crew, Cushing met with ensign Rudolph Sommers, of the *Otsego*, who had undertaken a number of small-boat reconnaissances of the *Albemarle*. The most recent had taken place the night before, during which part of his crew had been captured. Sommers gave Cushing the lay of the land: the *Albemarle* was moored on the waterfront of Plymouth, eight miles up the river. The width of the river at that point was about 150 yards. Camped on the riverbanks and in town were soldiers, maybe as many as 4,000, ready to protect the ram. There also seemed to be pickets on the wreck of the *Southfield*.

Around nine o'clock on the evening of October 26, Cushing picked up his men from the *Otsego*. A last-second addition, Acting Ensign Thomas Gay charmed his way into the cutter, appealing to Cushing's spirit of adventure. Progress was slow; the tide was running against them, and near the entrance to the river they ran aground. Freeing the cutter around two a.m., they proceeded a little farther along, when they were halted by Union pickets. Cushing then called off the mission, at least for the evening. If the Union pickets could hear the motor, so could the rebels.

The next day, as fleet carpenters boxed in the motor to muffle its noise, three escaped slaves swam to the fleet and were picked up. Cushing and Howorth questioned them for an hour. They confirmed that not only did the Confederates have pickets on the *Southfield*, they also had a schooner anchored near the wreck on which were stationed twenty-five men equipped with an artillery piece and signal rockets. After hearing the men out, Cushing and Howorth met with Macomb and Lieutenant Duer, executive officer of the *Shamrock*. They decided the cutter could tow behind it a launch holding a dozen or fifteen men; when they got near the *Southfield*, they could cast off the launch and the men could overpower the guard. Macomb was skeptical, but Duer was enthusiastic, and Macomb relented.

Again, the crew of the *Shamrock* was asked for volunteers to undertake a dangerous expedition, and once again the mission was amply subscribed. Duer selected the men and put Acting Gunner William Peterkin and Acting Master's Mate Wilson D. Burlingame in charge. Not until Cushing was once again under way that evening were they given their instructions. Another last-second addition, a mate from the

Minnesota, Assistant Paymaster Francis Swan obtained Will's permission by saying that he had never been in a fight. "This is a poor time for a start," said Will, relenting nonetheless.

Cushing left about a half hour earlier on the evening of the twenty-seventh, and reached the mouth of the Roanoke around eleven thirty. It was a rainy night, about 65 degrees, and the tall gum and cypress tress, forty feet high, crowding the shore, forced a feeling of closeness.

As they traveled, Will kept reviewing his plans.

His strong preference was to cut the ship out—rush the deck, eliminate the sentries, take out the crew sleeping on board. Cushing had almost thirty men. They could cut the ropes and go. Hopefully the rebels would have kept the furnaces banked so that the raiders could steam up quickly, but it hardly mattered; the Yanks could just button up and let the current carry them away. If the US Navy didn't have any cannon that could sink this ship, it's certain that the rebels didn't either. Cushing and his men could be back in time to invite Admiral Porter aboard for breakfast.

And if that didn't work? If they had to blow the ram? Then it would be up to the torpedo.

Modern fighter pilots have gone into battle not with weapons in hand but facing instrument panels full of buttons and levers. Cushing was a primitive version—so primitive that he was the instrument panel. As he stood in the prow of his cutter, Will held in his right hand three lines. One was attached to Engineer Stotesbury's ankle; one pull meant to speed up, two pulls to stop the engines. A second line connected Will to Howorth, who would be manning the howitzer; a tug would mean to start firing. The third line was attached to Ensign Gay, who would move the torpedo spar ahead if he felt Will's pull. Attached to Will's left hand were two lines by which he would arm and fire the torpedo. As they slowly cruised upriver, Will drilled himself, memorizing where each line reached his hand, rehearsing his response. There would be no room for hesitancy or error.

Two o'clock came; then two thirty. Cushing signaled with a handkerchief for the men to take their stations by their oarlocks and make ready, and the shifting of bodies he sensed behind him showed that the men had understood. They were getting close. Now there was an insistent jerk on his right hand from the line connected to Gay. He must have seen—yes, there it was, ahead—a dark shape angling awkwardly above the stream, the corpse of the *Southfield*, and the little Confederate ship lurking nearby. *Picket Boat No. 1* drew near, just twenty yards away. Will expected a rebel challenge at any moment—the click of a musket, a shot, but . . . nothing, not a sound, just the low, discreet murmur of his engine that piqued no interest.

And then they were through, floating past two enemy posts unseen. Will felt a sense of elation, a desire to whoop, which he immediately suppressed. They hadn't done anything yet.

Another five minutes went by; they passed another curve in the river. The low lights of Plymouth could be seen now, the dwindling campfires, the lamps in the windows of the sleepless.

And then, suddenly, there it was. Bulky, angular, squarely silhouetted against the wharf, somewhat more squat than any legendary beast ought to be, sleeping the calm, undisturbed sleep of a ruthless killer. Keep the launch, Will told himself. Keep the men. We'll cut this thing out, he thought. We'll steal it dead away.

But no sooner did Cushing move his launch toward the wharf than a sentry called. "Who's there? Who's there? Who goes there?" Then the shooting started.

CHAPTER 36

Now

I N JUST THAT SLIVER OF AN INSTANT, Cushing knew that the idea of cutting the ship out was finished. "Cast off, Peterkin," he shouted to the men being towed in the launch, "go get those pickets on the schooner!" He pulled hard on the engineer's lanyard, realized the need for silence was over, and shouted, "Ahead fast!" The engines roared, the launch fell away, the cutter shot forward toward the iron monster. Around them, the pop of muskets picked up, and bullets began to splash and zing. "Leave the ram, or I'll blow you to pieces!" Cushing shouted.

Suddenly from the shore there was a *whooomp*, and a tall pile of wood splashed with tar and turpentine ignited. A warning bonfire, built for this very contingency, leapt to life and turned the riverfront into a flickering, orange, shadow-dancing stage. As Cushing neared the ship, he could see by this illumination that the rebels had installed a line of defense he had not expected—a ring of logs, chained together, encircling the ram in a protective pen about thirty feet from her side, placed there for the very purpose of foiling a torpedo attack.

The presence of the timbers came as a complete surprise to Cushing, though ironically not to everyone on his team. Acting Master's Mate Woodman and four men had gone up the Roanoke in a dinghy on August 23, and reported that the *Albemarle* was protected by timbers. How word of this never reached Cushing is a mystery. Surely Cushing never would have held on to the idea of cutting the ram out if he had any notion that he would have been capturing a ship encircled by a timber boom.

Will ran the cutter up to the boom, oblivious to the increasing gunfire from the shore, and then ran alongside it, examining the chain for a weakness, a break, a piece of information that would unlock this obstacle. Turning the wheel hard, he traveled in a wide circle, running the cutter away from the ship, back near the tall gum and cypress trees and the darkness of the far side, and then spun again and aimed back at the *Albemarle*. "Full speed!" he shouted, and the light picket boat shot ahead. He would leap the boom, and once inside, he would blow the ship to hell, along with himself, his men, whoever was in the way. Ahead in the flickering of the flames he could see the rebels on the shore running in confusion, and in front of that the dark logs, silhouetted against the firelight, their wet mossy surfaces shining as he came.

Wham! Flying at full speed, the cutter smacked the logs. Cushing hoped that slime on the timbers would act as a lubricant, and that his momentum would carry him over. He made it only halfway; after impact there was a grinding, tearing sound, and then the launch hung there, stuck over the barrier. For a moment, the tableau was frozen, as raiders and rebels alike held their breath. Then Captain Warley, atop the casemate of the *Albemarle*, shouted, "What boat is that?"

"We'll soon let you know!" Cushing replied and yanked on the lanyard of the howitzer, sending a load of canister against the ironclad, clearing her deck.

And then, tumult. As gunfire erupted from all over the shore, Gay swung the spar around, and the torpedo was lowered below the surface of the water. The deliberate grinding of the winch testified that the torpedo was dropping as fast as possible—yet from the point of view of the men in the cutter, not nearly fast enough. Meanwhile, a race was developing: Will patiently waiting in his open boat for his torpedo to float below the edge of the ironclad's armor, where he could try to get it to explode; Captain Warley and a gun crew, inside the casemate of the

Albemarle, scrambling to load one of their Parrotts and blow Cushing to pieces.

Neither could make the weapons move the way they wanted. Borne on the current, the torpedo floated and bobbed, obedient to the laws of physics. Warley could see it come nearer. Will stood upright in the prow of his cutter, the epitome of cool. A bullet had already taken away the heel of his shoe, another creased his sleeve. A load of buckshot carried away the back of his coat, and still he did not flinch. The torpedo was at the hull of the ship now, just a few feet from going under, and the gaping mouth of Warley's gun was not ten feet from Will's head. But the rebels could not lower the mouth of the gun enough. Will could hear Warley yelling, "Lower! Lower! Lower!"

And then the torpedo dipped below the water and vanished under the ship.

Now!

Just as Will pulled the last lanyard in his left hand, he heard Warley scream "Fire!" and then all was lost in sensation: a tremendous earsplitting roar, a screaming hot wind above, the floor of the cutter seeming to vanish into pure air, and then a smashing wave of water.

Followed by throbbing quiet.

CHAPTER 37

Dead Gone Sunk

T HE TORPEDO EXPLODED at the same instant Warley discharged his gun. The canister flew over the attackers' heads like a swarm of iron bees, costing some their caps but none his life. Similarly, the torpedo went off imperfectly: much of the force of the explosion vented outside the ship and into the water and created a momentary vacuum that drew in Will's boat, then threw him and his men and a great blast of water flying back toward the surface. But if the explosion wasn't perfect, it was good enough. Warley sent his carpenter to inspect the damage; he reported "a hole in her bottom big enough to drive a wagon in." In minutes, the ferocious *Albemarle* was resting on the river bottom. The beast of the Roanoke River, the Confederacy's most effective ironclad, fell to a man standing in an open boat.

Cushing and his men, jostled and jarred, shakily held their places in the rocking picket boat, or treaded water in the drink. Calls from the shore and the ram commanded, "Surrender or we will blow you out of the water!"

"Never!" Cushing cried. "I'll be damned first!" Quickly he shed his sword, sidearm, coat, and shoes, and shouting "Men, save yourselves," he dived into the Roanoke.

Some of the crew, he knew, came in after him, but Will had no sense of who stayed or left. He swam hard for the far shore, disappearing deeper into darkness with each stroke. When he had the sense that he had gone a little distance, he came up, just in time to hear "a gurgling yell," the sound of the fireman, Samuel Higgins, slipping below the surface for the final time. The bonfire was still burning, but he could make out nothing of his men, just a lot of people milling, some of them boarding small boats with torches. They were going to be looking for something—survivors, bodies, most particularly him. The water was icy, but Will pushed on.

He traveled on the current for as long as he could. At one point he heard a man groaning, and paddled toward the sound. He found John Woodman, weak and fading. Cushing kept the man afloat for perhaps ten minutes more, but Woodman at last succumbed to the elements, and sank into the river.

Cushing, too, began to fade, and was finding it difficult to keep from going under. "My strokes were now very feeble, my clothes being soaked and heavy, a little chop-seas splashing [came] with choking persistence into my mouth every time I gasped for breath." Still he pressed on "with a mechanical motion long after my bodily force was in fact expended." Elated when at last his feet "touched soft mud," he collapsed on the riverbank.

Cushing couldn't have slept long—it was dawn when he came to. The rising sun rejuvenated him, and he felt strong enough again to look around. He reckoned that he was on the Plymouth side of the river, at about the point where the outskirts of town become less outskirts and more swamp. There seemed to be soldiers everywhere. He had to get into the swamp.

For five hours, Cushing made his barefooted, bareheaded way through the thick mud and rank ooze, pierced and sliced by thornbushes at every step. He finally stumbled onto a spot where the ground was solid enough to rest upon, but after only a few moments he realized that he was just yards from a rebel work party that was blocking the channel by submersing some old schooners. Will bellied away in a corn furrow that led to a small woods. There he encountered—it was hard to say who found whom—a tall black man. "I'm a Union officer," the bloody, muddy, half-drowned white man said, "and if you let out a sound Abraham Lincoln will come down here and skin you alive." The black man did not react, which Will took to be an encouraging sign. Reaching for his billfold, which had miraculously survived not only the collision but hours in the damp and wet, Will extracted twenty dollars and some texts of Scripture ("two powerful arguments with an old darkey"), and handed them to the man. "Go into town and find out what happened to the *Albemarle*," he directed. Hours had passed since the battle, and Will didn't know the outcome.

In less than an hour, the old man returned. "She is dead gone sunk, and they will hang you, massa, if they catch you," he reported.

Will slogged back into the swamp. He was moving, but not far and not fast. About two in the afternoon, he came up behind a spot where a picket party of seven soldiers was posted. Cushing could see that the platoon possessed a flat-bottomed, square-ended skiff, which was tied to the root of a cypress tree. Watching until the soldiers' attention was focused elsewhere, Cushing swam to the skiff, and snatched it.

Then he began paddling, and with nothing that he knew about between him and the federal fleet, he did not stop. Afternoon passed into evening, evening into night, and never did Will pause, not even at the mouth of the Roanoke, not even in Albemarle Sound.

"After steering by a star for perhaps two hours for where I thought the fleet might be, I at length discovered one of the vessels, and after a long time got within hail. My 'Ship ahoy!' was given with the last of my strength, and I fell powerless, with a splash, into the water in the bottom of my boat, and awaited results. I had paddled every minute for ten successive hours, and for four [of them] my body had been 'asleep,' with the exception of my arms and brain."

Until this point, the only news about the mission came from the men on the cutter that had neutralized the pickets on the *Southfield*, now back some twelve hours or so. Their account was scant at best and inaccurate. They reported hearing gunfire, an explosion, and shouting, but had no news of the outcome, or of casualties. But they had seen the explosion, they knew where Will would have been, and would have reported that Cushing must be dead.

Thus, at ten p.m. on October 28, when the officers of the watch of the *Valley City* heard an "Ahoy!" from the dark waters of the sound, they reacted with caution, thinking it might be an act of retaliation for the attempt on the *Albemarle* the night before. When they finally decided to investigate, Acting Ensign Milton Webster was sent to find an answer.

What he found was an unconscious officer, muddy, cut up, and bleeding. Carrying Cushing like a sack of flour, Webster hauled him onto the gunboat, where Acting Master J. A. J. Brooks, commanding officer of the *Valley City*, came closer. "My God, Cushing," he said, "is this you?"

Cushing nodded. "It is I."

"Is it done?"

"It is done."

Fortified by a little brandy, Cushing was carried to the *Shamrock* to report to Commander Macomb. Once the report was made, and the commander's admiration complete, Will went and sat on the deck. "As soon as it became known that I had returned, rockets were thrown up and all hands were called to cheer ship." Exhausted and exhilarated, Cushing watched the sky explode in tribute.

CHAPTER 38

Seldom Equaled, Never Excelled

EFORE NOON ARRIVED ON OCTOBER 29, the navy had begun
shelling Plymouth. The man of the hour, with bandaged feet
and hands, had the privilege of firing the first guns. It was one
of many honors that would be bestowed upon Will Cushing in the days
to come.

The country received news of the victory slowly. Admiral Porter
was informed on the twenty-ninth, and he telegraphed the story to
the newspapers, who had it in their headlines on October 30. Porter
included no information about the fate of the crew, so that when Howard Cushing read the news in the Washington papers, he held off sharing it with his mother. Not until the thirty-first did Howard learn that
Will was safe in Hampton Roads, at which point he telegraphed their
mother. Will followed up on the third with another telegram. "Mrs.
Cushing," it read, "Have destroyed the rebel ram *Albemarle*. Am all
right. Thanks of Congress, promotion and fifty thousand (50,000) prize
money. W. B. Cushing, U.S.N."

Plymouth fell on the thirty-first, after a shell from the *Shamrock*
exploded a rebel magazine. After that, the Confederates fled. The coat
Cushing was wearing on the night of the raid was found abandoned.
Half of a sleeve and its back were gone, but it was nonetheless taken to
Commander Macomb, who forwarded it to Will. Cutting the stitches

under the collar, Will found Mary Colman's gold chain and pendant, unchanged from the day he had removed them from her neck.

To celebrate Cushing's achievement, Admiral Porter issued General Order No. 34, which was to be read to the officers and crew assembled on the quarterdeck of every ship in the squadron:

> *It gives me pleasure to inform the officers and men of the squadron under my command that the rebel ram* Albemarle . . . *has been destroyed by Lieutenant William B. Cushing, who, in this hazardous enterprise, has displayed a heroic enterprise seldom equaled and never excelled. . . . The gallant exploits of Lieutenant Cushing previous to this affair will form a bright page in the history of the war, but they have all been eclipsed by the destruction of the* Albemarle. *The spirit evinced by this officer is what I wish to see pervading this squadron. He has shown an absolute disregard of death or danger.*

No message surpassed in eloquence that of Gideon Welles, whose personal connection to Cushing enriched the letter with a feeling of heartfelt and almost paternal pride:

> *When last summer the department selected you for this important and perilous undertaking, and sent you to Rear-Admiral Gregory at New York to make the necessary preparations, it left the details with you to perfect. To you and your brave comrades, therefore, belongs the exclusive credit which attaches to this daring achievement. The destruction of so formidable a vessel, which had resisted the continued attack of a number of our steamers, is an important event touching our future naval and military operations. The judgment as well as the daring courage displayed would do honor to any officer, and redounds to the credit of one of 21 years of age.*
>
> *On four previous occasions the department has had the gratification of expressing its approbation of your conduct in the face of the enemy, and in each instance there was manifested by you the*

same heroic daring and innate love of perilous adventure—a mind determined to succeed, and not to be deterred by any apprehensions of defeat.

The department has presented your name to the President for a vote of thanks, that you may be promoted one grade, and your comrades also receive recognition.

It gives me pleasure to recall the assurance you gave me at the commencement of your active professional career that you would prove yourself worthy of the confidence reposed in you, and of the service to which you were appointed. I trust you may be preserved through further trials, and it is for yourself to determine whether, after entering upon so auspicious a career, you shall by careful study and self-discipline be prepared for a wider sphere of usefulness on the call of your country.

Even the Confederates joined in. Captain Alexander Warley concluded his official report of the engagement by saying, "That is the way the *Albemarle* was destroyed, and a more gallant thing was not done during the war."

OF THE FIFTEEN men who were in *Picket Boat No. 1*, four made a break downriver after the explosion. Cushing found Samuel Higgins and John Woodman at or near the point of dying. They were the only fatalities incurred by either side during the raid. One other man, Edward Houghton, returned to Yankee hands after a week living in the rough. If there were records of his experience, they seem to have disappeared. He died less than a year later, on July 16, 1865.

The other eleven men were found in the water, most of them holding on to the logs, and were captured and held as prisoners of war. They suffered many deprivations, including, almost always, severely short rations and often inadequate shelter. After being marched from prison to prison during the month of November, they were permanently incarcerated in Libby Prison in Richmond, where they remained until February 21, when they were paroled. The ten enlisted men who accompanied Cushing and who survived were awarded the Medal of Honor (officers being ineligible for the award at that time, ensigns Gay and Howorth were not decorated).

In recognition for his exploits, Will was promoted a full grade, to lieutenant commander, and received the Thanks of Congress "for his important, gallant, and perilous achievement in destroying the rebel ironclad steamer." Only thirty army and navy officers earned this recognition during the war; of the fourteen naval officers who received this seldom-presented acknowledgment, Cushing is the only one who was not or did not eventually become an admiral. Will also received cash—his share of the prize money, a bounty paid to enterprising naval officers and their crews. The first installment amounted to $6,000, which he turned over to his mother.

Given some well-deserved leave after visiting Porter, Will spent a week in Fredonia, during which he was given a proud and raucous welcome at a meeting at the town's Concert Hall, cast his first presidential vote (for Lincoln), spoke at worthy gatherings, and received some useful motherly advice. "Ah, Willie," Elizabeth Cushing said, "beware of pride, for many is the time I have put you to bed while I have mended your only suit of clothes." After departing from Fredonia, Will also spoke at the Union League Club in Manhattan, serenaded the governor-elect of Wisconsin, and received a medal from the Union League of Philadelphia. His account of the sinking ran in papers throughout the country, there was a rush to get his photograph, and he was crowned by the press with a nickname that could not be refused or lost: henceforth, he would be known as "Albemarle" Cushing.

CHAPTER 39

Back in Action

A T OTHER TIMES IN US HISTORY, someone who has become a wartime hero was put to use in a place of relative safety; some Medal of Honor recipients during World War II, for example, went on bond tours before returning to the front. After his November sojourn, however, Will Cushing went back to work. As a reward, Lieutenant Commander Cushing was placed in charge of the *Malvern*, Admiral Porter's flagship. This honor was often given to a ranking officer with less seniority than the others in the fleet, showing that the position was not entirely an honor. On the flagship of an admiral, all things must be perfect, which must have caused more than a few headaches for a young officer accustomed to tugs and gunboats, hiding in cattails, and hiking through mud.

Porter was aboard the *Malvern* to help lead what was generally expected to be the last great battle of the Civil War. At this point, the Confederacy drew more strength from stubbornness than any strategy or hope. Lincoln had been reelected, killing the last chance of a negotiated settlement. Grant had Lee pinned down in the cold and mud of Petersburg. General William T. Sherman was marching to the sea, General Philip Sheridan was burning up the Shenandoah Valley, and Hood was about to sacrifice his army in a suicidal attack in Franklin, Tennessee. The ironclad rallying point, the *Albemarle*, was gone.

Still, as long as blockade runners were reaching Wilmington, as long as the last coil of Scott's Anaconda had not yet tightened, the Confederacy held on. A Confederate government report on the amount of goods that had been brought by blockade runners into Charleston and Wilmington harbors during a nine-week period in late 1864—and nearly all these goods went into Wilmington, for Charleston was tightly blockaded—totaled "8,632,000 pounds of beef, 1,507,000 pounds of lead, 1,933,000 pounds of saltpeter, 546,000 pairs of shoes, 316,000 pairs of blankets, 520,000 pounds of coffee, 69,000 rifles, 97 packages of revolvers, 2,639 packages of medicine, 43 cannon," and more. Wilmington was the last vein from the sea, and the last artery to Lee's army.

Taking Wilmington meant taking Fort Fisher, the largest and most formidable of the Confederate positions that protected the mouth of the Cape Fear River. As Cushing saw during his scouting adventure up the river, the rebels had lined both sides of the river with cannon, and clogged the waterways with sunken hulks and torpedoes. They devoted special attention to protecting the river's outlet to the Atlantic, fortifying a half dozen positions designed to prevent Yankee vessels from even getting into the river. By far the most important of these positions was Fort Fisher.

Fort Fisher sits at the end of a narrow peninsula shaped like an inverted triangle. Called Federal Point before secession, it was renamed Confederate Point (it is today known as Pleasure Island). Fort Fisher—named after a Confederate officer from the Sixth North Carolina Infantry, who died at Bull Run—protected New Inlet, the space between Confederate Point and Smith Island. By the time Union forces converged on it at the end of 1864, the fort was known as the Gibraltar of the South. Like its Mediterranean namesake, Fisher was surrounded by very rough waters, and was supposed to be impregnable.

That reputation would have been due to the intensity of Fort Fisher's commander, Colonel William Lamb, a twenty-seven-year-old former newspaper editor from Norfolk, who took command in 1862. At that time, Fort Fisher's defenses consisted of a few obsolete cannon optimistically lodged behind palmetto logs. Although Lamb had no formal training as an engineer, he was an avid student of military history and had taken a special interest in the Crimean War, where the guns atop the Malakoff Tower had enabled the Russians to withstand the French navy's siege of Sevastopol for almost a year. Lamb had also been present at Sewell's Point, near Hampton Roads, where early in 1862 Union gunboats swapped fire with a rebel battery on shore. The gunboats often found their mark, but the loosely packed dirt of the Confederate earthworks swallowed the shells and absorbed their impact. Walls of brick or stone might make a defender feel more secure, but shells fired by modern rifled cannon bore into defenses and quickly collapsed them. Lamb envisioned the defenses of Fort Fisher consisting not of towers but of mounds of sand—a substance he had in infinite supply—with bombproof chambers dug into them to safeguard men and ammunition during bombardment. Over the next two years, soldiers and slaves built thirty-foot-high hills of sand, crowned with a motley though deadly array of cannon—Columbiads, Brookes, an Armstrong 130-pounder, wheeled Whitworths—nearly two dozen in all.

Lamb arrayed Fort Fisher's defenses on two fronts: a land face, which stretched 1,800 feet across the peninsula west to east until it met the sea face at an oblique angle, then ran south along the coast for a mile to New Inlet. The land face was composed of fifteen mounds, which were connected by an underground warren of tunnels and ammunition vaults; the guns on top sat thirty-two feet above sea level. In front of the mounds stood a nine-foot-tall palisade fence, once the only impediment to invasion. At each end of the sea face were powerful batteries. The north end, where the faces intersected—the Northeast Bastion—was fortified by a powerful eight-inch Blakeley rifle; at the southernmost tip, right above New Inlet, on a mound sixty feet tall, was the powerful Buchanan Battery. In between were another twenty-two guns mounted on a dozen more twelve-foot mounds. How odd this must have looked from the sea: the flat, sandy peninsula, haphazardly decorated with patches of beach grass and a handful of wind-twisted trees, topped by these primitive, alien-seeming sand mounds bristling with guns.

Colonel Lamb not only improved the defenses of Fort Fisher; he brought a new pugnacity to it. Shortly after taking command, he spotted ships of the blockade fleet anchored a mile offshore. He was surprised to hear that it was a fairly typical arrangement that the Yanks would sit out there and once in a while drop a few shells into the fort just to liven things up. Lamb was appalled; from that point on, when federal blockaders ventured too close, Fort Fisher's gunners sent some iron their way and shooed them out to sea. In time, blockade runners began to look for the lights of Fort Fisher to tell them that the most perilous part of their journey was coming to an end. But Fort Fisher was always undermanned; at its peak, the garrison had just 1,600 men, and often there were many fewer.

In September 1864, General Grant finally freed up 6,500 troops from the Army of the James to join the North Atlantic Blockading Squadron for a combined land-sea operation to take Fort Fisher, placing them under the command of Major General Godfrey Weitzel, a twenty-nine-year-old native of Bavaria and graduate of West Point. To command the naval forces, Welles appointed Admiral Porter.

As the combined forces made their way to the fort, Weitzel received an unhappy surprise: his superior at the Army of the James, General Butler, had decided to come along. Benjamin Butler, the political general who whispered in Gus Fox's ear on behalf of ex-midshipman Cushing during that unhappy spring of March 1861, could usually be counted on to do what served his interests; in New Orleans, he was alternately called "Beast," because of his rude treatment of southern ladies who insulted Union officers, and "Spoons," because he allegedly pocketed silverware from the southern homes where he billeted himself. As 1864 waned, Butler was not much interested in spending the holidays in North Carolina, but he smelled in the attack on Fort Fisher one of the war's final chances to reap the glory of victory. Moreoever, Butler had an idea. He had a floating bomb.

CHAPTER 40

Secret Weapon

THE ORIGINAL PLAN OF ATTACK was straightforward: have Porter's fleet of fifty-seven assorted vessels—"big frigates of the Colorado type, iron-clads and monitors, double-enders, gunboats and merchant-vessels transformed into ships-of-war, and every one, according to the American custom, bristling with all the armament it could possibly carry," as future admiral George Dewey recorded—bombard the place until the sand fleas fled, then send the 6,500 soldiers to finish off the survivors of the 1,600-man garrison.

But once Porter arrived off the Carolina coast in mid-December and saw the sandy mounds, he realized that reducing Fort Fisher would be no simple task. The mounds, he realized, would absorb a lot of metal. Moreover, that "full speed ahead" dash under the Confederate batteries that he had used so effectively at Vicksburg would be impossible at New Inlet. At Vicksburg, Porter's flotilla blitzed down the river, challenging the rebel gunners to shell them accurately; only one ship was lost. At Fort Fisher, any boats that managed to get past the fort would probably have trouble finding the channel in the Cape Fear River, and would either run aground or back up and become easy targets for the Buchanan Battery. Porter may not have had much use for Butler—now that President Lincoln had been reelected, neither did the general's most powerful patron—but he surely wanted to hear more about Butler's secret plan.

Which was actually well past the planning stage. An aging gunboat, the *Louisiana*, had been stripped down and had its guns and part of its deckhouse removed. In Norfolk it had been loaded with 215 tons of gunpowder—more than fifty times the amount that produced the Crater in Petersburg just five months before—and then sailed for Beaufort, where the explosives were primed. The ship was now a giant bomb. Sitting low in the water, with her new, flattish profile, she also resembled a blockade runner. The plan was for a small crew to anchor her as close to Fort Fisher as possible, set three ninety-minute fuses aboard (a fuse, a backup, and a backup for the backup), and board an escort steamer that would dash to a zone of presumed safety. After that?

One school of thought believed Fort Fisher would be flattened; another thought the atmosphere would swallow the shock waves with no effect. Porter, like some congressional pol in a backroom conference committee meeting, split the difference. "I take a mean between the two," he said, rationally and pseudoscientifically. "I think the effect of the explosion will simply be very severe—stunning men at a distance of three or four hundred yards, demoralizing them completely, and making them unable to stand for any length of time a fire from a ship." That wouldn't be all: buildings would tumble, guns would be buried, houses would collapse. "If the rebels fight after the explosion," said Porter, "they have more in them than I give them credit for." And that would be just the opening act. Porter would follow up with a massive naval bombardment of the fort, and then Butler's troops would march in.

When Cushing was in Washington accepting his *Albemarle* triumph, Gus Fox had sounded him out about the possibility of captaining a floating bomb and being the one to set the fuses. As always, Will had agreed to do the job. In the event, however, the assignment went to Commander Alexander Rhind, a forty-three-year-old navy man who had several times been cited for bravery. Cushing had good friends in the operation assisting Rhind, including Lieutenant Roswell Lamson, Will's compadre on the Nansemond, and his academy classmate Samuel Preston. In the predawn hours of December 23, stealthily following the lights set out by Fort Fisher to guide blockade runners through New Inlet, the *Louisiana* was towed by the *Wilderness*, captained by Lamson, to a point 250 yards off Fort Fisher. The *Louisiana* anchored, and Rhind and his crew, including Preston, not only lit the fuses but, just to make sure, also set the boat on fire, before skedaddling onto the *Wilderness*.

And then they waited. Had the fuses, any of the fuses, burned as they had been designed, the *Louisiana* would have blown up at 1:18 in the morning. In the event, it wasn't until 1:40, an anxious half hour later, that the bomb blew up, thanks to the fire Rhind started as an afterthought. The ship erupted, producing a flash of light, a dust cloud, a low, heavy boom, and a sulfurous, malodorous cloud that passed over the fleet. "It was terrible," one young rebel later wrote laconically. "It woke up nearly everybody in the fort." In other words, it wasn't terrible at all. The sound, according to a reporter from the *New York Times*, "was not unlike that of the sound produced by the discharge of a 100-pounder," which at this point in the war was a fairly unexceptional noise. The expected shock wave had dissipated into thin air—literally. George Dewey summed up matters nicely: "The experiment was magnificent and spectacular but not helpful." In his diary, Gideon Welles wrote off the escapade as "a mere puff of smoke."

CHAPTER 41

Sitting Duck

MBARRASSED, EXASPERATED, NONPLUSSED, certainly angry—whatever Porter was feeling, he contained himself until noon, before steaming his fleet close to the coast and opening fire. Over the course of the next five hours, his 627 guns discharged approximately 10,000 rounds—some 115 a minute—onto the embracing, forgiving sands of Fort Fisher. The mighty discharge of ordnance resulted in one Confederate dead, twenty-two injured, and two guns disabled. The fort's comparatively puny reply—622 shells—inflicted considerably greater damage; eighty-three of Porter's men were killed or wounded, although more than half of them were injured in five separate instances when new hundred-pounder Parrotts overheated and blew up.

PORTER, OF COURSE, had unleashed his guns to cover Butler's invasion, but the general did not appear until nightfall, when he arrived with a few transports, and promises that the rest of the men would be along directly. With the hour too late to begin landing operations, a furious Porter sent him away; operations would have to commence in the morning. And indeed, on Christmas morning Porter resumed his bombardment, sending several more thousands of shells landward.

A few hours later, up the coast, General Weitzel managed to land a couple thousand soldiers on shore. The troops advanced to within a hundred yards of Fort Fisher's land face, where they were slowed by land mines and stopped by blasts of canister from guns that Porter believed his bombardment had destroyed. Weitzel reported what he had seen to Butler—"I told him it would be murder to order an attack upon that work"—and Butler did not disagree. Looking to the skies, Butler decided that the weather was changing against him and, disregarding General Grant's direct order to dig in after landing, ordered a withdrawal of his men while conditions permitted. Most got off; Butler abandoned the final seven hundred. "Nothing further can be done by the land forces," Butler informed Porter, and announced that he and his men were heading back to Hampton Roads. Porter, whose cooperation with Grant at Vicksburg was the very model of combined army-navy operations, was shocked and furious. He ordered his ships to continue the bombardment in support of the troops, and the next day, when the wind changed, he brought the wet, chilled soldiers off the beach. Overall, the army's casualties were light, suggesting that blood was not a factor in Butler's decision to go; the general simply lost interest once his floating bomb proved to be a dud. Having collected Butler's men, Porter, lacking any other option, withdrew as well. The rebels could not believe their luck. "You can now inspect the works and walk on nothing but iron," one officer remarked; none could understand why the Yankees had not attacked. At that moment, Fort Fisher's garrison numbered only five hundred men.

Before the fleet pulled out, Cushing had an opportunity to add a small exploit to his legend. Before Butler ordered his men to leave, he dispatched two officers to Porter to ask if the navy couldn't run a couple of ships through New Inlet, sail up the undefended Cape Fear River side of Fort Fisher, and bombard the land face from behind. After all, the rebels couldn't shoot at both Weitzel's troops and the ships in the river. Porter wasn't unwilling, but the Union charts were incorrectly marked, and the pilots could not find the channel. Cushing volunteered go look for a channel, and mark and buoy it if he could, checking for torpedoes along the way. Unaccustomed as he was to having the captain of his flagship request such duty, Porter nonetheless agreed, and at midday Will, another officer, and twelve seamen set off in the *Malvern*'s cutter. Flying the eye-catching blue-and-white pennant of a commanding officer, the cutter floated under the guns of the Buchanan Battery while Cushing, wearing the flashy four gold stripes of a lieutenant commander, sat in the stern directing the leadsman's activities.

For what seemed like ten minutes the rebels just gaped, but eventually they opened fire. Several Union boats came over to help Cushing, and marked torpedoes while Cushing and his crew continued the painstaking business of coast surveying. One shell hit a Union boat and sank it; the crew was rescued. Cushing's boat nonetheless drew closer to the shore. "Round shot, shell and shrapnel ploughed around us at every moment," Cushing wrote in his memoirs. When he was close enough that "a biscuit might be tossed from the boat to the beach," Cushing ordered his men to stop rowing and "stood up in the stern of his frail craft and took a cool and deliberate survey of the fort." In all, he remained under fire for six hours; shells splashed water into his boat so often that it had to be bailed out two or three times. Will returned to the *Malvern* after sundown, annoyed, he said, that the rebels had wetted his uniform; he had mapped out a narrow, crooked channel, one that Porter, unfortunately, decided was unsuitable for his plan.

CHAPTER 42

Return to Fort Fisher

S HORTLY AFTER THAT ADVENTURE, Porter relieved Will from commanding the flagship, and gave him back the *Monticello* ("Cushing was not so well adapted for the command of a flotilla . . . as he was for a single vessel," Porter later observed). The admiral had received a message from a lieutenant who was commanding an armed prize, reporting that there was a privateer called the *Chicka- mauga* off Smith Island in Old Inlet. Porter ordered Cushing to capture the privateer.

"Steaming around the shoal as rapidly as possible," Cushing wrote in his memoirs, "I found the vessel described, at anchor inside the bar under the guns of Fort Caswell, and fired a blank cartridge as a challenge." But the *Chickamauga* would not come out and fight, not even after Cushing opened fire on a large blockade-running steamer that blundered onto the scene. He sank the ship, even as Fort Caswell punched six holes into the *Monticello*. Cushing nonetheless lamented the *Chickamauga*'s decision. "Nothing was desired by us but a fair field and no favor," he later wrote. "With her extra men aboard she was much the stronger, and better to have finished her career in a gallant action on the ocean, than the way she did—sunk by a retreating crew in the Cape Fear River." Cushing returned to the fleet disappointed that he was denied a fight, but his mood was short-lived. A new attack on Fort Fisher was imminent.

In the aftermath of the failed attack, Grant, knowing the character of both Butler and Porter, had no doubt which man was at fault. "Please hold on to where you are for a few days, " Grant wrote to Porter, "and I will endeavor to be back again with an increased force and a new commander." Grant immediately pressed Lincoln to reassign Butler, and with his first order of 1865, Lincoln curtly dismissed his erstwhile ally, remanding him to Lowell, Massachusetts, to await orders. But Butler didn't go back to Lowell; he headed for Washington, where he met his old pals in Congress and complained about Welles and Porter and the impossibility of taking Fort Fisher. The Committee on the Conduct of the War invited him to come to Capitol Hill the following week and air his views in session.

THE COMMAND OF Butler's troops was given to General Alfred Terry, a thirty-seven-year-old Yale man, lawyer, and veteran of the First Battle of Bull Run. Called by Porter "my beau ideal of a soldier and a general," he is perhaps best remembered as the commander of a column that marched against the Sioux in 1876 and found the decaying bodies of Custer and his men at the Little Big Horn. Terry moved with efficiency; he and Porter had the army and the fleet reunited in Beaufort by January 8, and on the doorstep of Fort Fisher by January 12. From Petersburg, General Lee implored Colonel Lamb to hold on, telling him that his army depended on the goods that reached Wilmington under Fort Fisher's protection.

Just before dawn on the thirteenth, Porter ordered his five ironclad monitors to get as close to the shore as possible. His idea was to seduce the guns in the fort to shoot at these impregnable ships, and thus with their muzzle flashes betray their location on the shore. The plan worked perfectly, at which point the rest of Porter's 627 cannon unloaded. At

Christmas General Butler had complained about the accuracy of the navy's guns, and he had a point. On Christmas, the gunners had targeted Fort Fisher's flagstaffs, thinking that whatever was under a flag had to be important. This was hell on the flagstaffs, but did little damage to the guns.

This time, the gunners aimed at the parapets, and the results were stupendous; the fire devastated the defenses as the guns toppled over or collapsed into the mounds. The bombardment continued all day and into the night; Lamb lost more than half his guns, and though his forces had been replenished since the first assault, this cannonade cost him 100 of the 1,600 soldiers now under his command. Meanwhile, Terry landed his 8,000 men. Each brought forty rounds of ammunition and three days' rations, with six more days' worth of bread and another 300,000 rounds stockpiled in reserve. The first thing the troops did was dig trenches. Terry was no Butler; he would not be heading home when the weather changed.

Lamb continued to hope for reinforcements, but no more came. In some ways, Butler's dithering performance convinced General Bragg and the rest of the Confederate command of the fort's impregnability, a quality of which Lamb boasted but didn't entirely believe. Late on the thirteenth, Lamb's district superior, General William H. C. Whiting, showed up with his staff. "Lamb, my boy, I have come here to share your fate," Whiting said. "You and your command are to be sacrificed."

PORTER AND TERRY met aboard the *Malvern* on the fourteenth and scribbled out a plan of attack for the next day. The navy would bombard Fort Fisher until teatime, when the land forces would attack. Four thousand soldiers—half of Terry's men—would hit the west corner of the land face. At the same time, some 1,600 sailors and 400 marines under the command of Fleet Captain Kidder Randolph Breese, who fought with Porter on the *Mississippi*, would form a parallel force and charge the eastern corner, the so-called Northeast Bastion, the best-fortified and most strongly armed point in the place. Porter liked General Terry, but perhaps the only general he fully trusted was U. S. Grant. "I don't believe in anybody but my own good officers and men," he had written to Gus Fox on January 7, even before he met Al Terry. "I can do anything with them, and you need not be surprised to hear that the web-footers have gone into the forts. I will try it anyhow and show the soldiers how to do it." And so Porter and Terry agreed: four thousand soldiers in trained units carrying forty rounds of ammunition apiece would hit the west side of the land face, after which half that number, mostly sailors carrying only cutlasses and pistols, would attack the more formidably defended northeastern corner.

CHAPTER 43

Slaughter at
the Northeast Bastion

FTER SPENDING THE MORNING OF THE FIFTEENTH on the *Monticello* swapping shells with the suddenly emboldened *Chickamauga* and some other vessels, Cushing and forty of his men joined the naval assault forces. The navy's continuing bombardment provided a ceaseless accompaniment. "Such a hell of noise I never expect to hear again," Cushing later wrote. "Hundreds of shell[s] were in the air at once . . . all shrieking in a grand martial course that was a fitting accompaniment to the death dance of the hundreds about to fall."

While the detachments from ships were arriving, Will ran into two of his closest friends, lieutenants Samuel Preston of Illinois and Benjamin Porter of New York (no relation to the admiral), young officers who, like Cushing, were also building distinguished records and reputations for bravery. Preston and Cushing were both members of the Naval Academy's class of 1861, although Preston's experience was rather different from Will's: he graduated first in his class. He had accompanied Rhind aboard Butler's floating bomb on Christmas Eve, and he was cited for bravery. Ben Porter, twenty, graduated from the Naval Academy in 1863. The year before, while still a midshipman, he commanded a battery of howitzers at the Battle of Roanoke Island "with a degree of skill and daring," said the official report, "which not only contributed largely to the success of the day, but won the admiration of all who witnessed the display." So well regarded was young Porter that Admiral Porter named him to succeed Cushing as commander of the *Malvern*. Preston and Ben Porter had also shared the grueling experience of having been captured in a futile raid on Fort Sumter in September 1863, and spent the better part of a year in Richmond's Libby Prison before being exchanged.

Ben, Will found, was excited; as the commander of the flagship, he would have the honor of carrying the admiral's blue pennant during the assault. Preston, in contrast, would be commanding a group of pioneers, men who would precede the attack with shovels and, six hundred yards before the fort, quickly dig a trench that the rest of the force could use for cover. "Cushing," Preston said, with unusual gravity, "I have a prophetic feeling that I am not coming out alive."

"Nonsense," said Porter, trying to lighten the mood. "You bet I am."

"Cheer up, Preston," Cushing said, "and let's drink to success and little Nell." Little Nell was Ellen Grosvenor, a young lady popular with the Cushing family and their set, and later the wife of Will's brother Milton. The ever-resourceful Will pulled a bottle of beer from his pocket, and the three young officers drank the toast.

The navy briefly lifted its bombardment, and the pregnant silence that followed was suddenly filled with all the steam whistles of the fleet, bellowing and groaning and shrieking their terrible war cry. At this point, the marines and the sailors, "dressed as if for inspection," and their officers in all their gold braid, began making their way through a wooded area toward the Northeast Bastion, cutlasses ready and pistols drawn. The orders of their admiral—"board the fort on the run in a seaman-like way"—rang in their ears.

The sailors and marines met the same fate as Union soldiers at Fredericksburg, the same fate Alonzo dished out to rebel soldiers on Cemetery Ridge: they were cut to pieces. Lamb's men inside the Northeast Bastion first found their range with their cannon, tearing holes in the advancing ranks. "About five hundred yards from the fort," wrote Ensign Robley Evans, who later commanded the battleship *Iowa* during the Spanish-American War, "the head of the column suddenly stopped, and, as if by magic, the whole mass of men went down like a row of falling bricks . . . At about three hundred yards they again went down, this time under the effect of canister added to the rifle fire. Again we rallied them, and once more started to the front under a perfect hail of lead, with men dropping rapidly in every direction." By that point, Evans had been shot in four places.

Each time the sailors hit the ground, fewer of them got back up, leaving behind the dead, the wounded, and those who had given up. Those who advanced lumbered clumsily, their feet sinking to the ankles in the soft sand. They pulled their round, brimless caps over their eyes, trying to blind themselves to the blue flashes of the rebel muskets. There was a final mad dash to the palisade fence below the bastion. Maybe two hundred members of the two-thousand-man force reached that fragile stand, which, once upon a time, before Lamb's arrival, was Fort Fisher's only wall. Ironically, the paltry fence that never could have halted a Yankee attack probably ended up providing the attackers just enough protection to prevent them from suffering a total massacre.

The sailors paused. Their plan was a wreck. The bombardment had not destroyed the rebel guns, and the marines were not positioned where they should have been, in a place where they could chase off the rebel marksmen. The sailors had launched their attack too early. The soldiers should have gone first, but the sailors jumped off too soon, ensuring that the tars would face the full brunt of Lamb's men. Now the shot-up sailors were too few in number to continue the assault, and they had left too many casualties back in the woods to think that help might be on the way. "The enemy treated us to liberal doses of grape," said one participant in the charge.

Bobbing in the ocean with the rest of the fleet, George Dewey had a privileged seat. (Some thirty-three years later he would enjoy another privileged seat when, as admiral, his ships destroyed the Spanish fleet in Manila Bay.) But at Fort Fisher, the twenty-eight-year-old executive officer of the USS *Colorado* was little more than a helpless witness. "We could see very clearly the naval detachment which had landed under the face of the fort," he later wrote.

The seamen were to make the assault, while the marines covered their advance by musketry from the trenches which they had thrown up. For weapons the seamen had only cutlasses and revolvers, which evidently were chosen with the idea that storming the face of the strongest work in the Civil War was the same sort of operation as boarding a frigate in 1812. Such an attempt was sheer, murderous madness. But the seamen had been told to go and they went. In face of a furious musketry fire which they had no way of answering they rushed to within fifty yards of the parapet. Three times they closed up their shattered ranks and attempted another charge, but could gain little more ground.

"The sailors might as well have had broomsticks for all the good them pistols and cutlasses done," one seaman remarked.

Ben Porter tried to break the paralysis. Leaping forward, he seized the flag, and urged the men on. "Ben threw himself to the front, flag in hand, and the charge went on," Cushing told *Harper's* magazine. "By the ditch that surrounds the fort, Ben fell shot through the breast. His last words were 'Carry me down to the beach.' Four of the *Malvern's* and *Monticello's* men raised and tried to comply. Two were killed. He waved the others aside with a last motion and died."

Cushing then saw Sam Preston get hit in the thigh by a bullet that severed his femoral artery; he collapsed into a crater and bled out. As sharpshooters began to pick off the men huddled at the palisade, they broke and ran. Cushing tried to rally the few who wouldn't budge, but they were paralyzed. "I made up my mind that it was my duty to join my men and rally them," Cushing later wrote. "That retreat was a fearful sight. The dead lay thickly strewn along the beach, and the wounded constantly called for help to their comrades and prayed to God that they might not be left behind." Captain Breese had a similar experience; he was observed "ingloriously flying" to the rear, where he tried to rally his ravaged, ill-prepared men. Rather than remain at the rear, he then returned to the palisade. "How he managed to escape death is a marvel to me," observed a fellow officer.

Twenty-five minutes after it began, the assault was shattered, and at least 284 dead and wounded sailors and marines were bleeding into the sand. But as Colonel Lamb gazed upon the carnage his lovingly constructed defenses had wrought—"something we had never seen before—a disorderly rout of American sailors and marines"—he saw out of the corner of his eye a sight in the west that was out of place. It was the Stars and Stripes, and it flew over one of his mounds. It was not alone. There was another flag, and another, and a fourth—units of Terry's forces had conquered the slimly defended western point, and were now flooding into the fort.

At that moment, Lamb's men lifted their fire from the naval assault, and turned to face Terry's soldiers. The lifting of the gunfire was a huge relief, but Porter's shore party was now a shocked, disordered, throbbing mess. The dead needed burying, the wounded needed treatment, the shocked, dispirited men needed to be pulled out of their daze and re-formed into a group that could act, if necessary, as a fighting unit. There were other rebel armies in North Carolina; other troops might be coming to the relief of Fort Fisher.

Will Cushing stepped up and, for the rest of the day, asserted command over a broken force. He braked the retreat. He pulled wounded men off the beach and out of the danger of drowning in the incoming tide, and organized the unwounded sailors into an effective force. By evening, General Terry was able to use these men to hold his line of entrenchments, and to rotate units of the US Colored Infantry, who had been holding those trenches, into the fort. Fortunately, no rebel armies appeared to test the weary sailors. "Naval history may be searched in vain for another such instance of assault by sailors," wrote Lieutenant Commander James Parker in his memoirs. "There had been instances where sailors had landed close under small batteries (Tenerife, where Nelson lost his arm, is one such case), but never before had such a force been landed, without organization, or plan, or knowledge of the work to be done, to attempt such an assault. I don't believe it will ever be repeated."

The rebels fought valiantly on throughout the evening, but the North's advantages in manpower and firepower inexorably took effect. General Whiting had fallen at the western salient, gravely wounded; Colonel Lamb also was lost when a bullet broke his hip. Once night fell, the morale of the rebels disintegrated, and at ten o'clock, the rebels surrendered. They had lost about five hundred men defending the fort; the Union had lost nearly triple that number taking it.

Defeat, as we know, is an orphan; victory has a hundred fathers. The sailors who all too casually attacked the fort's still-ferocious defenders took a terrible licking, but between the navy's brilliant gunnery and the army's tactics and punch, the battle was won, and there was plenty of credit to go around. There was even enough to embrace Benjamin Butler, who on the morning of the sixteenth was in Washington, testifying before a congressional committee, saying that even if the navy's gunners were worth a damn, the mighty Fort Fisher was simply impregnable. At that moment there was noise on the street—cheering, newsboys crying "Extra!" The headline, it seems, was from North Carolina: Fort Fisher had fallen. "Impossible!" Butler blustered, but in no time the room was roaring with laughter. At least Butler had the wit to know that when you are the butt of the joke, make sure you laugh loudest of all. When things quieted, he raised his hand, and offered a benediction. "Thank God for victory!" he said.

Thank God for victory, for success, for the glory of triumph. That way, there is enough backslapping and drink buying and cigar lighting so that when a man felt like crying over the wasted futures of Ben Porter and Sam Preston and so many others, there were too many people around to indulge the emotion. And when they went away, and a man's thoughts became full of people who were no longer there—well, thank goodness there was still a war going on.*

---

* Butler could not maintain his facade forever. On January 18, Gideon Welles wrote in his diary, "The congratulations on the capture of Fort Fisher are hearty and earnest. . . . General Butler does not appear gladsome."

CHAPTER 44

Endgames

ORT FISHER MAY HAVE BEEN NEUTRALIZED, but the path to Wilmington up the Cape Fear River still lay under a number of smaller batteries, any one of which could clog up traffic and inflict casualties. Guarding the mouth of the river was Fort Holmes on Old Inlet; forts Campbell and Caswell as well as Battery Shaw on Oak Island; and Fort Johnson, east of Smithville. In the middle part of the river stood Fort Lamb and farther north, Fort Anderson and Fort Sugar Loaf covered the approach from opposite shores; still farther north was Town Creek Battery. If an invasion force reached the watery outskirts of Wilmington, attackers would have to deal with forts Meares, Campbell, Lee, and Stokes, and Eagle's Island Battery.

A weary Cushing spent the day after the attack, the sixteenth, clearing mines from the channel that he had coolly charted on Christmas. The next morning, members of his crew heard explosions from the area of Fort Caswell across Old Inlet, and sighted smoke. Porter told Cushing to investigate.

Will crossed to the fort with five men and an officer in a gig and landed unmolested. He was shocked to discover that the place had been abandoned, and his tiny force was now the new proud owner of a formidable installation with impressively high walls and thirty guns. With enough troops to defend it, the rebels might have caused Porter real problems; on the other hand, Fort Fisher, with its soft, smothering walls and formidable batteries, took but a couple days to fall. In any event, they were gone. Cushing raised the Stars and Stripes over Fort Caswell. For the next few hours, he had the pleasure of repeating that exercise at Fort Campbell, Fort Shaw, and Bald Head Battery.

He and his little force then left for Smithville, where he had gone general hunting the year before. It, too, was deserted, or at least was well along in the process. Cushing received the surrender of the town from the mayor, took possession of a large supply of muskets and provisions, and once again broke into the home of General Hébert, only to find that the general was still not home and did not seem likely to be returning. Some rebel cavalry on the outskirts of town appeared in no hurry to leave, however, so Cushing called for reinforcements, and the cavalry moved on. By the nineteenth, Cushing had two hundred men under him, had named himself the military governor of Smithville, and was living in General Hébert's large white house with the generous veranda.

For the next month, Cushing cruised up and down the Cape Fear River, chasing blockade runners, seizing rebel goods, and outsmarting his adversaries. It was less a war than schoolboy pranking.

The very first thing he did at Smithville was to arrest the pilots who had guided blockade runners through the tricky shoals and up the elusive channels of the Cape Fear River. Cushing's grander scheme was to capture any blockade runners who remained at sea. He thought that he might have a small window during which news of the Union's victory at Fort Fisher might not have traveled to the Bahamas or to Cuba, and that there might be some ships still at sea that hadn't heard anything since Butler ignominiously decamped before the walls of Fort Fisher. To lure the ships in, he would need the pilots to hang out the proper signal lights that the blockade-running captains needed to see before heading into the inlets. So Cushing told the pilots, *Hang the proper signal lights, or I'll hang you*. If his threat was serious will never be known. The lights were lit, and on the second night, two ships, heavy with goods, slipped unsuspectingly into the trap.

The first was the *Charlotte,* a reasonably fast but unusually capacious ship, which was bringing in small arms, blankets, shoes, liquor, lace, silks, and women's hats from Paris. She slid over the bar at Old Inlet and anchored next to the ship that was already resting there—the *Malvern,* the flagship of Admiral Porter, who looked on with pleasure as his men boarded the vessel. The *Charlotte'*s captain and his five passengers, all British, several of them army officers, had just begun a champagne supper to mark their safe arrival when they were interrupted by Cushing, who called for another case of champagne.

"Gentlemen," he said, "we will drink to the success of those who succeed."

"Beastly luck!" exclaimed one of the passengers. "An unmitigated sell!" added another.

Before long, an encore performance was held, this time with the *Stag,* one of the largest of the blockade runners that had been built in England for the Confederacy. Her captain had orders to burn her rather than allow her to fall into Yankee hands, but instead he pulled in and anchored her into captivity.

For the next week or so, Cushing followed Porter's orders to search for blockade runners, but came up empty-handed. After a profitless week, Cushing decided to explore the Little River, the tributary of the Cape Fear that he had so memorably raided in January 1863. Eight miles up, he landed the *Monticello* in All Saints Parish, rounded up the mayor, and rather high-handedly demanded a hot breakfast for himself and his four boatloads of men. As an inducement, he told the citizens that he was just the tip of an invasion force. Naturally he was fed a good breakfast, along with a lot of assurances that All Saints Parish loved the Union and was eager to be free from military rule. Cushing nonetheless burned $15,000 worth of cotton, and took off with twenty-three more bales and some now-liberated black men who wanted to go north. Later he sent back another detachment to burn a storehouse full of cotton in a neighboring inlet. The war was ending, but Cushing was still making the rebels pay.

Cushing reported back to Porter after a couple of weeks, handing over the prisoners he had taken. The admiral told Will that unlike the rebels who had abandoned their guns on the lower Cape Fear, the defenders at Fort Anderson were hanging tough. Cushing went out on a couple of forays to scout the position, once bringing along his brother Milton, an acting paymaster; Will had promised him "a lark," and together they examined some obstructions in front of Fort Anderson and then went upriver nearly to Wilmington. (Reading between the lines fifteen decades later, one wonders if Will treated his deskbound brother to a thrill or two without actually placing him in danger.)

The second time Will checked out the obstructions, on the following evening, he went without Milton, and conducted a much closer, more businesslike examination. He found the fort was protected by three layers of piles, cemented with sand and earth, too formidable an obstacle to be overcome by ramming. He also saw plenty of torpedoes.

"One night," he recalled in his memoirs, "I found a band of music playing in Anderson, and speeches being made by enthusiastic confederates, who were picturing in glowing terms the victories of the chivalrous South; and heaping whole continents of scorn upon the base and cowardly North. The confederacy was about to tumble but they were blind to that fact. Their armies were all beaten, but one Southerner was still the sure conqueror of five Yankees." Cushing didn't record on what date this happened, nor did he seem to know what the occasion might be ("What do you suppose they have to cheer about?" he asked a comrade). But this scouting party was surely made after the fifth and before the eighteenth; February 8 would have been the fourth anniversary of the founding of the Confederate government in Montgomery. Perhaps Cushing stumbled upon an anniversary celebration.

The cheerfulness irked Cushing, and as the band played "Dixie," he took his carbine and sent "a bullet amidst the crowd." The revelers returned fire, and Will and his men dashed back to their ship. It's not clear whether the shot Will put into the crowd found flesh.

Cushing's findings about Fort Anderson came as a disappointment to Porter, who had hoped for better news. With his fleet redistributed to move against Charleston and other objectives, Porter no longer had the naval forces to capture the fort. It was then that Cushing had a brainstorm. *Build a mock monitor, sir! Just like you did on the Mississippi!*

Porter indeed had used an unmanned wooden monitor to draw the fire of Confederate guns in Vicksburg and to panic them. Porter, of course, loved the idea—little flatters an old performer more than being reminded of one of his hits—and very soon Old Bogey was being built on a flatboat out of barrel staves and canvas. "It was not possible," wrote Cushing, "to tell the difference at two hundred yards." The proof came on February 18, when Cushing launched his Trojan ship. The rebels poured fire on it, but the plucky Old Bogey skirted the obstructions and sailed past the sight of the fort before running aground.

Cushing could not have hoped for a more complete success. With a monitor upriver, the Confederates abandoned Fort Anderson, with its ten guns and piles of ammunition, without offering a fight.

Union forces entered Wilmington on February 22, but by then the navy's part of the job was finished and Cushing assigned a new task. Confederate agents in Denmark had at long last achieved Stephen Mallory's dream and purchased a European ironclad, the *Sphinx*, a sluggish ship built in Bordeaux and sold to the Danes, who rechristened her the *Staerkodder*. Now in the hands of the rebels, she was once again renamed the *Stonewall*; according to the American consul at Nantes, she had been sighted at the island of Houat, and was on her way to America. Admiral Porter was notified, and although it wouldn't take a Napoleon to realize that the rebels were beaten, another ironclad loose on the Atlantic coast could cause a lot of pointless bloodshed. Porter ordered Cushing, now the navy's resident dragon slayer, to leave the Cape Fear River and take the *Monticello* to Norfolk to have a torpedo attached to it. No matter that Cushing barely escaped with his life in his assault on the *Albemarle*; no matter that the torpedo was a conspicuously unpredictable weapon; no matter that the navy was full of men eager for glory—*get Cushing to do it!*

Not that Cushing seemed to mind.

CHAPTER 45

Victory

A FTER BERTHING THE *MONTICELLO*, on February 22, Will
headed to the Navy Department to update Secretary Welles.
He arrived just as the capital was learning that Union troops
were taking possession of Wilmington. "While the heavy salutes at
meridian were firing," Welles later wrote in his diary, "young Cushing came in with the intelligence of the capture of Fort Anderson."
Delighted with the news, Welles asked Cushing to come with him
to the White House. "While there General Joe Hooker came in, and
[Secretary of State William] Seward, for whom the President had sent,
brought a dispatch from [American consul in Paris John] Bigelow of
a favorable character. General H. thinks it is the brightest day in four
years. The President was cheerful and laughed heartily over Cushing's
account of the dumb monitor which he sent past Fort Anderson." Lincoln also offered his personal congratulations on Cushing's destruction
of the *Albemarle*, and on his subsequent promotion.

Was this the apex of Will Cushing's life? Certainly it would have
to rank among the most sublime moments—sitting with the president
and other great men of the nation, receiving their congratulations on
his victories, amusing them with tales of his cleverness, telling them
how he'd handle the *Stonewall*, and discussing the other developments
of the day. Perhaps it was the high point, although for a man like

Cushing, the great moment might have come the moment the torpedo exploded, or when he whispered "It is done" to Acting Master Brooks of the *Valley City*, or any number of other times when he had achieved a perfect validation of his existence. But wherever that moment with Lincoln ranked, no more than two years later, when he composed his memoirs while on duty in the Pacific, he did not bother to bring it up.

Two days after meeting Lincoln, he was separated from the *Monticello* and told to await orders. Nearly three months passed before orders came from the Navy Department. During that time, Robert E. Lee would surrender, the *Stonewall* would sit impotently in Havana harbor, the Confederacy would perish, Abraham Lincoln would be killed, and the war would come to a close. Peace had broken out, and Welles needed to find a suitable place for his young hellcat.

Cushing celebrated the Union victory in Fredonia. The night that Richmond fell, April 3, a crowd that had already been saluting the news at the Concert Hall in town marched by torchlight to Elizabeth Cushing's house. In response to their jubilant, insistent serenade, the resident hero stepped onto the porch and added some brief remarks to the patriotic clamor. "Three cheers for the old flag!" he ended, then joined the throng, which boisterously paraded to the Johnson House hotel, where everyone capped the glorious evening with a late supper. Cushing, his mother, and his sister were honored with seats at the head table. The victory party lasted all night, the celebrants making a fair bid to exorcise four years' worth of woe and worry with one great shebang. Outside the hotel, Fredonians took the rebel flag that Cushing had captured in Fort Caswell in January, spread it on the street, and took turns trampling on it. At first light the rebel rag was found flying upside down at the courthouse, beneath a glorious Stars and Stripes. A week later, when Lee's surrender was announced, the whole party replayed at greater length and louder volume, although with something of a more mechanical feel. Cushing spoke again, the main speaker in what was now a formal program, and he no doubt did his rousing best. He did not, however, reprise his revelry, but instead spent the night hiking in the hills. It isn't hard to imagine what might have been on his mind. This was a night to celebrate with comrades, with the men whose sacrifices had purchased this victory, and to raise a glass to absent friends, to Alonzo and Charlie Flusser, to Ben Porter and Sam Preston, to John Woodman and Sam Higgins, and maybe even to the rebel officer with the ringlets whose men Will had blown apart on the banks of the snaky Blackwater, and more, so many more. Instead, he was left with the poltroons of Chautauqua County, reckoning with the realization that the conflict in which he had invested all of his creativity and ingenuity and bravado, and which in return had rewarded him with honor, wealth, and glory, had come to an end.

In *War Is a Force That Gives Us Meaning*, his brilliant book of 2002, the veteran war correspondent Chris Hedges acknowledges that war can be exhilarating and even addictive: "It gives us purpose, meaning, a reason for living." The Civil War had revealed Cushing to be a genius of war, an artist of military action. Now his easel had disappeared. No wonder he preferred to be alone in the hills. The apple farmers may have been ordinary men, but in the morning, when they opened their bleary eyes, they would know who they were.

CHAPTER 46

On the West Coast

C USHING KNEW HE WANTED TO STAY in the navy, a safe and unimaginative choice. The second half of the nineteenth century was going to bring vast rewards to those audacious enough to seize the moment. He could have been an explorer, a lawman, an adventurer, a revolutionary, an imperialist, a progressive, a well-compensated captain in another country's navy. How much would his good name have been worth on a company's board of directors, or on a political party's ticket? He could have gone anywhere and brought war with him. Instead, he remained in the navy, where he would wait for war to come to him.

Lee surrendered in April, and Cushing, without an assignment since February, grew restless. The large navy that Gideon Welles built in 1861 and 1862 rapidly began demobilizing. If the prewar service was going to be any kind of a model for how the navy would be reorganizing itself, officers' berths were going to be assigned to the most senior men. Will, not yet twenty-three years old, a man with a high rank but little tenure, was concerned that he would be left out. In May he finally received temporary orders to report to New York Navy Yard—the arrival of Lieutenant Commander William Cushing was noted by the *New York Times* in its daily report of notables who had entered or exited the city—but this assignment did not completely alleviate Will's anxiety. Not until mid-June, when he was named the executive officer of the *Lancaster*, the flagship of the Pacific Squadron, could Will rest easy. The *Lancaster* was a plum assignment; Welles and Fox could not have done more to show their confidence in Cushing and his future. The ship was a large, modern vessel whose commander headed a squadron; clearly, Cushing would have many opportunities to sharpen his management skills and learn the fine points of command, and he would have them in the Pacific, a new ocean for him, and one that the Navy Department had alertly recognized as a key arena for the fulfillment of America's—and the navy's—destiny.

True, there would be some sacrifice. For the first time in almost three years, Cushing would not be the master of his own vessel, but would report to a superior, in this case George Pearson, a sixty-six-year-old acting rear admiral, whose solid if unspectacular success patrolling the Pacific during the Civil War was the capstone of a solid if unspectacular career. The *Lancaster*'s most dramatic service during the war was thwarting the so-called Salvador Pirates, a group of Confederate sailors who aimed to capture one of the steamships belonging to the Panama Railroad, turn it into a raider, and seize a gold-laden vessel belonging to the Pacific Steamship Company. In the coming months, when the captain and the other officers swapped war stories in the wardroom, Cushing no doubt had to exercise a fair amount of self-discipline in order to avoid monopolizing the conversation.

Cushing spent nearly two years on the *Lancaster*. He joined the ship's company at Aspinwall, a city on the Atlantic coast of Panama, whose "quaint streets and houses all remind me of history and romance," as he wrote his mother, but whose dilapidated churches and pocky walls "illustrate the decay of Spain's glory and fame as well as anything could." The country was populated predominantly by "Spanish negroes," and he disapproved "that such a miserable people should be able to hold this magnificent country, and to call themselves a nation." A natural-born American imperialist, Cushing contended that "we could land a good ship's crew and take the whole of Central America." From some men, such talk could be dismissed as idle boasting; with Cushing, a plan was probably half sprung.

The *Lancaster* next sailed to the Sandwich Islands, soon to be relabeled Hawaii. With the Civil War occupying the navy's attentions, no American warship had visited the islands for seven years, and the British used the period of distraction to court King Kamehameha V, going so far as to invite his mother to visit Queen Victoria in London. Cushing's interest in Hawaii was less a diplomat's than a tourist's. Captivated by the volcanoes, he tried to reach the rim of Kilauea, but he broke his shoulder when his horse stumbled and fell on him. He had to be carried back to the *Lancaster* on a litter, an excruciating thirty-five miles.

A personal high point for Cushing was marked in March 1866, when the *Lancaster* docked in San Francisco, and the man who sank the *Albemarle* was given a hero's welcome. The Board of Supervisors voted him the "freedom of the city," an earlier version of being given the key to the city, an honor dating back to medieval times. He became, for the time he was in port, the beau of the social season, the sine qua non of a successful soiree. "I find that it is impossible to keep out of flirtations," he wrote in a letter to his mother. "The ladies here are exceedingly pretty." One beautiful young woman and the dashing war hero seem to have been especially drawn to one another. "The admitted belle of the city is exceedingly charming in every way. I am therefore engaged in the dangerous amusement of escorting her everywhere and have cut out all competitors." Customarily, the object of such a flirtation was marriage; Cushing was not interested in a relationship, but he did not feel that he was taking advantage of an ingenue. "If she were not a young lady who knows full well how to look after herself, I would not even enter the lists," he wrote his mother. "As it is, no harm can come either way."

Cushing's concerns nominally had to do with money; he didn't want to enter into marriage with nothing but an officer's salary to sustain his family. He had anticipated a sizable reward for sinking the *Albemarle*, perhaps $50,000. Instead, he had been paid a $6,000 installment of an $18,000 award that he gave to his mother. The navy suspended hearings on other claims, for ships like the *Stag* and the *Charlotte*. Will didn't think his bounty would be enough—not enough, anyway, to court this unnamed belle of San Francisco. Meanwhile, the *Albemarle* settlement was under legal review.*

In 1867 his tour of duty with the *Lancaster* was over. Will went back east on leave, and to await orders. Passing through Norfolk, he visited the hulk of the *Albemarle*. She had been raised from the Roanoke and towed by the *Ceres*, once one of the gang of seven she had fought to a draw, to the Norfolk Navy Yard, where she was moored in ordinary storage. Constructed without exterior-surface worm protection, and provided no protection at the Navy Yard, the once ferocious leviathan sat ignored, decaying in the sun. "She'd been stripped of her iron and machinery, and . . . left to rot down. *Sic transit gloria mundi*."

Was he also thinking of himself? What role is there for a dragon slayer once the dragon is dead?

---

* Prizes were awarded to encourage energy and enterprise on the part of naval officers and their crews. Everyone involved in capturing or sinking an enemy vessel, ranking from a powder monkey to the admiral of the fleet, got a share of the value of the ship and its cargo, with most going to the captain. In August 1865, a prize court in Washington determined that the *Albemarle* was worth $79,944; Will's share was calculated under a complicated formula to be just under $18,000. (Admiral Porter got $4,000 just for thinking that Will couldn't do it.) Will was unhappy—he expected to get about $50,000—but he never complained on the record. In 1873 Congress reevaluated the proceedings, and found that Cushing and his men should have been credited with $200,000 worth of property that fell into US hands after the raid, raising Will's share to $56,000. Ensign Howorth ultimately collected $35,887.50, and Ensign Gay took $24,710. Later, Charles Steever, a third assistant engineer who was among the picket boat's crew, sued, saying that the most recent calculations had not been performed according to the navy's rules. In March 1885, the Supreme Court decided that Steever was correct, and that Cushing, Howorth, and Gay had been overpaid, and the others underpaid. Under this opinion, Will was entitled to a flat 10 percent of the value of the prize, which in this case amounted to $25,126, slightly more than half of what he had been awarded. The rest would be distributed proportionally based on salary, meaning that three of the men—acting assistant paymaster Swan and third assistant engineers Stotesbury and Steever—would have earned more than Cushing, the engineers about $10,000 more each, and Swan about $20,000 more. No effort was made to recoup the overpayment the officers received, but the others were made whole. The practice of awarding prizes began to be phased out after the Civil War, and was ended by Congress during World War I.

CHAPTER 47

Love and Duty

CUSHING SPENT A GOOD PORTION OF 1867 on leave, much of it in Fredonia. Like many vacations, his was spent relatively uneventfully. He sat for a bust by a local sculptor, Rufus W. Lester. He worked on his Civil War memoirs. He took two cousins from Boston sailing on icy Dunkirk Bay, despite warnings about the chunks of ice and tricky winds. "I have not gone through all the ocean peril I have to be drowned in a mill pond," he supposedly said. Given that his boat capsized and that he and his charges had to be rescued by the very natives who had shared their warnings, one hopes his tone was self-effacing rather than haughty. After the rescue, he was incapacitated for two days with a severe pain in his hip. His mother chalked it up to his exposure to the extreme cold of the bay, but this was perhaps wishful thinking. These pains had started a couple months after the sinking of the *Albemarle*; this was the worst attack by far.

Easily the most significant development of the time, however, was that he fell in love. The fortunate young lady was twenty-year-old Kate Forbes, the daughter of a prosperous and well-regarded merchant who also commanded the Sixty-eighth New York regiment. Kate has been described as vivacious, charming, tall, slim, and possessing "youthful beauty"; she was said to hold herself proudly, "like a soldier." In her photograph, which like all nineteenth-century photographs deprives her of color, animation, or a smile, she looks a little like the actress Mary Louise Parker. Moreover, she had had something of an education: she learned languages and mathematics.

The beginning of the courtship is a little murky. Although Will had, in effect, moved away from Fredonia when he was fourteen, they might have been distantly known to one another all that time. Or they might have met when Will was in Fredonia when the war ended; among the people with whom he celebrated was David Forbes, the merchant-general, and eighteen-year-old Kate might have caught the hero's eye then. A handful of occasions presented themselves over the course of the summer. In May, he came to town to negotiate the terms of the sale of his mother's house; in June, he attended the wedding of his sister Mary Isabel, a wedding in which her friend Kate served as a bridesmaid. A month later, he came to Fredonia to close on the sale of the house, and proposed.

His decision seems both sudden and surprising. First, Will made it clear that he would not marry until he had enough income to support a wife and family in comfort. Second, he was a very eligible bachelor. Although he did not come from wealth, he was Albemarle Cushing, a national hero who had been feted by the most powerful, wealthiest, and most prominent people in Washington, Boston, New York, Philadelphia, and San Francisco, and who had enjoyed flirtations with young ladies in those cities. Instead, he plucked a country flower.

They must have been in love; what else would excuse the predicament their engagement created? Gideon Welles was still the secretary of the navy, and still Cushing's patron. Will had been lobbying him hard for command of his own ship, and although it took Welles the better part of the summer to find him the right slot, Will's orders finally came through. He was given command of the *Maumee*, a three-masted gunboat with an Ericsson engine and twelve guns that was being assigned to the Asiatic squadron. Will was pleased. "She is a beauty; and in every respect, a good one," he said. His assignment, however—to take the *Maumee* for an extended cruise to the Far

East—would surely last for many months and perhaps as long as five years. He had to have been very confident in his young love to believe that his and Kate's commitment would endure a separation of that length; it surely was a lot to ask of her. And yet they did not marry before he shipped out, an obvious option. They decided it would be best to wait.

"I intend to see every nook and corner of this little world that is to be seen, if I live," he had written to a cousin several years earlier, and this expedition on the *Maumee* would cover a good part of the atlas. The ship left Fort Monroe in Hampton Roads on November 11, and reached Rio de Janeiro on the day after Christmas. Cushing stayed three weeks and then set out for Cape Town, South Africa.

Will was in both places an enthusiastic tourist. In Brazil he studied Sugar Loaf mountain; relished the mangoes, pomegranates, and other exotic fruit; gazed upon the beautiful "black-eyed Spanish delilahs"; and was fined by the authorities for breaking city ordinances against driving a wagon too fast. He met the emperor of Brazil. He bought Kate earrings made of polished green beetles in gold mounts, which he claimed were very popular in Rio. For himself, he bought a monkey.

In customary fashion, Cushing also stirred up a bit of trouble. Riding in his official cutter in Rio harbor while wearing civilian clothes, Will was slighted—that is, accorded insufficient respect—by a Brazilian naval officer. Will treated this as an insult to the flag, and demanded satisfaction. When Captain Melancthon Wooley, the senior US naval officer present, heard of the affair, he issued orders to Cushing to go to sea as soon as possible, muttering, "If that young man stays here, he will bring on an international war!"

The *Maumee* left Rio on January 9, 1868; Cushing departed unhappily. "I am disgusted with the big city of Rio and its 500,000 people, because of numerous things," he wrote in his diary, "and I don't want to see it again." Twenty days and thirteen hours later, the *Maumee* reached Cape Town, a notably fast passage. For several days during the crossing he suffered a high fever that left him confined to bed and tormented by "the fictitious infinity of delirium." On the upside, his crew caught an albatross, something sailors regard as good luck.

The three weeks Cushing spent in Cape Town seem to have been intensely social. Wearing full dress, he visited the governor general of the colony, called on other notables, swapped shipboard visits with British officers, and entertained local dignitaries aboard the *Maumee*. The highlight of this reception, which would be repeated numerous times as the ship made its way through the waters of the Far East, was a performance by some of the more musically inclined members of the crew. In December, Will had given some of the men permission "to organize a troop [*sic*] of 'Nigger Minstrels' for the entertainment of guests, etc." The troupe called itself the *Maumee* Christys, a reference to Christy's Minstrels, the era's most famous blackface minstrel act, one that performed on the stages of the United States and the United Kingdom for more than sixty years. Performances were consistently well received, and Cushing not only approved of the act, he underwrote the group with the purchase of a dozen musical instruments. In return, he was able to parlay his crew's abilities into greater popularity for himself and, by extension, the United States, among the European diplomatic and military communities that he encountered on his voyage.

Modern audiences would undoubtedly blanch in shock at the casual racism of these minstrel shows, the first distinctly American musical form, which depicted black people as lazy, dim-witted, buffoonish, and eager to perform catchy, delightful music. It would be nice to report that Cushing transcended the prevailing thinking of his age, that he was more enlightened about matters of race, but he wasn't. In no sense did he believe anything but what most men of his station believed— namely, that white European and American males should rule the world. Encounters with people of color, particularly those who were poor, brought out a smirky superiority in Cushing. For example, when he arrived in Africa, he published a kind of travel article in the *Fredonia Censor*. "Africa is quite a tract of land," he wrote.

I could not see all of it on account of a large tree that stood directly in the way, but from the view I got I should judge it to contain 60 or 70 acres more than North America. The native African is very dark complexioned, and not very delicately perfumed, especially in hot weather. They are not at all extravagant in dress, a red handkerchief or half yard of sheeting constitutes the wardrobe of most of them. Their principal accomplishments are throwing the boomerang and eating missionaries. A well brought up African will eat his brother with the greatest nonchalance, and consider a Christian done up in a pot pie a great luxury.

Cushing obviously wrote this tongue in cheek, but many a truth is revealed in jest. Cushing was a product of his times, raised to lead. The idea that the races might be equal was one that he never seriously considered.

More than eleven weeks would pass before the *Maumee* reached Hong Kong on May 1, with stops at St. Paul Island and Batavia on the island of Java in between. During the first leg of the trip, Cushing suffered a relapse of his fever, but he had recovered by the time the ship reached St. Paul on March 14. The *Maumee* stayed at the uninhabited (by humans) volcanic island for six days, while the crew replenished the supply of fresh fruit and stocked up on fish. They also relaxed, in their way; on one day, Cushing personally shot 47 penguins and caught 187 fish. On April 20 they reached Batavia; on the way Cushing was again bedridden with the fever for a few days. The Batavians welcomed Cushing enthusiastically—"I am well-known here, a 'great lion,'" he wrote to Kate. "They call me 'the second Nelson'"—but he stayed only two days before heading for Hong Kong, taking the most direct route possible and skipping Singapore. Almost certainly he should have paid more attention to his stores; he was nearly out of fruit and fresh water when on May 1 he finally dropped anchor in Hong Kong, the headquarters of America's Asiatic Squadron.

CHAPTER 48

Love Letters

NOTHING SUSTAINED WILL during those last few difficult days of his cruise more than the expectation that there would be a pile of mail waiting for him. "I do long for them," he wrote to Kate on the eve of his arrival. "I can hardly wait til tomorrow. Every minute is a long year, until I hold fast your letters." Imagine, then, his incredible disappointment when he arrived to find from Kate only two letters. One, written in December, was caring and affectionate; the second, mailed a month later, shocked him to the marrow, for instead of eloquent declarations of love, it rather casually suggested that Kate was considering bringing their engagement to an end.

Cushing was an ardent and disciplined correspondent, especially to Kate. His notes to her fall into several general categories, but they all reveal him to be what he was: a young man still coming into his maturity, a young officer still learning how to command, a young beau still learning how to sustain a relationship, and a long-distance one at that. There is a reason that young men in love are often treated as comic characters: their efforts to be serious and sincere contrast sharply with their ardor and emotional intensity. Will could be highly romantic ("Oh Kate, dear darling Kate! God bless and keep you—yes—us—until we meet again. All my hopes are bound upon you, and with all my heart, I ask you to love and remember"); petulant ("[You say in your letters] either you have been losing your love for me—or have been flirting—or, as in your last, you coolly inform me that I am a great egoist—and once made you angry, while at the same time you fail to tell me what I said and leave me in danger of offending you in the future"); condescending ("If ever I saw a dirty, mangy dog I would name it 'Fredonia,' if I discovered any low, mean, creeping trick or lie I would make 'Fredonia' the adjective to describe it"); paternal ("Aren't you a foolish, nervous girl to write so earnestly about your music[al studies]?"); and pompous ("Time will prove whether a gentleman and man of honor can rise above the fetid and envenomed clouds of falsehood and malice").

Will wasted no time in replying to her cool letter. "How shall I commence? What shall I say? My heart is like lead in my bosom, and I am sick with disappointment. Oh! Kate—my own precious girl. I do not know what to think or to write to you."

She hadn't given him very much to go on, and the letters were months old besides. He harped on one phrase, in which she said she had "forced" herself to write to him. "I could not help thinking that you grudge me the little time you give to me amidst the daily gaiety you mention—and I know that my heart tells me that the favor of love was not there." Most of the rest of the letter consists of Will howling at the moon. "Do you not, indeed, love Oh my darling! Say that you do! I cannot bear to lose you!"

This was the first letter he sent in response. He wrote many more. All of them contained repeated expressions of his love and devotion and the pain he felt at not being with her. He also attempted to show, with the very limited options he had at his disposal, that he was thinking of things that were important to her. He strongly rejected having an interest in any women in Fredonia with whom he may once have been associated, especially one Sally Wheelock. He expressed an interest in joining a church, once they were married, and worshipping there, rather than asking her to change her affiliation. He asked about what colors of silk might flatter her and her sister, since he was thinking of having dresses made for them. And far from complaining about the rubes of

Fredonia, he inquired respectfully about her father. He also from time to time offered a coy reference to "feeling in fine flirting condition," and the young ladies he encountered at one official function or another, just to make sure she didn't think that she was the only starfish in the sea. Admiral Porter had a less elaborate strategy for taking Fort Fisher than Cushing possessed for keeping Kate Forbes.

Mostly he played his ace, over and over. Surely a number of good young men with fine prospects were present body and soul on the sidewalks of Fredonia, birds virtually in hand, closer than Will was and for the foreseeable future could be. And the reason for that was simple: he was Will "Albemarle" Cushing, a national hero, the youngest lieutenant commander in the navy, and he wasn't around not because he was hauling apples to Albany but because he was commanding an American warship in distant China. He shared with Kate everything he was experiencing—the palaces, the people, the exotic cuisine that offered dog, owl, and chicken heads, the inexpensive treasures, his experiment with opium. Kate Forbes would have to endure with painful patience a tremendous amount of loneliness before she would ever see her investment in Will Cushing mature into profitability, but he tried to show her as best he could that their future life together would be filled with status, income, and adventure, if only she would wait.

Perhaps it was the emotional disappointment he was feeling after receiving Kate's letters, or the aftereffects of his long and feverish journey, or his inherent obstinacy about rules and protocols, but Will committed a faux pas upon his arrival in Hong Kong that caused him enormous embarrassment. It was a British colony; by custom and tradition, Will, as the commander of a visiting ship, should have paid a visit to the officer who commanded the British fleet in China. The commander was Admiral of the Fleet Sir Henry Keppel, member of an eminent family, who was at that time in the forty-sixth year of a distinguished naval career that saw him fighting Malay pirates before Will was born and commanding a naval brigade at Sevastopol during the Crimean War when Will was a schoolboy. Instead of presenting himself, Will sent his card to the admiral via an ensign named William Emory, who was surely one of the ship's junior officers, if not actually the youngest.

The very next day, Admiral Keppel—with his broad girth, abundant whiskers, and plumed bicorne, a model of Victorian military grandeur—came to the *Maumee* to pay a call. Keppel was met by Cushing and the ship's other senior officers, and he and Will then exchanged the customary greetings. Then, as protocol instructed, Will invited Keppel to his cabin. But the admiral surprised everyone by politely declining, and asked instead for Ensign Emory. "I have come to return his call," said the admiral, who was escorted to the junior officers' wardroom, where he paid a lengthy visit to the young man. Oh, how this silken rebuke must have stung Will! (Emory was the son of army general William Emory, a distinguished cartographer, and would go on to become an admiral and, like Robley Evans, command one of the legs of the Great White Fleet's trip around the world.)

His left-footed landing notwithstanding, Cushing's arrival was welcomed enthusiastically by the other Americans in China. The commander of the China Station was Admiral Stephen Clegg Rowan, the man who had declined the opportunity to lead the mission to sink the *Albemarle*. This might have produced awkward feelings in a lesser man, but Rowan was pleased to have Cushing's talents at his disposal. He assigned Will to cooperate with the British fleet in ridding the area of the pirates who had been plaguing trade vessels on the Pearl River and the Gulf of Tonkin.

Cushing was delighted; the prospect of suppressing those predators conveyed his first chance of seeing real action in four years. He set up operations off the island of Hainan. Assigned to Admiral Rowan's flagship was Ensign Robley Evans, the young officer who was still recovering from the four gunshots he sustained at Fort Fisher. He implored Rowan to reassign him to Cushing, but was turned down on medical grounds. As Evans recounted in his memoirs, however, he missed nothing. "Cushing went after the pirates," he wrote, "and in a few days they began to arrive at Hong Kong by the dozens. He found, as we all suspected he would, that every Chinese junk was a pirate when it suited the owner to be so. The war junks were the worst of the lot. So Cushing ran in everything that he came across and only stopped when the authorities asked that he be recalled, as he was capturing the entire Chinese merchant fleet."

After suppressing, if only temporarily, the pirates of the South China Sea, Cushing proceeded in November 1868 to Yokohama, where he would begin an extended stay in Japan. There, to his great delight, he found two letters from Kate, the first he had received since that chilly January letter received in Hong Kong in May. Will spared no exclamation points in expressing his happiness and relief. "Thank you! Bless you! My love—my own dear sweetheart—the whole World, life—all things—seem brighter and better since I have read [your letters]. . . . [Y]ou are so good in these sixteen pages that my heart is content—and the clouds are all blown away. You do love me—I am not forgotten—that is enough for me. Oh how I do love you for your trust and constancy!"

So ENDED WILL Cushing's spell in romantic purgatory. He would remain in the Far East for another year; although he and Kate would sometimes poke or provoke each other in a letter, the fevered feelings of confusion and doubt never again dominated the relationship. It is hard to tell how calculating Kate was being when she wrote to Will that her social calendar was so busy that she practically had to force herself to find time to write to him. If, in the bright light of day following their whirlwind courtship, she wanted more reassurances from this fiancé she hardly knew, she got them. If she wanted the war hero/world traveler to take his eyes off the lush landscapes and black-eyed Delilahs he was encountering and turn them back to boring little Fredonia, she succeeded. And whether or not Will was consciously playing the same game, his references to flirtations at official balls or to seeing naked women and men together at Japanese bathhouses struck a jealous chord in her. At one point he felt compelled to send her a half-filled dance card to prove that he wasn't excessively enjoying himself at the social functions he was obliged to attend. In this couple's case, a little friction seemed to help keep the fires of affection burning.

CHAPTER 49

In the Orient

L ATE IN AUGUST 1868, Cushing returned to China. He had
been ordered to take the *Maumee* up the Pei Ho River, and to
evaluate the security of the numerous missionaries and other
Americans in the vicinity of Tientsin. During this stay, Cushing and
several of his officers availed themselves of the opportunity to indulge
in some tourism in nearby Beijing. Staying at the American legation,
they visited the Forbidden City. Discovering an unguarded point of
access, they snuck in and prowled around. Eventually they were discovered and held by about a hundred guards, who cried and moaned
that they now faced decapitation because the walls had been breached.
Instead of taking the Americans into custody, they begged the foreigners who had subjected them to such shame to be gone, and Cushing and
his friends obliged.

They visited other sites, practicing a kind of imperial tourism. They
visited the Temple of Yung-Ho-King, formerly the palace of the heir
to the throne. Dominated by a large statue of Buddha carved from
one tree, the temple was also decorated with hundreds of other statues.
Will tried to buy one—"one of the brass ones, about a foot high, a
female, tastefully dressed in a necklace and pair of bracelets"—but was
told that they were not for sale. He then tried to bribe one of the priests
to make an exception, but was refused. As a final gambit, Will moved

one of the small statues of Buddha that was in easy reach. When a shaken caretaker demanded to know what had happened to the statue, Will showed the frightened old man where it had been misplaced. "While he was replacing it," Will wrote, "I managed to pocket a very pretty idol of stone—about 300 years old—which he did not miss." Perhaps remembering the deed brought on a tiny pang of conscience, for he then tried to exculpate himself for this act of temple-lifting. "This was a case where stealing is a virtue," he wrote. "I stole an idol, and so aided the cause of Christianity." He also smuggled home a stone from the Great Wall.

While Cushing was in the Far East protecting American interests, he was acquiring an advanced tutorial on Asian goods, their value, and their going rate, as well as customs rules and regulations. Silks, furs, silver, jewelry, lacquered boxes, bamboo birdcages, bespoke suits—Cushing's letters are full of references to splendid things he thought of buying, almost all of them evaluated according to one principle: would Kate like them?

Part of this, of course, was conjuring in Kate's mind the payoff that awaited his Fredonian princess. "I will not tell what I bought," he wrote to her in a letter in which he had already admitted that his wallet was much lighter, "for if I tell you everything I shall have nothing to surprise you with when I get home, but . . . if I did get a large suit of sable, that was the finest in Peking, [that] had belonged to the emperor's brother . . . Ah! But I am breaking my resolution."

As 1868 drew to a close, Cushing's future was far from clear. Inspections revealed that the *Maumee* was suffering from dry rot and was no longer seaworthy; the Navy Department had to decide what to do with her, and with her commander. Would Will get another ship? Or serve under another captain? He was tantalized by the prospects of going to work for the armed forces of Japan. They were building up their fleet, and someone with Cushing's credentials could write his own ticket. On the other hand, there was his health, which, he said, had been "unstable."

What Will really wanted was to go home. "Brother officers say to me, 'Why Cushing—What on earth do you of all men want to go home for?' You have a splendid position abroad. Travel, do just as you please, live afloat or ashore as you see fit, are lionized, dined and wined. What more could you want.'" But the answer was no enigma. "[L]ove is Nature itself," he wrote to Kate, "and as necessary to my happiness and life as is the blood coursing in my veins. . . . It had been a latent power in me until I met you."

Will spent part of 1869 back in Japan, mostly observing the ebb and flow of tensions between the declining shogun of Yeddo and the newly assertive, more modern imperial court at Kyoto. This was a conflict that the emperor was destined to win, but at that moment Cushing's function was to show the flag, and subtly remind all parties that the United States had commercial interests at stake and would protect them, regardless of who was in power. One duty that fell to Cushing during this time was to take custody of the *Stonewall*, the erstwhile Confederate ironclad that Will had once, briefly, been charged with sinking. When the war ended, the *Stonewall* ended up in Havana harbor, the property of the United States. Sold to Japan, she sailed to Yokohama, where both Japanese factions vied for control of the potentially game-changing weapon. Prudently, Cushing babysat the ship until events played out, at which point the Kyoto government accepted control of the rechristened *Kotetsu*, the first ship in the Japanese imperial navy.

This was one of Will's final responsibilities in Asia. He returned to China for the latter half of the year; perhaps the most notable event of that period was the dinner he attended in honor of the Duke of Edinburgh, Queen Victoria's second son. His host was Admiral Keppel, whom Will described as "a jolly old sea dog." Apparently no more lessons in protocol had been required.

But one other may have been given. In Cushing's file at the Naval Academy is a decidedly unofficial report, written by Lieutenant Commander Roy C. Smith sometime during 1909–1910, when he was cap-

tain of a gunboat that was part of the Yangtze Squadron, the USS
Villalobos. In the report, Smith, who in 1917 would be appointed governor of Guam, recounted a story told to him in Shanghai in 1908:

> *In 1869 Commander William B. Cushing, of ALBEMARLE
> fame, commanded the small gunboat USS MAUMEE on the China
> Station. Shanghai, then as now, was a favorite port for men-of-
> war of all nations. Relaxation and amusement were in order in the
> International Settlement.*
>
> *The usual landing place for ship's boats was alongside the Bund,
> on the main waterfront, where several floats were moored for the
> purpose. Cushing was off for shore one afternoon in his gig, and was
> making for one of these floats. As he approached, he noticed a foreign
> captain's gig occupying most of the float. [Cushing] lay on his oars for
> a few minutes and then politely requested the Captain to move ahead
> a few feet and give him room to come alongside. The answer to this
> request was:*
>
> *"Oh, keep your shirt on, you'll get ashore in plenty of time."*
>
> *Cushing answered very quietly. "I'll keep my shirt on, but I'm
> coming alongside now."*
>
> *"Give way together," was his command to his crew [to pull in an
> easy rhythm].*
>
> *Arriving near the float, he gave "Way enough," [stop pulling and
> remove the oars from the water] and the oars were boated. Now the
> foreigner had left his outboard oars in the water, and as the Ameri-
> can boat, with considerable way on, came alongside, these oars were
> neatly chopped off, one by one. Cushing then calmly stepped out of his
> gig, across the foreigner's, and ashore. Handing the speechless captain
> his card, the American went on uptown without comment.*
>
> *Later, at a club near the Bund, the foreign captain related his
> unusual experience with a rude American captain.*
>
> *"Who was he?" his listeners asked.*
>
> *"I don't know," he replied, "but here is his card. I was too aston-*

ished to look at it." Fishing the card out of his pocket, he handed it to
one of his friends, who read it to the others:

    "Commander

          William B. Cushing,

             United States Navy,

      Commanding U.S.S. MAUMEE"

    "You've drawn a winner," they said.

    "Why, what have I got to do about it?" he asked.

    "Well you will probably have to challenge him, and he's a terror.
It would be much better for you to forget the whole affair."

    And so the incident was forgotten.

As it happens, there is a nearly identical document in the US Navy
Library in Washington. The discrepancies are few but interesting. Both
call Cushing a commander, although he was not promoted to that rank
until he returned to the United States, but the account in Annapolis
plausibly places him in command of the *Maumee* in 1869, while the one
in Washington has him commanding the *Saco* (this never happened) in
1870, by which point he was back in the United States. The variations,
the length of time between the telling of the story and its recording,
the fact that the recorder wasn't an eyewitness and that no one knows if
the teller was an eyewitness or heard it fiftieth hand—all these things
are good reasons to be skeptical of the story. But it sounds like Will.

CHAPTER 50

Howard

I N NOVEMBER 1869, Cushing finally received orders that he was being transferred back to the United States. With a final serenade of "Home Sweet Home" from the *Maumee* Christys, Will departed from his ship, and made for Kate Forbes and America.

At six o'clock on February 22, 1870, at Trinity Episcopal Church in Fredonia, William Barker Cushing and Katherine Forbes were married. The church was packed with family, friends, naval officers, and curious onlookers who weren't invited but who nonetheless wanted to participate in the event. Kate wore a gown of "elegant and costly Japanese crape trimmed with point lace," and Lieutenant Commander Cushing wore all his gold braid and all his medals. Guests drank two-hundred-year-old rum said to have belonged to Miles Standish (Pilgrim pal of Cushing ancestor John Alden) and some kind of liquor taken from the recently opened grave of the so-called Cardiff Giant, which had to have been expensive even if its provenance turned out to be entirely bogus. Will gave Kate a jeweled watchcase, a sapphire ring, an emerald cross, and a set of furs, valued at $3,000, that presumably once belonged to an emperor's brother.

It is said there are only two stories in journalism: build 'em up and tear 'em down. While the *Fredonia Censor* celebrated the joyous wedding of the hometown Cushings for the fabulous local event that it was, just thirty miles away, the *Jamestown Journal*, the big newspaper in Chautauqua County's biggest town, tried to sell papers by being snide rather than celebratory. In the March 11 edition of the paper, editor C. E. Bishop weighed in on the recent nuptials. "The Fredonia papers contain full accounts of the marriage of Lieut. Com. W. B. Cushing, U.S.N. and Miss Kate Forbes of Fredonia on the 22nd ult," Bishop wrote.

> *The papers could be in better business than such toadying. Cushing is the most ineffable, idiotic young snob that ever trod leather. He could have secured on ten minutes notice a free ride out of F. from a delegation of his former friends and school-mates whom he has snubbed. For a little upstart like him, who by an act of insubordination in the navy [the sinking of the Albemarle] blundered into notoriety, to pompously order older and better men than himself to address him as "Lt. Com. Cushing, Sir," is disgusting. . . . Flunkeyism is born in a servile soul, and will show itself.*

Bishop was quite proud of this attempted character assassination: he sent copies of the article to officials in the navy and prominent residents of Fredonia.

On April 21, after the happy couple returned from their honeymoon, Will and his father-in-law visited the offices of the *Journal*. When they encountered Bishop, Cushing produced a rawhide whip, with which he thrashed Bishop about the head and shoulders until a group of the paper's employees subdued Will and ushered him out, to the delight and amusement of General Forbes. Cushing and Forbes then went to nearby Jamestown House, where they ordered dinner while waiting for the arrival of the police.

Nothing more came of the incident. Bishop pressed no charges, and Will ignored Bishop's ongoing insults. That soon became easier to do, when the Navy Department assigned Will to ordnance duty at the Boston Navy Yard; having had sea duty essentially since 1861, Will was entitled to a good long stretch in port. "I am enjoying my quiet married life very much," he wrote to his cousin Elliot Pillsbury, "and am completely domesticated. My bachelor habits have gone to the winds—a great saving of dollars and an improvement in health."

Kate and Will seem to have had a very happy newlywed life. He worked; she kept house. They went out to dances and visited friends; they also stayed home, where the action hero read to his wife from Thackeray, Dickens, and Tennyson. Sometimes they entertained. In the front parlor Will kept a model of the torpedo that sank the *Albemarle*, a gift from the navy, and when visitors asked, he would show them how the thing worked: the spar and the hinge and the pulley, the trigger, and the thin lanyard that he held tightly in his hand.

A year later, the Cushings moved to Medford, Massachusetts. They were still very happy. Kate was expecting, Will's back had stopped aching, and his mother had come to Boston to visit relatives and help with the baby when it arrived.

The mood changed abruptly when Will learned that his eldest brother, Howard, had been killed in action fighting against Cochise and the Apaches in Arizona.

Only in a family like the Cushings would the exploits of Howard Cushing be mentioned third. His parents' second child, Howard was closer to his elder brother, Milton, than to the younger pair of Lon and Will. The most independent of the brothers, Howard left home at sixteen to work at a printer in Boston, and was a typesetter at a Chicago newspaper when the South fired on Fort Sumter. Despite having been diagnosed with tuberculosis, Howard quit his job and enlisted as a private in Captain Ezra Taylor's Battery B, First Illinois Light Infantry. For the next decade, he wore his country's uniform with distinction.

Howard saw more than his share of fighting during the war: he manned his guns at Fort Henry, Shiloh, and Vicksburg while battling dysentery and tuberculosis. After Alonzo's death, President Lincoln, by now acquainted with the younger Cushing brothers and their deeds, approved a proposal to promote Howard to lieutenant and to assign him to what remained of Lon's old unit, Battery A, Fourth US Artillery. The unit was involved in many engagements in 1863 and 1864, including the ferocious battles of the Wilderness and Cold Harbor. Howard and his men spent the final months of the war occupying defensive positions near Washington.

Howard's military career continued after the war. Appointed a lieutenant in the Third US Cavalry, he served briefly in Texas and then in Arizona. There, some of the Native American tribes who resented the growing influx of white settlers opposed it with violence. The cavalry's job was to protect the whites, and Howard, like his brothers, was very good at his job. John Gregory Bourke, a fellow officer whose diaries of soldiering in Arizona were later published under the title *On the Border with Crook*, said that Howard was the bravest man he ever saw. "I mean just that," he repeated; "the bravest man I ever saw."

Howard spent two years based in Tucson, the territorial capital, considered at the time to be "one of the dirtiest of little Spanish-American towns." The Apache practiced a kind of guerrilla warfare; among the acts of which they were accused were killing a party of thirty people going to work on a ranch; stealing or driving away livestock; attacking wagon trains and settlements; killing a stagecoach driver; and killing a party of travelers en route to Sonora, Mexico. Howard specialized in leading punitive expeditions, tracking and killing those he thought responsible for these acts. Throughout history, army campaigns against those who engage in guerrilla-type warfare, whether they represent tribes, ethnic groups, partisans, political ideologies, terrorist organizations, or criminal gangs, have been ugly, ruthless, and prone to excess and error. Cushing, Bourke tells us, "killed more savages of the Apache tribe than any other officer or troop in the United States Army had done before or since." One hopes all those lives were taken as righteously as Bourke would have us believe they were.

Of course, it goes without saying that the Apaches Howard was hunting were fierce and clever warriors. They had devised a tactic by which they conducted simultaneous raids against distant targets, forcing the cavalry to divide its forces, which left its forces exposed and weakened as they responded hither and yon. "Cushing was most active at this time, and kept his troop moving without respite," wrote Bourke. "There were fights, and ambuscades, and attacks upon Indian rancherias, and night marches without number, several very successful."

On May 5, 1871, Cushing was at the head of a twenty-two-man scouting party chasing the Apache chief Cochise. At Bear Springs in the Whetstone Mountains, the detachment was ambushed. Howard, a few civilians, and three soldiers were cut off, and although they held off their attackers for about a half hour, they were eventually killed. The rest of the troop, now under the command of Sergeant John Mott, repelled the attackers after a hand-to-hand battle. The event became known as the Cushing Massacre, and Howard as the Custer of Arizona. Sergeant Mott received the Medal of Honor.

"There is not a hostile tribe in Arizona or New Mexico," wrote Sylvester Maury in a letter to the New York *Herald*, "that will not celebrate the killing of Cushing as a great triumph. He was a beau sabreur, an unrelenting fighter; and although the Indians have got him at last, he sent before him a long procession of them to open his path to the undiscovered country. . . . He has left behind him in Arizona a name that will not die in this generation." (Maury would be pleased to learn that Cushing Street in Tucson is named for Howard.)

It was through Maury's letter, published May 15, that Will learned of his brother's death. He broke the news to a cousin who worked in a nearby bank, and then carried the sad report to his mother. Later that day he wrote to his brother Milton, who was soon to depart for duty with the Pacific Squadron.

My only and very dear brother: With a heart full of agony I write to you of our terrible misfortune. Dear, brave Howie is no more. . . . We are left alone now—the last of four; and let us swear to stand by each other and our noble Mother in all things. Let our old boyhood vows come back with full force and meaning, and let us cling together in truest and most unselfish love and friendship. . . . We must be doubly loving and attentive to little Ma now. Write often to her. One thing is certain of her Sons; they cannot be beaten. You can kill but not conquer them.

Stanton Loring, the cousin whose bank the grief-stricken Will walked into after he read of Howard's death, later described Will's actions that morning. "He could scarcely command himself to speak, but he dimly muttered: 'Howard is killed,'" Loring recalled.

His grief was such that I could not talk to him in the public office, and I took him into a private room, where he remained with me an hour before he was sufficiently composed to go to his home. His first thought was of vengeance, and he insisted that he should apply for leave of absence, so that he might go out to Arizona, and fight the Indians, but after we had talked a while he took a more rational view. I have been in the presence of grief many times during my life, but never have I witnessed anything like the emotion shown by this strong man. In that hour that I spent with him I got an entirely new insight into his character, and with all his impetuous bravery, I found him possessed of the tender heart of a little child.

The intensity of Will's reaction seems unusual, an extreme response from a man who had lost in the war people to whom he was much closer than he seemed to Howard. Will was four years younger than his brother, who left home to work when Will was twelve, meaning that more than fifteen years had passed during which they saw each other only infrequently. But perhaps those factors intensified his feelings. He had lost so many friends without properly grieving them, had survived so many terrifying circumstances while keeping the appearance of cool; perhaps Howard's death opened feelings long repressed, and for a while, they took possession of him.

CHAPTER 51

The World Stage

WILL SPENT THE MONTHS after Howard's death in poor physical and emotional condition. The pain in his hip intensified, and he contracted pneumonia. Instead of relief, his work in the harbor was a burden. "We have nothing to do but sit in our office chairs and swear at 'dull Time,'" he wrote to a cousin, and the navy's postwar retrenchments meant that there would be fewer ships to command for a twenty-nine-year-old officer of high rank and short tenure. (Between 1865 and 1870, the navy went from nearly seven hundred ships to fifty-two.) There were some bright spots for Will: the birth of his daughter Marie Louise on December 1, 1871, and his promotion in January 1872 to the rank of commander, making him the youngest at that time to hold that rank. But between the pain in his hip and the melancholy in his mood, the pleasures were short-lived.

He wanted to go to Pensacola, where the warm weather might alleviate the chronic hip pain, but there were no open billets. He spent time during 1872 in Washington, in Norfolk, and finally back in Fredonia, much of the time in the hands of doctors. None offered anything more than temporary relief. The war had not seen a bullet magical enough to kill Will Cushing, but during his life there must have been countless leaps, tumbles,and falls that could have damaged his nerves or ruptured his disks, injuries that could have grown progressively worse. Will may also have had a slow-growing infection. He spent years performing on a daily basis duties that could have left him with nicks, cuts, and scrapes that would soon be exposed to the bogs and swamps and rivers of North Carolina; no telling what stung him or bit him or swam into his bloodstream. He may have had tuberculosis of the pelvis, a slow-developing infection; or cancer of the prostate gland. Whatever he had, nobody knew how to cure it, and as 1872 melted frighteningly into 1873, Will's health and career both began a long, slow decline.

In June 1873 he was offered command of the USS *Wyoming*, a steamer of six guns and 997 tons then in the Caribbean station. The assignment was just the restorative he needed, and although his hip still hurt and Kate, again pregnant, was worried about the toll that another command would take on him, there was no question that this was a blessing. After two years of drift, William Cushing had been given back his purpose, and he was ready for a new adventure.

Cushing and the *Wyoming* spent about seven weeks together at Aspinwall, in Panama, where a civil war had broken out. Cushing was ordered to protect the Panama Railway, an essential link between the east and west coasts. While doing so, he worked his men hard, conducting landing exercises and taking target practice with the *Wyoming*'s two eleven-inch and four nine-inch guns. It was a good period. Will's crew, fattened on peace, grew sharper, and Will's health, cosseted by the warm weather, improved.

On November 8, the *Wyoming* received several telegrams from the United States consul at Kingston, Jamaica, desperately calling for the help of a US warship. An American vessel had been captured by Cuban authorities, he reported. Americans had been executed, and more were in danger.

Cushing, having no orders to intervene (and clear orders to protect the Panama Railway), resisted an impulse to dash off. Instead, he worked the telegraph to obtain more information. By the tenth, how-ever, he had heard enough that he felt he couldn't wait any longer, and decided to act on his own authority. "Am now coaling," he telegraphed the Navy Department. "Will leave to-night or early to-morrow morn-ing for Santiago."

CHAPTER 52

The *Virginius*

T HE POTENTIAL FOR AN INCIDENT of this sort in Cuba had been brewing for some time. Spain owned Cuba, but since 1869 there had been an active independence movement, which Spain ruthlessly attempted to suppress. Many Americans, President Grant among them, generally supported the Cuban rebels. In February 1870, Grant appeared ready to endorse a Senate resolution that would have recognized independence. It seemed like an easy decision. Just as the Americans of 1776 wanted to free themselves from European control, so did the Cubans of 1870. They wanted to exercise their inalienable rights.

But Grant's secretary of state, Hamilton Fish, objected. He believed that approving the resolution would inevitably lead to war with Spain. In addition, one of his major priorities was to settle the *Alabama* claims, a grievance held by the United States against Great Britain. The *Alabama* was the Confederate raider that had seized or sunk sixty-five US merchant ships before being sunk by the USS *Kearsarge* off Cherbourg in 1864. Because the *Alabama* had been built by British shipbuilders, the United States maintained that Britain had violated neutrality acts, and ought to pay something for the ships and cargoes that were taken or destroyed. This was just one of a number of issues between the United States and Britain that Fish wanted to settle, and he feared that if Washington could claim that it was within its rights to aid Cuban rebels against their Spanish masters, Westminster could claim that it was within its rights to aid the Confederate rebels against the North. It wasn't a bulletproof argument, but Fish didn't want to risk a settlement with Great Britain, the world's leading power, just to help a bunch of Cuban peasants.

Fish prevailed. The resolution failed, and the United States kept silent about the Cuban rebellion. In 1871, the United States and Great Britain signed the Treaty of Washington, which settled the *Alabama* claims and other issues. Fish was praised for his diplomatic skill.

But the residue of these issues, Grant's position of nonbelligerency, remained. Many Americans didn't care; out-of-work soldiers of fortune—Civil War veterans, true believers in manifest destiny—saw an opportunity to enrich themselves by helping the movement overthrow the Spanish government. As the rebellion heated up, efforts to contain it intensified as well. And one day, straight into this conflict, right at the heart of a settled administration policy, sailed William Cushing.

BY THE TIME Will left Panama, the crisis in Cuba was already eleven days old. On October 31, an American steamer, the *Virginius,* outbound from Kingston and flying the US flag, had been chased down in international waters by the *Tornado,* a Spanish man-of-war. The *Tornado* had received a tip from a source in Jamaica that the *Virginius* had been purchased by backers of the rebellion, and was coming to Cuba carrying rebels and supplies. Certainly that seemed more plausible once the *Tornado* spotted her; the *Virginius* sat heavy in the water, and throughout the ensuing ten-hour chase, her crew was observed heaving cargo into the sea. Despite these efforts to lighten her, the *Virginius* began to take on water and, finally, around ten p.m., in brightly moonlit waters about twenty miles off Jamaica, the *Tornado* closed on the ship and put several shots across her bow; the last took out the ship's smokestack. The *Virginius,* still flying an American flag, surrendered.

The captain of the *Virginius*, Joseph Fry, vociferously argued that his ship was neutral, but of course he was lying; along with the weapons, most of which had been dumped, he was carrying 103 rebels, including four of their leaders—generals Bernabe Varona, Pedro Cespedes, Jesus Del Sol, and Washington Ryan. Fry, a fortyish man with a full beard, had served in the US Navy for fifteen years before joining the Confederacy. He ran the blockade off Wilmington and fought at Mobile Bay, but found it hard to get work after the war. In 1873 he threw in with the Cuban revolutionaries and became master of the leaky *Virginius*. He recruited a crew of fifty-two Americans and Britons, most of them inexperienced and quite young—three were not yet thirteen years old. It's highly unlikely that many, if any, understood that they were getting involved in something political. And for all his experience, it's possible Fry didn't entirely grasp the implications either. A US consul at Kingston had warned him that he would almost certainly be shot if he was captured, but Fry was skeptical; in his experience, blockade running was always treated as a revenue crime, he told the consul, never punished with death.

Whether or not Fry was whistling past the graveyard when he said that, he quickly realized that his captors weren't treating him like an ordinary blockade runner. The *Virginius* was secured and brought to Santiago, Cuba, where the next day he and his men were frog-marched away with their elbows pinioned behind them; the authorities charged all of them with piracy. The charge was obviously spurious—there wasn't a shred of evidence indicating piracy—but it was a capital offense. Suddenly it was clear that the men of the *Virginius* were to be executed in a legalized lynching aimed to send a message not only to the rebels but to anyone who would arm or shelter or even transport them.

Immediately, the local consuls stepped up their efforts to obtain legal representation for their citizens who were behind bars, but those efforts were quickly squelched. Fortunately, a resident of Jamaica who was in Cuba, hearing of the British citizens under arrest, contacted

British commodore A. F. R. de Horsey of the Royal Navy's Atlantic Squadron, who ordered HMS *Niobe*, a frigate under the command of Sir Lambton Loraine, to proceed directly to Santiago and halt further executions. Loraine departed immediately, going with such haste that he left several members of his crew behind.

CHAPTER 53

The Butcher

THE TRIALS OF VARONA, Cespedes, Del Sol, and Ryan were held the next day, November 3, 1873, and the court wasted no time in convicting the four Cuban generals of treason. The following morning, as a large crowd rained insults and derision on them, the revolutionaries were paraded about a mile from the jail to a courtyard lined with adobe buildings, where they were to be executed. Varona smoked a cigar with flamboyant ease as he strolled. At the courtyard, the guards forced Cespedes and Del Sol to kneel, then shot them in the head; Varona and Ryan refused to kneel and struggled. The guards killed the rebels where they stood. Varona fell easily; an officer had to finish off Ryan with a sword thrust. Cavalrymen then rode up and allowed their horses to trample the bodies. Descending into the gore, the mob severed the heads from two of the dead men, placed them on pikes, and marched them about the city. "I regret vehemently that this is not the last occasion I [will be] called upon to fulfill this painful task," said the executioner, General Juan Nepomuceno Burriel, whose nickname was "The Butcher." A native Cuban who rose up from the ranks to become military governor of Santiago, Burriel said, "The rebels must be punished in the interests of our country and its salvation. Let us hope that this may serve as a lesson to wandering bands of disaffected men now in the island of Cuba. They will see to what end their misdeeds will bring them."

When word reached Spain that Americans had been charged with piracy, the American consul in Madrid, Daniel Sickles, a former Union army general, reportedly met with the president of Spain, Emilio Castelar, who issued orders to the authorities in Cuba to suspend all proceedings involving the crew until the facts could be obtained. If his orders were actually sent, they were not followed. The legal proceedings continued, with no representation for the accused. Other diplomatic approaches were pursued. The British consul escalated his protests on behalf of the sixteen British crew members who were in prison, pointing out their rights to an attorney under treaty obligations, and asking that any sentences be delayed until the arrival of the *Niobe*. But General Burriel, who was described in *Frank Leslie's Weekly* as "bombastic, violent, tyrannical, bloodthirsty, cruel and selfish," declined the request, saying that the law must be fulfilled. Burriel not only ignored similar protests filed by the American vice-consul E. G. Schmitt, but even refused Schmitt's requests to use the telegraph lines to communicate with the State Department. Burriel meant to teach the rebels, and anyone who would aid them, that the reward for rebellion was death.

THE *NIOBE* ARRIVED in Santiago on the seventh. Sir Lambton Loraine urgently requested an interview with the military governor but was put off. He finally saw Burriel the next day, when he appealed for the lives of the British subjects who were in custody, and more generally sought clemency for all. Whatever was said between the men, Burriel's actions spoke more loudly, for on that same day, a dozen prisoners, including Fry, were shot dead.

The next day Loraine put his position in writing:

> *Military Commander of Santiago—Sir: I have no orders from my government, because they are not aware of what is happening; but I assume the responsibility and I am convinced that my conduct will be approved by Her Britannic Majesty, because my actions are*

pro-humanity and pro-civilization, I demand that you stop this dreadful butchery that is taking place here. I do not believe that I need to explain what my actions will be in case my demand is not heeded. [Signed] Lambton Loraine

After three days went by without further executions, the hope was that Loraine had been persuasive. On the thirteenth, however, Burriel clarified his position: thirty-seven more members of the crew were shot dead, sixteen Britons among them.

CHAPTER 54

Face-off

CUSHING PAUSED IN KINGSTON to pick up a pilot and learned of the latest developments, including the additional executions. He decided to use his entrance to make a statement. When he brought the *Wyoming* into Santiago late on the fifteenth, she was stripped and ready for action, and so was Cushing, His plan was to enter the harbor and, if possible, immediately seize the *Virginius* and take her away. Unfortunately, the Spanish moved the ship the day before.

Instead, Cushing met with the American vice-consul and with officers of the *Niobe*. They said that they had been put off and treated dismissively by Burriel, and that he continued to threaten further executions.

Such a reply would never satisfy Cushing, but he was willing to follow protocol, so he wrote to Burriel calling for the release of the prisoners. Delivered on the sixteenth, the long letter was eloquent and learned; somewhere along the way, Will Cushing had picked up a fair amount of international law. He scoffed at the idea that *Virginius* was a pirate, and persuasively argued that its worst crime was smuggling. The *Virginius*, he wrote, "if offending at all, was simply a neutral vessel carrying contraband of war," and was not a "pirate." Then, in blunt and stirring language, he condemned the trials and executions that had taken place. "In the eye of the nations of the earth and their well-defined laws, sanctioned by the tests and trials of centuries, such trial and execution is simply murder." He concluded on an ominous note: "The Government of the United States will know how and when to protect its honor."

Cushing followed up his letter with a request to see Burriel, to make sure that his message was received and understood; more to the point, it was probably to ensure that he received a response. When Burriel continued to dodge, Cushing answered with his customary straightforwardness. "If I do not see General Burriel by the day after tomorrow, and if any more prisoners are executed," he informed the general's aide, "I shall open fire on the Governor's palace." As Burriel pondered the message, he could see the crew of the *Wyoming* sighting its guns on Spanish warships, rigging boarding netting, and adding a layer of protection by spiking chain cable to her hull outside her engine and boilers.

Cushing was granted the interview. Joined by his executive officer, Lieutenant Charles Hutchins, he entered the governor's palace. The legend of Albemarle Cushing was by now known far and wide, especially among military men, and though Burriel may have been a butcher, he was obliged to pay his respects. He approached Will with a smile and an outstretched hand, but Cushing wouldn't shake. The closer Burriel extended his hand, the further Will withdrew his, as though he believed that simply touching the man would corrupt him.

Burriel recognized the insult, yet went on with the matter at hand. At that moment, Will had already defeated Burriel, who began to fidget and shake. All the while, Will looked at Burriel with a steady, unbroken gaze, which Burriel could not meet; he kept averting his eyes. Finally, he managed to mumble; he wanted Will's assurance that he would behave peaceably while in Santiago harbor.

Cushing ignored the question. "Have I *your* assurance that no more prisoners will be executed?"

Hemming and hawing, Burriel failed to answer.

"In that case, sir, I must request that all the women and children be removed from the city. I would not harm them."

It was as though Will had detonated a torpedo under Burriel's waterline. The Butcher made some more noises, but the bold man who could execute unarmed sailors was too timid to invite a war with the United States—especially one in which he might be among the first casualties. Cushing believed he was right, and was therefore prepared to act accordingly. Back on the *Wyoming*, he and his officers had drawn up plans for assaulting the jail, releasing the prisoners, and capturing the city from Burriel's control. War had its terrors for William Cushing, but none to compare to allowing this small-time martinet to push around the United States.

Under Will's unbroken gaze, Burriel cracked. No more killings, he promised, nor would he remove the prisoners from Santiago unless ordered to do so by Havana.

"It was a grand sight," Lieutenant Hutchins later said, "when Cushing stood up and looked 'The Butcher' down."

The next day, Burriel left for Havana.

It has not been recorded whether Cushing spoke in Spanish or in English. Evidently he made himself understood.

THOUGH BURRIEL'S CONCESSION ended the crisis, tensions did not immediately disappear; instead, a kind of confusion prevailed. The prisoners were still held, but with Burriel gone, no one had the authority to release them; with no imminent threat to the prisoners, the *Wyoming* and the *Niobe* had no immediate cause for action. Neither did they have reason to step down. Cushing stayed in Santiago, where his presence kept pressure on the governments in Washington, Havana, and Madrid. He visited the killing grounds where the sailors had been executed and paid respects at their common grave. The sight deeply affected him; he observed that every time a government resorts to such acts of despotism, it undermines its claim to legitimacy. "The shots which killed the passengers and crew of the *Virginius* have sounded the death knell of Spanish power in the Western Hemisphere," he told Loraine one night on the *Niobe*; he was off by a few decades, but he wasn't wrong. Meanwhile, he continued to tweak his rescue plan; he badly wanted to go in.

But Hamilton Fish had never wanted war with Spain, not even in the last couple of weeks, when editorials in the big city newspapers howled over Spain's insult to the flag, and demonstrations demanded the release of the prisoners. He wanted a negotiated settlement fast, and kicked the responsibility for managing Cushing over to Secretary of the Navy George M. Robeson. "For God's sake hurry on to Santiago de Cuba," Robeson ordered his subordinates. "We are afraid that Cushing will do something." First Burriel, then Fish, then Robeson—and then even the French—were worried about what Cushing would do. At one point, a French man-of-war responded to diplomatic calls for help. Arriving in Santiago after her British and American counterparts, the ship's captain sought to intervene with Burriel on behalf of the prisoners, but was brushed off. What should I do? he asked Cushing. "Bombard the place or go back to Martinique," said Cushing. The captain accepted the advice. "I will let you do the bombarding, and I will go back to Martinique," he replied, another in a long line of people who couldn't tolerate Will Cushing's idea of a risk. On November 26, Commander D. L. Braine, a Civil War comrade—he relieved Cushing as military governor of Smithville in 1865—arrived in Santiago harbor and assumed command. Within days, an agreement was signed between the United States and Spain. Cushing headed back to Panama, and things returned to normal in Cuba, at least for those who hadn't been executed.

Oddly, in most accounts of the story the usually hero-worshipping press missed the role played by the twenty-four-carat hero, and the ordinarily xenophobic House of Representatives ignored the all-American Cushing to pass a resolution offering the Thanks of Congress to Captain Sir Lambton Loraine of the Royal Navy. Perhaps Cushing was ignored because he acted without orders, although the navy ruled that he acted properly. In the end, the House Committee on Foreign Affairs, examining the whole affair, got the story right. Loraine may have reached Santiago before anyone else, but he hadn't done much to protect American lives, or for that matter English ones. But as the congressional report put it, Cushing "did his duty completely and gallantly in asserting the rights of the American government and its citizens, and upholding the honor of the American flag."

CHAPTER 55

At Rest

THE WINTER FOLLOWING the settlement of the *Virginius* affair was kind neither to the *Wyoming* nor to her captain. The balky boilers that provided such a lumbering trip from Aspinwall to Santiago broke down twice, and Will continued to suffer back and hip problems. In April the *Wyoming* put up in Norfolk for an overhaul, and Will was placed on a list for reassignment. He went to Fredonia to meet his newborn daughter, Katherine Abell, who had been born in October. Kate was shocked by his appearance. He had lost weight, and looked drawn and exhausted and much older than his thirty-one years. His mood, too, was darker and he was short-tempered, perhaps the result of his pain. But while in Fredonia, he received the good news that he had been named executive officer of the Washington Navy Yard, second in command under Admiral Thomas H. Patterson. He reported for duty in August; Kate and the girls soon joined him.

September and October passed, Cushing's professional life uneventfully and his household life pleasantly. In November his mother came for a holiday visit. On Thanksgiving Day she and Kate and Will went to church; Will noted that President Grant sat nearby. After lunch, the three Cushings took a carriage ride and visited the Corcoran Gallery of Art, which had opened earlier in the year. They saw pieces from the British Museum, the Vatican, and the Louvre, as well as modern

American works. "I was intensely interested, as I had never been there before," he wrote to Milton that night. "I was perfectly amazed at the treasures of art [Corcoran] has bestowed on this fortunate city." One wonders what he liked best. The busts of Washington and Napoleon, of Ajax and Agrippa? The bronzes of wolves and stags and tigers and crocodiles locked in fierce combat? Or the lush, serene Hudson River landscapes, reminiscent of the fields and orchards of his youth? When he saw the marble *Daughter of Niobe*, was he reminded of events in Santiago? Did the *Borghese Gladiator*—a first-century BC statue of a warrior standing upright, head upturned, eyes looking above him— offer a flashback to a night just over a decade before, when Will stood upright in a small boat on the Roanoke and, with his head upturned, saw Warley lowering his six-inch cannon, and did not flinch?

The Cushings drove home in a harsh rain, and at five-thirty enjoyed a full Thanksgiving dinner. Afterward, Will's back began acting up. The pain intensified throughout the weekend, and on Monday, although he had hardly slept, he pushed himself out to work. Kate not only protested his decision but sent a message to his aide, the same Lieutenant Hutchins who had been with Will on the *Wyoming*, urging him to bring her husband home. Hutchins was surprised to receive such a message from Kate, so unusual for her, but he could see that Will was wracked with pain, so he attempted to oblige. Overruling his wife, Will worked past dark.

That was Cushing's final day on active duty. His deterioration accelerated. The pain grew more agonizing; not even morphine killed it, and he turned delirious. "It was pitiable to see the bright young mind drift rapidly away in delirium," said Lieutenant Commander Lester Beardslee, a neighbor and future rear admiral and commander of the Pacific Fleet, "but I can say that through his disconnected talk and ravings there never was once to my knowledge a profane or immodest word or act, and the principal burden of his thoughts seemed to be the anger and disgust he had for conduct on the part of others which he deemed dishonorable."

After a week of such pain, Kate knew she could not care for Will at home, and he was taken to the Government Hospital for the Insane, as St. Elizabeth's Hospital was then known. Will slipped into a coma. Apparently he regained consciousness in the afternoon of the seventeenth, long enough to take his mother's hand and recite after her the words of "Our Father." When they reached "amen," he closed his eyes and died.

Epilogue

THE SAD SPECTACLE OF WILL CUSHING falling into delirium before a premature death was no doubt shocking to many, and just as the death of a famous young person in our own time often invites gossip and speculation, the absence of a clear cause of death and the presence of a little-understood mental illness might have brought out the worst in some individuals. Perhaps Lester Beardslee's report of Will's last moments should be read at least in part as his warning to the naval community to cease the dishonorable gossip about one of America's great heroes.

Beyond the gossips, however, there were others who were predisposed to believe the worst about him. "Cushing had his enemies," the faithful Lieutenant Hutchins, who would go on to become a rear admiral and commander of the Pacific Fleet, told Charles Stewart, the author of a 1912 biography of Cushing. "Some from fancied ill-treatment, others from a failure to understand his character, and last but not least, enemies who were jealous of his success." Fairly or unfairly, mental illness is often seen as evidence of another illness or depravity—drug addiction, sexual libertinism or deviance, perversion, feeble-mindedness, and so on.

What actually killed Will Cushing? What was the cause of his delirium? Decades after his death, his biographer was still investigating these questions. In 1910, Stewart wrote to William Alanson White, the superintendent of the Hospital for the Insane, inquiring about Cushing's case. Looking at thirty-five-year-old records, White could not determine if Cushing suffered from "sciatic tuberculosis"—the listed cause of death. Absent tissue or blood samples, no doctor today could say any more, other than to confirm that this diagnosis would account for the chronic and severe hip pain that Will suffered. Alternatively, cancer might have been the cause.

Regarding "acute mania," White explained that it was a term "used in those days to cover a multiplicity of things." Though the actual cause of Will's death is uncertain, White was sure pain caused the delirium. "Technically, a delirious person is insane," wrote White, but "you are quite right in assuming that he did not suffer what is generally understood as insanity." White was unable to confirm "that there was any rational period at the end of the commander's residency here"—that is, that period spent in prayer that Lester Beardslee and Mary Cushing and others mentioned. "I know you are trying to do the right thing in regard to a brother officer whom you highly respect," wrote White, "and although it is no disgrace to be insane, unfortunately there is a stigma attached to it, and it is as well if it could be left out of the record you are preparing." Stewart handled his information straightforwardly: he reported that Cushing was delirious, but he refused to speculate about insanity. But at least one later writer couldn't resist sprinkling Cushing's story with the tragically poetic perfume of madness.

"Before he was thirty . . . he would become the youngest commander in the United States navy," wrote Shelby Foote in his great narrative, *The Civil War*. "But that was as far as he went. He died at the age of 32 in a government asylum for the insane, thereby provoking much discussion as to whether heroism and madness, like genius and tuberculosis, were related—and if so, had insanity been at the root of his exploits?"

Madness probably had less to do with Cushing's death than sciatic tuberculosis, or cancer, or a bacterial infection contracted while wading through parasite-rich swamplands of the Roanoke or the Cape Fear or the Yangtze. But as glib as the masterly Foote seems at this moment, he may have unwittingly caught the thread of an idea; Cushing's heroism may not have had to do with madness per se, but with what today we call a personality disorder.

Recent developments in brain scanning and neuroscience suggest that along with the murderous psychopaths who hold a place of honor in our prime-time television programming, there are many "functional psychopaths" among us, including some whose detached, unflinching, charismatic personalities help them attain enormous success in mainstream society. The eminent psychologist David Lykken contended that "the hero and the psychopath are twigs from the same branch," and that certain heroic types, such as astronauts, mountain climbers, business executives, and world leaders, might come from the same biological type as antisocial personalities. Both have the same disregard for authority and disdain for limits, and some share the qualities of narcissism and indifference to the feelings of others. The difference, Lykken speculated, between those who threaten society and those who contribute to it is upbringing. Parents who try to control the excesses of behavior through punishment are likely to fail, because psychopaths don't fear pain and are therefore relatively immune to its effects. Lykken said that positive, loving controls are more effective, which naturally brings to mind a comment by Will's mother: "Will was particularly daring," said Elizabeth Cushing, "impatient of restraint but easily governed through his affections; very truthful, loving and sympathetic; quick to feel and prompt to act."

Lykken's work dovetails with that of Theodore Millon, arguably the world's leading expert on personality disorders. He has identified the risk-taking individual as one of the five main subtypes of the antisocial personality disorder. He describes the risk taker as consistently "dauntless, venturesome, intrepid, bold, audacious, daring; reckless, foolhardy, impulsive, heedless; unbalanced by hazard; pursues perilous ventures." Sound familiar?

The key quality behind Lykken's hero and Millon's risk taker is fearlessness—a quality that occupies the far end point on a spectrum psychologists call the "approach and withdrawal dimension." For most of us, survival depends on striking the right balance between being risk-averse and taking risks. Sometimes, however, survival—of an individual or of a people—requires fearlessness of a higher order.*

Of course, Will may not have had a personality disorder; he might just have had a personality in which impulsiveness and a quick temper and a taste for fun dominated for a time, and then diminished as he matured. And his success may have had nothing to do with a disorder, but with genius.

In a cover article in 1985, *Time* magazine's Tom Callahan discussed two great superstars then in their prime, basketball's Larry Bird and hockey's Wayne Gretzky: "Though neither is highly educated, in the study of their games they were prodigies as children, and are intellectuals now. By some similar force of instinct and understanding—maybe Chess Grand Master Bobby Fischer would know about this—they see and play the game several moves ahead of the moment, comprehending not only where everything is but also where everything will be. Shown a photograph of a nondescript instant on the ice, Gretzky can replace the unpictured performers here and there about the periphery and usually recall what became of them the next second."

One feels the same was true of Cushing: he was extraordinarily intuitive and fast on his feet, someone with a grasp of the big picture who could anticipate changing conditions and adapt instantly and unexpectedly. We see it again and again: his quick thinking during the battle on the Blackwater River; his audacious frontal attack against cavalry at Chuckatuck; his unhesitating decision to vault the log pen

---

* Some studies have shown that many psychopaths have unusually low blood pressure. One would think that hypotension would be useful if someone was trying to aim a cannon at your head while you're standing in an open boat manipulating five lanyards, while buckshot was clawing away the back of your coat.

protecting the *Albemarle*; and, perhaps most astonishingly, the moment in the Cape Fear River, where he read the current and the momentum of his adversaries, and zigzagged his vessel away from nine boatloads of soldiers. As the psychologist K. Anders Ericsson has shown, what we often perceive as innate talent in people is actually the result of intense practice conducted for a decade or more. Perhaps the hundreds if not thousands of hours young Will spent roaming Chautauqua County, racing wagons, outrunning farmers, tiptoeing along fence rails, scrapping with the local boys, speeding about on the lake—not to mention pulling creative, imaginative stunts, sometimes misinterpreted as a talent for buffoonery—turned out to be just the preparation he needed to become a virtuoso in his daredevil brand of warfare.

Cushing had one other quality: desire. This may or may not have scientific validity as a concept, but at least one expert observer thought it was a real factor. In his memoir, Admiral David Dixon Porter defended the reputation of the officers and men of the North Atlantic Blockading Squadron, who had less opportunity to achieve distinction than their counterparts who fought at Vicksburg and New Orleans and Mobile Bay enjoyed. However, noted Porter, "in war, the true secret is to make the opportunity. It is what seldom comes to any one. It must be sought for, and though it is a shy spirit, not easily wooed and won, yet it puts itself in the way of those who are determined to pursue and overtake it in spite of all obstacles. The proof of this was demonstrated in the case of Lieutenant Cushing."

THE DEATH OF Commander William Barker Cushing was officially announced to the nation by Secretary of the Navy Robeson, a onetime Union general from New Jersey. An elaborate military funeral was held in Washington, after which Cushing's body was placed in a vault in the Congressional Cemetery. It remained there for nearly three weeks, until it was officially interred at the Naval Academy Cemetery on January 8. Will's tomb sits on a small bluff overlooking the Severn River, not ten feet from the graves of Charlie Flusser and Sam Preston. On one side of his marker is carved the word "Albemarle," on the other "Fort Fisher."

Will's brother Milton maintained the family tendency to die prematurely, passing away on January 1, 1886, a few months short of his fiftieth birthday. He had been invalided out of the navy, and spent the last year of his life in Dunkirk, three miles from his boyhood home. He is buried at the Forest Hill Cemetery in Fredonia, where there is also a marker to all four Cushing brothers.

Elizabeth Cushing outlived the last of her sons by five years. She moved to Missouri to live with her daughter Mary Isabel and her husband and four children. After Alonzo's death, Mrs. Cushing received a government pension of $17 a month; in 1891, the year of her death, the monthly sum was raised to $50. Little Ma was eighty-five when she died.

Kate Cushing did not remarry. She devoted a considerable amount of the ensuing decades to maintaining her husband's memory. In 1890 she attended the commissioning of the USS *Cushing*, a torpedo boat that was the first of five vessels the navy would name after Will; four destroyers followed, the most recent of which was decommissioned in 2005. In 1898, she asked Theodore Roosevelt to write Will's biography. Roosevelt, who as a freshly minted Harvard graduate had written a highly regarded naval history of the War of 1812, and was then serving as the assistant secretary of the navy, graciously declined, saying, "No one could help being pleased at being singled out to write a history of a man who, in my opinion, comes next to Farragut on the hero roll of American naval history, but it is not possible for me to undertake such a work at this time." This was probably true: before the year was out, he had quit his job, organized the Rough Riders, and led the assault on San Juan Hill. Kate then approached Captain Alfred Thayer Mahan, whose books about sea power had begun to influence naval policy around the globe. Mahan, too, declined, and it's just as well; a bloodless theoretician who didn't actually like being in the navy, he and Will do not seem simpatico. Kate died in 1932, in Fredonia. Neither Marie Louise nor Katherine Abell, Will and Kate's daughters, ever married; both became schoolteachers.

After the war, Gilbert Elliott worked as a banker and lawyer in Norfolk and St. Louis. In 1893 he and his son opened a law firm in New York City where, two years later, an attack of erysipelas killed him at fifty-one. He is buried in Green-Wood Cemetery in Brooklyn. The illness that caused Captain James Cooke to resign the captaincy of the *Albemarle* continued to plague him after the war, and he died in Portsmouth, Virginia, in 1869 at the age of fifty-seven. Alexander Warley's military service ended with the *Albemarle*. He returned to New Orleans and worked for the city in various capacities until his death in 1892.

After the attack on the *Albemarle*, *Picket Boat No. 1* fell into Confederate hands, and could be seen moving about the Roanoke in the few days between Cushing's attack and the recapture of the city. Later she was sent to Annapolis to be used by midshipmen as an instruction boat. The *Albemarle* was stripped and sold for salvage in 1867.

Like the men who joined Will in the assault on the *Albemarle*, Sergeant Frederick Fuger, who stood so valiantly with Alonzo at Gettysburg, was awarded a Medal of Honor. He stayed in the army, rose to the rank of lieutenant colonel, and died in 1913. After a prolonged citizens' campaign and congressional action, Alonzo, too, was awarded a Medal of Honor in 2010.

After Lincoln's assassination, Gideon Welles remained secretary of the navy through the presidency of Andrew Johnson. His diary is regarded as a peerless sources of information about Lincoln's administration. After leaving public life, Welles wrote several books. He died in February 1878 at the age of seventy-five.

Captain George S. Blake was superintendent of the Naval Academy throughout the war. He was promoted to commodore, and died in 1871 at the age of sixty-eight. Admiral David Dixon Porter, Cushing's commander at Fort Fisher, succeeded Blake as superintendent. Outspoken and ambitious, Porter made enemies, who eased him into a semiretirement that lasted twenty years. He died in 1891, at age seventy-seven. Porter is the only man to receive the Thanks of Congress three times, the last for Fort Fisher.

Christopher R. P. Rodgers, the man who focused on Will Cushing's talent for buffoonery, left the academy and was assigned to the South Atlantic Blockading Squadron. He served with distinction in various command positions throughout the war. After his promotion to rear admiral in 1874, he returned to the Naval Academy and served two stints as superintendent that were separated by his command of the Pacific Squadron. He was seventy-two when he died in 1892.

It's interesting to imagine what Will Cushing might have made of his life had he been allotted a healthy three score and ten. Had he stayed in the navy, more glory might have been in the offing. After all, he was senior to George Dewey; it might have been Admiral Cushing who vanquished the Spanish fleet in Manila Bay in 1898 or led the Great White Fleet in 1907. But there were so many other opportunities in the world: the broad West, the beckoning Pacific, the booming markets—there is no telling the heights that might have been achieved by a man of such energy and proven ability. Four American presidents in the second half of the nineteenth century were generals, two of them of no special military distinction; the country might not have had to wait until 1960 for a handsome naval hero to enter the White House. At the dawn of the twentieth century, Will would not yet have been sixty years old.

And yet, little good can come from imagining what might have been. Cushing was one of those rare men who met his moment, and the result was sublime. As David Dixon Porter put it, in sinking the *Albemarle* Will "displayed a heroic enterprise seldom equaled and never excelled." Who could ask for more?

Acknowledgments

O N JANUARY 6, 1961, *LIFE* MAGAZINE, the most popular weekly magazine of its era, and a great patron of illustration and photography, began a six-part series marking the centennial of the Civil War. In that issue, the editors published ten full-color paintings of notable moments that took place during the war. Among the ten, spread across two pages, was C. E. Monroe Jr.'s dramatic painting of the moment William Cushing exploded the torpedo under the *Albemarle*. That was my introduction to Will Cushing, and I vividly remember sitting in my parents' basement studying that painting. I am thrilled that it has been included on the cover of the book. Mr. Monroe, who died in 1998, was best known as an accomplished illustrator of hunting, fishing, and nature scenes, but I'm grateful that he accepted this assignment (he also contributed a brilliant painting of a cavalry charge at Brandy Station for the issue's cover). I thank him for the inspiration, and I also thank his son, Buck Monroe, for agreeing to let us use the picture.

Thanks to Tom Mayer and the team at W. W. Norton for their work in making this a better book. Thanks also to my agent, David McCormick, for the dedicated support and wise advice he has given me over the years.

Thanks very much to the resourceful and conscientious Katelyn

Fossett, who undertook a number of research assignments for me. She delivered every time. Thanks to my friend Ken Smith, for his excellent work on the Web site.

David D'Onofrio, Special Collections Librarian of the Nimitz Library at the United States Naval Academy, responded swiftly and patiently to what must have seemed like ceaseless pestering. Very helpful as well were Randall Fortson of the Navy Library, Chris Killilay of the National Archives, Simone Munson of the Wisconsin Historical Society, and Mimi Carter and Lisa Strong of the Corcoran Gallery of Art. I am grateful to all of them for their assistance.

Many thanks to Kim McCray, the curator of the Port O'Plymouth Museum in Plymouth, North Carolina, who led me through the museum's collection of *Albemarle* relics, and to Jimmy Hardison, a member of the board of directors of the Washington County Historical Society, who took time out of his day to share his extensive knowledge of Plymouth, the Roanoke River, and the *Albemarle*.

Finally, thanks to my wife Ginny and daughters Molly and Cara. It's all for you.

Notes on Sources

WHEN I SET OUT, I did not intend this book to be a work of original scholarship, but a retelling of an exciting story about a remarkable individual whose name had begun to fade. But along the way, I discovered letters regarding Will Cushing's resignation from the Naval Academy that I have not seen mentioned in previous biographies. These letters should change our understanding of what happened to Will.

In the rather large file kept on Cushing at the Navy Library in Washington was a tantalizing letter dated November 6, 1951, written by Admiral John Heffernan, the director of naval records, to Mr. Granville Tilghman of Norfolk, Virginia. The letter stated that there were eleven documents in the National Archives related to Cushing's dismissal, which Heffernan enumerated. Among them were the two letters from Commandant Rodgers to Superintendent Blake that are quoted in this book, as well as a petition calling for Cushing's reinstatement signed by his classmates, a letter from Congressman Ely, a letter to Blake from a mathematics professor, John Huntington Crane Coffin, and a note from Captain Magruder written on the back of Congressman Ely's letter. None of these letters were in the file at the Navy Library.

The letters from Rodgers, however, showed up in the National Archives, along with the letters between Blake and Palmer, the Naval Academy surgeon. Rodgers's letters were highly critical of Cushing's conduct. The first shows that he thought Will "had a talent for buffoonery." The second expressed his opinion that Will was simply not officer material, and warranted dismissal.

After that, the library at the Naval Academy was able to produce the series of letters between Blake and Navy Secretary Toucy documenting Will's absence for most of the month of January, the time when the "He bit the hoss" incident allegedly took place.

The letters from Ely, Magruder, and Coffin, and the petition from the midshipmen, alas, have yet to appear—maybe someday. But reading between the lines, one sees that Will had provoked the ire of Commandant Rodgers early in the academic year. Did Will's extended absence in January sharpen that ire? Was Rodgers sharing suspicions about Will's excuses with Blake? Hard to say, although the absence weighed sufficiently on Blake's mind that he wrote the suggestive letter to Palmer and perhaps tried to get information from Commandant Smith. When Cushing flunked his Spanish midterm, I believe, Rodgers stepped up his criticism and, using the failed grade and Will's high number of demerits, pressed Blake to call for Will's resignation. The new material presents a far more realistic view of Cushing's dismissal, and, for the first time, reveals Rodgers's role.

ALL OF THE works listed below were helpful to me, and I thank the writers not just for the fruit of their efforts but for their inspiration and for the pleasure of reading their books. I would like to cite several that I found particularly useful. Earlier Cushing biographers Charles Stewart and Ralph J. Roske and Charles Van Doren established the fundamentals about Cushing's life and activities. No one knows more about Alonzo Cushing's life and career than Kent Masterson Brown, just as no one has dug deeper into Cushing's courtship of Kate Forbes and Will's years in the Far East than Julian McQuiston. William S. Dudley's research about naval resignations was irreplaceable, just as was Robert G. Elliott's work on Gilbert Elliott and the construction of the *Albemarle*. Gene A. Smith's book about the *Monitor* and the *Merrimack* was enormously informative, as were the books Mark Hunter and Charles Todorich wrote about the Naval Academy. Thanks again to all.

Bibliography

Documents and Papers

United States Naval Academy, Annapolis, MD:
Documents related to William Cushing's undergraduate career and resignation from the
  Naval Academy
National Archives, Washington, DC:
Documents related to William Cushing's resignation from the Naval Academy
United States Navy Library, Washington, DC:
Documents related to Cushing's military service
Wisconsin Historical Society, Madison, WI:
Cushing family papers and letters

Books and Articles

Bradford, Richard H. *The Virginius Affair*. Boulder: Colorado Associated University Press,
  1980.

Brown, Kent Masterson. *Cushing of Gettysburg: The Story of a Union Artillery Commander*.
  Lexington: University of Kentucky Press, 1993.

Browning, Robert M., Jr. *From Cape Charles to Cape Fear: The North Atlantic Blockading
  Squadron During the Civil War*. Tuscaloosa: University of Alabama Press, 1993.

Carr, Dawson. *Gray Phantoms of the Cape Fear: Running the Civil War Blockade*. Winston-
  Salem, NC: John F. Blair, 1998.

Carter, Alden R., ed. *The Sea Eagle: The Civil War Memoir of Lt. Cdr. William B. Cushing
  U.S.N.* Lanham, MD: Rowman and Littlefield, 2009.

Dudley, William S. *Going South: U.S. Navy Officer Resignations & Dismissals on the Eve of
  the Civil War*. Washington, DC: Naval Historical Foundation, 1981.

Edwards, Eliza Mary Hatch. *Commander William Barker Cushing, Of the United States
  Navy*. Memphis, TN: General Books, 2012.

Elliott, Robert G. *Ironclad of the Roanoke: Gilbert Elliott's Albemarle*. Shippensburg, PA:
  White Mane Publishing Co., 1994.

Foote, Shelby. *The Civil War: A Narrative.* New York: Vintage Books, 1986.

Goodwin, Doris Kearns. *Team of Rivals: The Political Genius of Abraham Lincoln.* New York: Simon & Schuster, 2005.

Hunter, Mark C. *A Society of Gentlemen: Midshipmen at the U.S. Naval Academy 1845–1861.* Annapolis, MD: Naval Institute Press, 2010.

McFeely, William S. *Grant: A Biography.* New York: W. W. Norton, 1981.

McPherson, James M. *War on the Waters: The Union and Confederate Navies, 1861–1865.* Chapel Hill: University of North Carolina Press, 2012.

McPherson, James M., and Patricia McPherson, eds. *Lamson of the Gettysburg: The Civil War Letters of Lieutenant Roswell H. Lamson, U.S. Navy.* New York: Oxford University Press, 1997.

McQuiston, Julian R. *William B. Cushing in the Far East: A Civil War Naval Hero Abroad 1865–1869.* Jefferson, NC: McFarland & Company, 2013.

Miller, William Lee. *President Lincoln: The Duty of a Statesman.* New York: Alfred A. Knopf, 2008.

Musicant, Ivan. *Divided Waters: The Naval History of the Civil War.* New York: HarperCollins, 1995.

Naval Enterprise, Illustrative of Adventure, Heroism and Endurance. London: Frederick Warne and Co., c. 1860.

Parker, David. *A Chautauqua Boy in '61 and Afterward.* Boston: Small, Maynard, 1912.

Quarstein, John V. *A History of Ironclads: The Power of Iron over Wood.* Charleston, SC: History Press, 2006.

Roske, Ralph J., and Charles Van Doren. *Lincoln's Commando: The Biography of Commander William B. Cushing, U.S.N.* Annapolis, MD: Naval Institute Press, 1957.

Schneller, Robert J., Jr. *Cushing: Civil War SEAL.* Washington, DC: Brassey's Inc., 2004.

Slotkin, Richard. *The Long Road to Antietam: How the Civil War Became a Revolution.* New York: Liveright, 2012.

Smith, Gene A. *Iron and Heavy Guns: Duel Between the Monitor and the Merrimac.* Abilene, TX: McMurray University, 1998.

Stempel, Jim. *The CSS Albemarle and William Cushing: The Remarkable Confederate Ironclad and the Union Officer Who Sank It.* Jefferson, NC, and London: McFarland, 2011.

Stewart, Charles. *William Barker Cushing.* Annapolis, MD: Proceedings of the United States Naval Institute, vol. 38, issues 1–2 (June 1912).

Still, William N. *Iron Afloat: The Story of the Confederate Armorclads.* Columbia: University of South Carolina Press, 1988.

Sweetman, Jack. *The U.S. Naval Academy: An Illustrated History.* Annapolis, MD: Naval Institute Press, 1979.

Todorich, Charles. *The Spirited Years: A History of the Antebellum Naval Academy.* Annapolis, MD: Naval Institute Press, 1984.

Wert, Jeffry D. *General James Longstreet: The Confederacy's Most Controversial Soldier.* New York: Simon & Schuster, 1993.

———. *Gettysburg Day Three.* New York: Simon & Schuster, 2001.

INDEX

"acute mania," use of term, 276

Adams, John, 22

Adelaide, 103

admirals, 56*n*

Alabama claims, 260–61

albatrosses, 238

Albemarle, 161, 182, 280

building of, 162–63, 165

defenses of, 191–92

dominance of, 170–75, 182

final disposition of, 281

first battle of, 167–70

invincibility of, 172–73, 175, 176–77

launching and maiden voyage of, 165–67

prize money for, 234*n*

Roanoke River battle of, 171–75, 177

shortcomings of, 166, 177

sinking of, 18, 194–97, 198, 202, 207, 233,
235, 243, 249, 252, 253, 274, 278*n*, 279,
281, 282

small prey for, 178

specifications of, 166

strategies for destruction of, 176–79,
180–82, 188–89

WC's grueling escape from, 194–97

WC's mission against, 187–90, 191–93,
194–97, 227, 228

wreckage of, 234

alcoholism, 29, 52

Alden, James, 51

Alden, John, 22, 251

Alden, Priscilla, 22

Alert, 119

Alexander, Porter, 132–33, 135

All Saints Parish, 225

American Party (Know-Nothings), 25

American Revolution, 28, 46*n*

Anaconda strategy, 55, 142, 203

Anderson, Fort, 223, 226–27, 228

Anderson, Richard, 114

Antietam, Battle of, 95, 113–15, 132

Apaches, 253, 254–55

approach and withdrawal dimension, 278

Arizona, 253, 254

Arkansas, 161

Armistead, Lewis, 136

Armistead (slave), 85

Armstrongs (cannons), 204

Army, Confederate, 93, 142

see also specific battles

Army, U.S., 55, 129, 265

in attempt to recruit WC, 107

in campaigns against guerrilla warfare,
254–55

casualties of, 61, 92

Corps of Engineers, 55

Army, U.S. (*continued*)
  in joint operations with Navy, 62–63,
    97, 163, 185, 205, 210, 221
  strategical errors of, 115
  see also specific units and battles
Army of Northern Virginia, 132
Army of the James, 205
Army of the Potomac, 24, 70, 113, 124,
  128
Army of the Tennessee, 127
Army of Virginia, 113
Asiatic Squadron, 236, 239
Aspinwall, Panama, 232, 258, 272
asymmetrical warfare, 74, 181
Atlanta, 161

Bache, Alexander, 55–56
Back River raid, 61–65, 66
Bahamas, 224
Baker, Laurence, 178
Bald Head Battery, 224
Baldwin (coal heaver), 176
Ball's Bluff, Battle of, 33
Barnard, John, 55
Barton, Samuel, 64
Batavia, Java, 239
Battery A, Fourth US Artillery, 60, 116,
  124, 128, 133, 254
Battery Shaw, 223
Beardslee, Lester, 273, 276
Bear Springs, 255
Beaufort, N.C., 82, 91, 97, 106, 112, 207, 213
Beauregard, Pierre Gustave Toutant,
  59–60, 92–93, 171
Beijing, China, 246, 247
Big Bethel, Battle of, 63
Bigelow, John, 228
Bishop, C. E., 252
Black, John, 17–18
blackface minstrelsy, 238
Blackwater River, 98–99, 230, 278
Blake, George S., 29–31, 34, 38
  death of, 281

WC admonished by, 20–21, 32, 36
WC recommended by, 71–72
in WC's expulsion from the Naval
  Academy, 39–42, 47
Blakeley rifles, 204
blockade, 51–52, 55, 57, 62–65, 76, 137, 161,
  164, 182, 205
  shortcomings of, 203
  successful strategy of, 143–44
  WC's boredom with, 66–67, 98, 147–48
Blockade Board, 55–56, 62
blockade runners, 58, 74, 75, 91, 103, 117,
  137, 142–43, 146, 147, 149, 178, 203, 205,
  207, 262
  WC's strategy for, 224–25
blood pressure, 278*n*
Bogue Inlet, 103
Bombshell, 167, 171, 172–73
Borghese Gladiator, 273
Boston, Mass., 50, 54, 57, 83, 127, 236, 253
  WC's ordnance duty at, 252–53, 257
Bourke, John Gregory, 254–55
Bragg, Braxton, 113, 118, 214
Braine, D. L., 270
Breckinridge, John C., 59
Breese, Kidder Randolph, 214, 220
Brooke, John, 74, 78
Brookes (cannons), 204
Brooklyn, N.Y., 85, 86, 87
Brooklyn Navy Yard, 70, 180
Brooks, J. A. J., 197, 229
Brown, John, 50, 59
Buchanan, Franklin, 78–80, 88
Buchanan, James, 55
Buchanan, McKean, 80
Buchanan Battery, 204, 206, 211
Buckingham, Catharinus Putnam, 115
Buddha statue, 246–47
Bull Run, First Battle of, 60–61, 66, 70,
  95, 213
Bull Run, Second Battle of, 113
Burlingame, Wilson D., 188
Burnside, Ambrose, 115–16

Burriel, Juan Nepomuceno "The Butcher,"
264–66, 267–69, 270
Bushnell, Cornelius, 84–87
Butler, Benjamin "the Beast," "Spoons,"
48, 61, 62–64, 163, 164–65, 205–6,
209–10, 213–14, 222n, 224
in hearings on Fort Fisher, 213, 221

Callahan, Tom, 278
Cambridge, 72, 75–76, 77, 80–82, 91
Campbell, Fort, 223–24
cancer, 276
Cape Fear, 111, 117
Cape Fear River, 277, 279
reconnaissance mission on, 149–50,
151–53, 154–56, 157, 177
strategic importance of, 108–9, 111,
142–47, 161, 185, 203, 206, 208, 212,
223–27
Cape Hatteras, 142, 185
Cape Henry, 88
Cape Town, South Africa, 237–38
Caswell, Fort, 109–10, 111, 143, 149, 155, 212,
223–24, 229
Cemetery Ridge, 129–30, 132, 135, 217
Censor, 121
Ceres, 172
Cespedes, Pedro, 262, 264
Chancellorsville, Battle of, 123–26, 128,
132, 166
Charleston, S.C., 33, 49, 91, 92, 227
Union blockade of, 52, 57, 142, 203
Charlestown Navy Yard, 50, 54
Charlotte, 225, 234
Chase, Salmon, 22
Chatauqua Boy in '61 and Afterward, A
(Parker), 24–25, 125n, 139
Cherokee, 156
Chickamauga, 212, 216
Chicopee, 178, 187
Chicora, 161
China, WC stationed in, 246–47, 248–50
China Station, 243, 249

Chinese junks, 244
Chowan River, 98
Christy's Minstrels, 238
Chuckatuck, Va., 122, 278
Civil War, The (Foote), 276
Civil War, U.S.:
Confederate decline in, 202–3, 225–27
end of, 229–30, 231
four-part Anaconda strategy for, 55, 142,
203
onset of, 48, 49, 59–60, 63, 253
prelude to, 19–21, 33–34, 35–36, 45–47
see also specific battles, persons, and units
Clarendon Foundry, 163
Clark, Fort, 62, 64, 163
Cochise, 253, 255
Code Duello, 67
Cohasset, 119
Cohen, Michael, 163
Cold Harbor, Battle of, 254
Coleman, Mary, gold pendant of, 182, 198
Colorado, 57
Colorado, USS, 219
Colored Infantry, US, 220–21
Columbia, S.C., 19, *161*
Columbiads (cannons), 204
Committee on the Conduct of the War,
213
Commodore Barney, 117–23, 125, 127–28
Commodore Hull, 172, 174, 187
Commodore Perry, 97–100
Confederacy:
Civil War as unwinnable by, 164, 202–3,
225–27
culture of, 73
fall of, 229, 231
feats of daring by, 141–42
formation of, 34, 35, 226
Great Britain and, 158, 225
industrial inferiority of, 160–61
strategy of, 74, 113, 115, 128, 133, 164–66,
181
Union coastal blockade of, *see* blockade

Confederate Point, 203

Congress, 79–81

Congress, U.S., 55, 56*n*, 96, 186, 201, 213, 221, 234*n*, 270–71

WC as page in, 25–26, 31

Congressional Cemetery, 279

Continental Hotel, 139

Continental Shipyards, 85

Cooke, James W. "Ironmonger Captain," 162–63, 165–68, 171–74, 177

death of, 281

Corcoran Gallery of Art, 272–73

Corps of Topographical Engineers, 115

cotton, Confederate dependence on, 54, 55, 74, 103, 104, 142, 225

Cotton Plant, 171, 172

Couch, Darius N., 96, 116, 124, 128

Crayon, Porte, *see* Strother, David

Crimean War, 63, 74, 86, 204, 242

Crosby, Pierce, 61

Crumpler's Bluff, Battle of, 99–100, 112

Cuba, 224

independence movement in, 258–59, 260–63

Cuban crisis, 250–63

corruption and atrocities in, 264–66, 267, 269, 270

WC's role in, 258–59, 260–61, 267–71

Cumberland, 50, 52, 56, 57, 79–80

Curtin, Andrew, 139

Cushing, Alonzo "Lon," 22–24, 107, 117, 253

acclaim for, 116, 124–26, 128, 130, 146–47, 281

as artillery commander, 116

Civil War service of, 66–67, 68, 70, 77, 93–94, 95–96, 113–16, 123–24, 127–30, 132–36, 139, 217, 254, 281

heroism of, 93, 130, 134

mourning of, 137, 138–39, 182, 230

personal characteristics of, 60

posthumous Medal of Honor of, 281

promotions of, 60, 130

as topographical engineer, 115

at West Point, 28–29, 59–61

wounding and death of, 134–36, 253, 280

Cushing, Benjamin, 22

Cushing, Elizabeth "Little Ma," 22–25, 116, 127, 139, 182–83, 201, 229, 236, 253, 255–56, 272, 274, 277

later years and death of, 280

WC's correspondence with, 57, 64, 75, 81–82, 96, 98, 119, 120–21, 137, 198, 232, 233

Cushing, Ellen Grosvenor "Little Nell," 217

Cushing, Howard, 22, 92–93, 127, 139, 198

death of, 253, 255–56, 257

military career of, 253–55

Cushing, Kate Forbes, 272–74

death of, 281

marriage of, 251–53

pregnancies of, 253, 258

WC's engagement to, 235–36, 237, 239, 240–42, 244–45, 247

WC's memory maintained by, 280–81

Cushing, Katherine Abell, 279, 281

Cushing, Marie Louise, 257, 281

Cushing, Mary Isabel, 22–24, 229, 236, 276, 280

Cushing, Milton, Jr., 22, 70, 116, 117, 125, 136, 217, 226, 253, 255–56, 273

death of, 280

Cushing, Milton Buckingham, 22, 115

Cushing, USS, 280

Cushing, William Barker "Will":

adventure pursued by, 26, 47, 57, 66–67, 71, 98, 103, 106, 118, 139, 143–48, 149–50, 156, 188, 210–11, 212–13, 223–24, 226, 227, 230, 237, 243, 270, 279

and Alonzo, 66–67, 68, 70, 95–96, 97, 107, 117, 127–28, 137, 138, 182, 253

as appealing to women, 182, 233–34, 236, 242

appearance of, 18, 27, 272

appetite for risk of, 53, 108–12, 149–50, 179, 270, 277–78
arrest of, 139–40
Atlantic cruise of, 31–32
as audacious and insolent, 157–59, 249–50, 268
birth of, 22
Black's tribute to, 17–18
casual racist attitude of, 76, 232, 238–39
childhood of, 22–26
chronic hip and back pain of, 235, 253, 257–58, 272, 273, 276
courtship and engagement of, 235–36, 237, 239, 240–42, 244–45, 247
delirium and death of, 273–74, 275–76, 279
disparagement of, 252, 275
embellishment and exaggeration by, 20, 39, 67, 148
engagement of, 235–36, 237, 239, 240–42, 244–45, 247
enthusiastic tourism of, 233, 237, 246–47
fearlessness and bravery of, 25, 101, 103, 105, 107, 110–12, 143–48, 193, 194, 199–200, 211, 273, 278
financial concerns of, 233–34, 236
Flusser admired by, 97–98
as forgotten American hero, 17–18
Fredonia's tribute to, 229–30
funeral and burial of, 279–80
as fun-loving prankster, 28, 30–31, 36–39, 67, 145, 224, 278, 279
heroism sought by, 46, 54
Howard's death and, 253, 255–56, 257
ill health of, 76, 92, 237–38, 239, 247, 257–58
imagined future of, 282
initiative and ingenuity of, 28, 100, 103–6, 108–10, 138, 155–56, 224–25, 227, 278–79
as irrepressible, 22, 23–25, 48, 71, 181, 244
leadership qualities of, 23–24, 28, 103, 106, 110, 112, 219–20

love letters of, 240–42, 244–45
marriage of, 251–53
maturing of, 182, 240, 278
melancholy and moodiness of, 257, 272
peacetime transition of, 230, 231–32, 234
personal Civil War losses of, 230
popularity of, 23–24, 27
pugnacity of, 24–25, 27, 139–40, 148, 237, 252
quick temper of, 68, 122, 139–40, 158, 184, 226, 237, 252, 256, 278
rebellious streak of, 18, 42, 67, 71, 96, 138, 144
recklessness of, 68–69, 110–11, 192, 235
restlessness of, 231–32, 257
sculpted bust of, 235
speculation over possibility of mental illness in, 275–77
speculation over possibility of personality disorder in, 277–79
Cushing, William Barker "Will," naval career:
acclaim for, 57, 65, 82, 100–101, 106, 112, 124–26, 138, 145, 157, 197, 198–201, 202, 207, 228–29, 233, 236, 239, 242, 248, 271, 280, 282
Albemarle attacked and sunk by, 18, 187–90, 191–93, 194–97, 198, 227, 228, 233, 234, 235, 252, 253, 274, 278n, 279, 282
Albemarle strategies of, 178–79, 180–82, 188–89
appointed to Navy, 48, 53, 54
in attack on Fort Fisher, 210–11, 216–20, 281
blockade duty of, 57–58, 66–67, 98, 147–48, 224–25; *see also specific missions and battles*
on *Cambridge*, 72, 75–76, 80–82, 91
Cape Fear River search and reconnaissance missions of, 149–50, 151–53, 154–56, 157, 177, 223–27
as captain of *Delaware Farmer*, 56–57

Cushing, William Barker "Will," naval
    career (*continued*)
    captives taken by, 150, 152, 154
    as commander, 18, 119–20, 250, 257
    Commodore Barney commanded by,
      117–23, 125, 127–28, 137
    on *Commodore Perry*, 97–100
    creative and daring battle strategies
      of, 91–92, 108–10, 122–23, 143–44,
      146, 148, 154, 224–25, 227, 267–70,
      278–79
    in Cuban crisis, 258–59, 260–61, 267–71
    dubbed "Albemarle" Cushing, 201, 236,
      242, 268
    Ellis commanded by, 101, 102–7, 162
    at end of the Civil War, 230, 231–34,
      235
    excitement of battle for, 63–64, 93, 156
    as executive officer of Washington
      Navy Yard, 272
    global cruise as commander of *Mau-*
      mee, 236–39, 240–45, 246–50, 251
    greatest moments of, 228–29
    Hong Kong faux pas of, 242–43
    Lancaster commanded by, 232–34
    as lieutenant, 18, 96, 97, 112, 117
    as lieutenant commander, 18, 201, 202,
      211, 242, 251, 252
    Malvern commanded by, 202, 211, 212,
      217
    memoirs of, 229, 235
    as military governor of Smithville, 224,
      270
    on *Minnesota*, 54, 56–57, 61–65, 66–67,
      70–72, 94
    Monticello commanded by, 137, 142, 146,
      156, 157–58, 212, 216, 225, 227, 228, 229
    on *Pioneer*, 57
    pirates hunted by, 243–44
    prize money awarded to, 198, 201,
      233–34
    promotions of, 18, 96, 97, 112, 198, 200,
      201, 228, 250, 257

    ships named in honor of, 280
    Shokoken commanded by, 137–38
    uncertain future of, 247–48
    as war correspondent, 121
    wounding and injuries of, 81, 92, 94, 197,
      198, 258
    Wyoming commanded by, 258, 267–69,
      272, 273
Cushing Massacre, 255
Cushing Street, Tucson, 255
Custer, George Armstrong, 17–18, 213
cutters, 211
    in *Albemarle* mission, *see* Picket Boat
      No. 1
    loss of, 184–86

Dahlgren guns, 50, 87, 168
Daughter of Niobe, 273
Davenport, H. K., 103, 106, 108, 170, 176
Davis, Charles, 55
Davis, Jefferson, 31, 73–74, 118–19, 121, 165
de Horsey, A. F. R., 263
Delafield, Wis., 22
Delamater, Cornelius, 85
Delaware Farmer, 56–57
Del Sol, Jesus, 262, 264
Deming, Lorenzo, 187
Dewey, George, 27, 206, 208, 218–19, 282
Dix, John A., 98
"Dixie," 226
Doubleday, Abner, 114
Douglas, Stephen, 31
"Dueling in the Old Navy" (Paulin),
    67–68
duels, 67–68, 70
Duer, Lieutenant, 188
Dunker Church, 114
Du Pont, Samuel, 55

Eagle's Island Battery, 223
Early, Jubal, 114
Edinburgh, Duke of, 248
Edwards, Francis Smith, 25–26

Edwards, Mary, 25
    WC's letters to, 19–20, 34, 54, 61, 103,
        118
Edwards Ferry, 162–63, 166
elections:
    of 1860, 31, 55, 59
    of 1864, 164, 201, 202, 206
    mock, 59
    Pennsylvania gubernatorial, 139
Elizabeth City, N.C., 97, 102, 161–62
Elizabeth River, 50, 51, 53, 77, 79
Elliott, Gilbert (father), 161
Elliott, Gilbert (son), 161–62, 167, 168,
        173–74, 281
Ellis:
    as Confederate ship, 162
    as WC's first command, 101, 102–7, 111,
        162
Ely, Alfred, 44–45
Emancipation Proclamation, 95
Emory, William (ensign), 243
Ericsson, John, 85–88, 176
Ericsson, K. Anders, 279
erysipelas, 281
ethnocentrism, 238–39
Evans, Robley, 33, 218, 243
Everett, Edward, 139
Ewell, Richard S., 128–29

Fair Oaks, Battle of, 93
Far East:
    value of goods from, 247
    WC's departure from, 251
    WC's extended cruise to, 236–39,
        240–45, 246–50
Farley, Henry S., 49, 59
Farmer's Advocate, The, 92
Farragut, David, 17–18, 56*n*, 173, 181, 185,
        280
Fawn, 178
Federal Point (subsequently Confederate
        Point, Pleasure Island), 203
Feterhoff, 146

First Illinois Light Infantry, Battery B,
        92, 253
Fischer, Bobby, 278
Fish, Hamilton, 260–61
Fisher, Fort, *see* Fort Fisher; Fort Fisher,
        Battle of
flag officers, 56
floating bomb, *Louisiana* as, 207–8, 216
Florida, CSS, 177
Flusser, Charles, 45–46, 48, 97–101, 102,
        163, 170, 197, 280
    death of, 168–69, 230
Foote, Shelby, 276–77
Forbes, David, 236, 252
Forbes, Kate, *see* Cushing, Kate Forbes
Forest Hill Cemetery, Fredonia, 280
Fort Anderson, 223, 226–27, 228
Fort Campbell, 223–24
Fort Caswell, 109–10, 111, 143, 149, 155, 212,
        223–24, 229
Fort Clark, 62, 64, 163
Fort Fisher, 143, 150, 152, 155–56, 185
    defensive fortifications of, 203–5, 206,
        209, 224
    failed attacks on, 209–11, 213, 217–20
    strategy for, 205, 206–8, 213, 215, 242
    Washington hearings on, 213, 221
Fort Fisher, Battle of, 95, 212–15, 216–22,
        223, 243, 280, 281–82
    Union victory at, 221–22, 224
Fort Hatteras, 62–65, 66, 68, 69, 163
Fort Henry, Battle of, 253
Fort Holmes, 223
Fort Jackson, 178
Fort Johnson, 223
Fort Lamb, 223
Fort Lee, 223
Fort Meares, 223
Fort Monroe, 51, 88, 98, 237
Fort Philip, 178
Fort Pickens, 47, 51
Fort Shaw, 224
Fort Stokes, 223

Fort Sugar Loaf, 223

Fort Sumter, 33, 35–36, 47
  Confederate bombardment of, 48, 49, 51, 59–60, 78, 92, 253

Foster, John G., 107

Fox, Gustavus, 48, 64n–65n, 92, 109, 176, 178, 181, 205, 207, 215
  WC supported by, 96, 97, 106, 146–48, 232

France, 74, 270

Frank Leslie's Weekly, 265

Franklin, Tenn., 202

Franklin, Va., 98–99

Franklin, William, 115

Fredericksburg, Battle of, 115–16, 124, 217

Frederick Warne and Co., 46

Fredonia, N.Y., 45, 244, 257, 272
  Alonzo's leave in, 116
  Cushing brothers' marker at, 280
  end of Civil War celebrated in, 229–30
  WC's disparagement of, 241–42
  WC's family in, 19, 22–23, 35, 121, 236
  WC's leaves in, 92, 94, 181–83, 201, 235
  WC's wedding in, 251–52

Fredonia Censor, 238, 251–52

"freedom of the city" honor, 233

French, Charles, 168

From Sail to Stern: Recollections of Naval Life (Mahan), 28

Fry, Joseph, 262, 265

Frying Pan Shoals, 111

Fuger, Frederick, 134–36, 281

"functional psychopaths," heroic types of, 277

Galena, 85, 86

Gay, Thomas, 188–90, 192, 200, 234n

Gemsbok, 91–92

General Order No. 34, 199

Germantown, 50

Getty, George W., 121

Gettysburg, Battle of, 95, 129–31, 132–36, 164, 182, 281

Gettysburg, Pa., national cemetery at, 139

Gettysburg Address, 95

Gibraltar of the South, 203

Girault, Arsène, 38

Goldsborough, Louis M. "Old Guts," 80, 94–96, 101, 109

Gosport Navy Yard, 74, 78, 84, 94
  debacle and loss of, 50–53, 62

Government Hospital for the Insane (St. Elizabeth's Hospital), 274, 276

Grant, Ulysses S., 127, 202, 205, 210, 213, 215, 260–61, 272

Gray Ghost, see Mosby, John Singleton

Great Britain, 91, 158, 225, 233
  in Cuban crisis, 262–63, 265–66, 270
  in the Far East, 242, 243, 248
  tensions between U.S. and, 157–59, 260–61

Great White Fleet, 243, 282

Green's Battery, 61

Green-Wood Cemetery, Brooklyn, 281

Grosvenor, Ellen, see Cushing, Ellen Grosvenor

guerrilla warfare, 254–55

Hadfield, Joseph, 146, 157–58

Hainan Island, 243

Halleck, Henry, 95

Hamilton, Richard, 187

Hampton Roads, 51, 56, 57, 66, 77, 92, 94, 95, 112, 117, 138, 184, 198, 204, 210, 237
  Back River raid on, 61–65
  Battle of, 77–84, 88–90
  Monitor vs. Merrimack at, 88–90

Hancock, Winfield, 124, 128, 129–30

Hardman, W. D., 144–45

Harley, Barnard, 187

Harper's, 219

Harper's Ferry, arsenal at, 50

Harper's Weekly, 87

Harrington, Master's Mate, 57

Harvey Birch, 91
Hatteras, Fort, 62–65, 66, 68, 69, 163
Hatteras Inlet, Union victory at, 62–65,
    66, 68, 69
Havana, Cuba, 229, 248, 269
Hawaii (Sandwich Islands), 233
Hebe, 137–38
Hebert, Hilary, 133
Hébert, Louis, 144–45, 224
Hedges, Chris, 230
Henry, Fort, 253
Higgins, Samuel, 187, 195, 200, 230
Hill, A. P., 128–29
Hirst, Benjamin, 133
Hoke, Robert, 166–68, 171
Holden, Edgar, 172–73
Hollins, George, 45–46
Holmes, Fort, 223
Holt, Joseph, 59
Hong Kong, 239, 242–43, 244
Hood, John, 114, 202
Hooker, Joseph, 96, 115, 118, 123–24, 228
Houghton, Edward J., 187, 200
Houghton, Lawrence and Jane, 127
Houghton, M. B., 133
Hound, 157
House of Representatives, U.S., 270–71
    Committee on Foreign Affairs of, 271
Howorth, William L., 144, 149, 151, 181,
    184, 187–89, 200, 234*n*
Hudson River, 181, 273
Hunchback, 98
Hunt, Henry, 133
Hutchins, Charles, 268, 269, 273, 275

imperialism, American, 232–33
Iowa, 218
ironclads, 147–48, 150, 202, 206, 213,
    248
    Confederate commitment to, 74,
        160–63, 227
    Confederate failures of, 160–61, 166
    designs for, 74–75, 84–88

European, 227
    first battle between, 88–90
    strategy for, 171–72
    Union superiority in, 160, 180
    U.S. Navy's opposition to, 29, 84
    see also specific vessels

Jackson, Fort, 178
Jackson, Stonewall, 113, 118, 124, 128
Jacksonville, 104
James, George S., 49
James Douglass, 147, 186
James River, 79, 84, 85, 118–19
Jamestown Journal, 252
Japan:
    opening of, 28
    WC in, 244–45, 247, 248
Johnson, Andrew, 281
Johnson, Fort, 223
Johnson House hotel, 229
Johnston, Albert Sidney, 92
Jones, Colonel, 145, 152–53
Jones, J. E., 144–45, 149
Jones, Catesby ap Roger, 80–81, 89–90

Kearsarge, USS, 260
Kelly, Patrick, 144–45
Keppel, Henry, 242–43, 248
Key West, Fla., 56, 73
King, Robert, 187
Kingston, Jamaica, 261, 267
Know-Nothings (American Party), 25
Kotetsu (formerly *Stonewall*), 248
Kyoto, Japan, 248

Lamb, Fort, 223
Lamb, William, 203–5, 213–14, 217–18,
    220, 221
Lamson, Roswell, 120–21, 125, 208
Lancaster, 232–34
Lawton, Alexander, 114
Lay, John L., 180
Lee, Fort, 223

Lee, Robert E., 108–9, 113, 115, 118, 121, 123, 128–31, 132–33, 136, 164–65, 202, 203, 213
  surrender of, 229, 231
Lee, Samuel P., 101, 106, 108, 112, 116, 123, 125, 138, 146–48, 163, 170, 171, 176–77, 185
Lester, Rufus W., 235
Libby Prison, 200, 217
Lincoln, Abraham, 44, 47, 49, 51, 64n–65n, 70, 74, 76, 83, 86, 94–95, 113, 139, 196, 200, 213, 253
  assassination of, 281
  contemplated capture of, 128
  elections of, 55, 59, 164, 201, 202, 206
  WC's meetings with, 125–26, 228–29
Lincoln's Commando (Roske and Van Doren), 37
Little Big Horn, Battle of, 213
Little River, 109–10, 122, 225
Longstreet, James, 113, 117–23, 125, 128–29
Loraine, Lambton, 263, 265–66, 270–71
Loring, Stanton, 255–56
Louisiana, as floating bomb, 207–8, 216
love letters, 240–42, 244–45
loyalty oath, 59–60
Ludlow, Captain, 137–38
Lykken, David, 277–78
Lynch, William, 150

Macomb, W. H., 185, 187–88, 197, 198
Maffitt, John, 177–78
Magruder, George, 42, 47
Mahan, Alfred Thayer, 28–29, 280–81
Malakoff Tower, 204
Mallory, Stephen G., 73–74, 160, 162, 177, 227
Malvern, 202, 211, 212, 214, 217, 219, 225
Manassas, CSS, 171, 178
manifest destiny, 261
Manila Bay, 210
Mansfield, Joseph, 80
Martin, William, 161–62

Maryland, as conflicted about secession, 50, 78
Mattabesett, 172
Maumee, 236–39, 240–45, 246–50, 251
Maumee Christys, 238, 251
Maury, Sylvester, 255
McCauley, Charles, 51–53
McClellan, George, 70, 93, 94–95, 113, 115, 156
McPherson, James P., 142
Meade, George, 114, 129–31, 132
Meares, Fort, 223
Medal of Honor, 201, 202, 281
Medford, Mass., 253
Melville, George W., 180
mental illness, 275–77
Merrimack (CSS Virginia), 50–51, 161, 163
  in battle at Hampton Roads, 77–82, 84, 160, 165
  in battle with Monitor, 88–90
  fear engendered by, 83, 94
  Monitor compared to, 87
  redesigned as ironclad, 74–75, 78, 87–88
  scuttling of, 94
  shortcomings of, 78–79, 83, 89–90
Mexican-American War, 56
Meyer, Ensign, 174
Miami, 167–68, 172, 174
Millon, Theodore, 277–78
Milne, Lieutenant, 135
mines, underwater (torpedoes), 74, 161, 166, 172, 176, 178, 189, 192–93, 211, 223, 226, 229, 253
Minnesota, USS, 48, 54, 56–57, 61–65, 66–67, 70–72, 80–81, 84, 88–90, 94, 177, 189
missionaries, 246
Mississippi, 214
Mobile Bay, 279
Monitor, 82, 94
  in battle with Merrimack, 88–90
  design and construction of, 84–88

monitors, 160, 170, 176, 206, 213
   mock, 227, 228
Monroe, Fort, 51, 88, 98, 237
Monticello, 56, 138–40, 142, 146, 156, 157–58, 212, 216, 219, 225, 227, 228, 229
Mosby, John Singleton (Gray Ghost), 141, 144–45, 156
Mosquito fleet, 97, 162
Mott, John, 255
Mount Washington, 119–20
Mumma, Samuel, 114
"Muss Company, The," 24

Nansemond River incident, 118–24, 147, 208
Napoleon III, Emperor of France, 86
Napoleons (guns), 114
Nashville, 91–92
Native Americans:
   violence by, 254–55
   see also specific tribes
Naval Academy, Annapolis, Md., 94, 120, 173, 216, 281, 282
   attempts to restore WC to, 44–47, 70–71
   Confederate resignations from, 33, 36, 45, 59
   reform attempts at, 29–31
   strict discipline and academic program of, 27–28, 30, 32
   WC's education at, 19, 26, 27–32
   WC's expulsion from, 18, 34, 35–43, 47, 71
   WC's file at, 248–50
   West Point compared to, 29
Naval Academy Cemetery, 279
Naval Enterprise, Illustrative of Heroism, Courage and Duty, 46
Navy, Confederate, 79
   casualties of, 81, 100, 169, 209, 221
   disadvantages of, 73–74
   see also specific battles
navy, Japanese imperial, 248

Navy, Royal British:
   in Cuban crisis, 263, 270
   in Far East, 242–43, 248
   heroes of, 46
Navy, U.S.:
   Albemarle destruction strategies of, 176–77
   casualties of, 16, 81, 100, 119, 200, 209, 217–21
   after Civil War, 231
   commitment to ironclads by, 160–61
   dueling in, 67–68
   enlargement of, 96
   incompetent officers in, 28–29, 42, 52–53, 70, 92, 94–95, 210, 213, 214, 224
   in joint operations with Army, 62–63, 97, 163, 185, 205, 210, 221
   Library of, 250
   postwar shrinking of, 257
   ranking system of, 56*n*, 68*n*, 96
   strategical errors of, 65
   unprepared state of, 47, 51
   WC's appointment to, 48
   WC's temporary resignation from, 68–72
   see also specific units and battles
Nelson, Horatio, Lord, 221
Neuse, 161, 171
Neuse River, 62, 65, 165, 171
New Bern, N.C., 62, 65, 97, 103, 107, 170–72, 174
   Confederate raid on, 164–65, 176
New Inlet, 109, 137, 143, 147, 153, 203, 204, 206, 207, 210
New Orleans, La., 48, 52, 142, 173, 184, 205, 279, 281
Newport News, Va., 79
New River Inlet, 104, 162
New Topsail Inlet, 103–4, 137
New York, N.Y., 57, 66, 83, 85, 91, 201, 281
   WC in, 231–32, 236
New York Navy Yard, 231
New York Times, 208, 231

Niobe, HMS, 263, 265, 267, 269–70

Niphon, USS, 137

Norfolk, Va., 50–53, 94, 96, 117, 142, 146, 162, 187, 203, 207, 227, 234, 257, 272, 281

North Atlantic Blockading Squadron, 77, 94, 101, 106, 146, 176, 205, 279

North Carolina, 147, 161

Northeast Bastion, 204, 214–15, 217–20

Old Bogey (mock monitor), 227

Old Inlet, 212, 225

On the Border with Crook (Bourke), 254

Oregon (gun), 85

Otsego, 187–88

Outer Banks, N.C., 62

Owl, 178

Pacific, WC's duty in, 229, 232–34

Pacific Fleet, 273, 275

Pacific Squadron, 232, 255, 282

Pacific Steamship Company, 232

Palmer, James, 39–40

Palmetto State, 161

Pamlico Sound, 62–63, 65, 171

Panama, 232, 261, 270

Panama Railway, 232, 258

parasitic infection, 277

Parker, David, 24–25, 125*n*, 139

Parker, James, 221

Parker, William, 75, 91–92

Parker, William H., 106

Parrots (guns), 114, 193, 209

Pasquotank River, 161

Patterson, Thomas H., 272

Paulding, Hiram, 52–53

Paulin, Charles, 67–68

Pawnee, 52–53

Peacemaker (gun), 85

Pearl Harbor, 81

Pearl River, 243

Pearson, George, 232

Peck, John, 118–19, 121, 123–24, 170

Pegram, Robert, 91

Pei Ho river, 246

Pemberton, John, 127

Pendleton, William, 132–33

Penninsular Campaign, 77

Pennsylvania, Civil War action in, 127–31

Perry, Matthew C., 28

Perry, Oliver Hazard, 28

personality disorders, 277–79

Peterkin, William, 188, 191

Petersburg, Battle of, 202, 207

Philadelphia, Pa., 139–40, 148, 236

Philip, Fort, 178

Pickens, Fort, 47, 51

Picket Boat No. 1:

    in *Albemarle* mission, 180–81, 185, 187–90, 192, 193, 281

    casualties of, 195

    primitive technology on, 189–90

    volunteer crew for, 187–89, 194, 200

Pickett, George, 132, 165, 176

Pillsbury, Elliot, 253

pilothouse raid, 110–11

Pioneer, 57

pioneers, 217

pirates, in South China Sea, 243–44

Pleasure Island, 203

Plymouth, N.C., 62, 165–69, 171, 174, 182, 188, 190, 195

    fall of, 198

Plymouth, USS, 31, 50

Plymouth River, 62

pneumonia, 257

Pope, John, 113

Porter, Benjamin, 214–15, 219, 230, 234*n*

Porter, David Dixon, 97, 110, 184–85, 189, 198–99, 201, 202, 205, 206–7, 209–11, 212–15, 217, 220, 223–24, 225, 227, 242, 279

    later years and death of, 281–82

Porter, John, 74, 78, 222

Preston, Samuel, 208, 216–17, 219, 222, 230, 280

Princeton, 35
prisoners of war, 200–201, 217, 226
Proceedings, 36–37
"psychopaths, functional," heroic types
    and, 277–78

Quaker City, 56

racism, 76, 232, 238–39
railroads:
    limitations of, 160
    Panama, 232, 258
Raleigh, CSS, 147–48, 149–50, 152, 161
rams, ramming, 80, 148, 163, 166, 167–68,
    170, 171, 173–74, 178, 189, 198, 226
Rappahannock River, 75–76, 118, 123, 124
Republican party, 139
Reynolds, John, 129
Rhind, Alexander, 207–8, 216
Richmond, CSS, 119
Richmond, Va., 62, 75, 77, 93, 113, 118–19,
    163, 200, 217, 229
Richmond Enquirer, 133
Rio de Janiero, Brazil, 237
Roanoke, 80
Roanoke Island, 65, 97, 142, 162, 170, 187
Roanoke Island, Battle of, 216–17
Roanoke River, 162–63, 164, 166, 171–75,
    177–78, 182, 191, 194, 196, 234, 273,
    277, 281
Robert Gilfillan, 91
Robeson, George M., 270, 279
Rodgers, Christopher Raymond Perry,
    28–31, 38
    later years and death of, 282
    WC admonished by, 30–32, 36, 282
    in WC's expulsion from the Naval
        Academy, 40–43
Roe, Francis, 173–75
Roget, E. A., in WC's expulsion from the
    Naval Academy, 30–31, 36–39
Roget, Eugenie, 38
Roosevelt, Theodore, 18, 280

Roske, Ralph J., 37–38
Rough Riders, 280
Rowan, Stephen Clegg, 176, 243
Ryan, Washington, 262, 264

Saco, 250
St. Elizabeth's Hospital (Government
    Hospital for the Insane), 274, 276
St. Lawrence, 80–81
St. Paul Island, 239
saltworks, 104, 138, 144
Salvador Pirates, 232
sand mound fortification, 204–6, 209,
    224
Sands, Captain, 143, 148
Sandwich Islands (Hawaii), 233
San Francisco, Calif., 233–34, 236
San Juan Hill, 280
Santiago, Cuba, 69, 259, 262–63, 265, 267,
    269–70, 271, 272
Sassacus, 172–74, 177
Savannah, Ga., 52
Schmitt, E. G., 165
sciatic tuberculosis, 276
Scott, Winfield, 55, 134, 142, 203
Scott's Anaconda, 55
screw propeller, 85
Sea Bird, 97
secession, 19–20, 33–34, 35, 45, 46, 59, 76,
    95
    of Virginia, 49–51
Seddon, John, 118
Sedgwick, John, 96, 114
Seminary Ridge, 130, 132, 234
Senate, U.S., 260
Seven Days, 93–94
Severn River, 279
Seward, William, 31, 86, 159*n*, 228
Sewell's Point, 204
Shamrock, 187–88, 197, 198
Sharpsburg, Md., 113–14
Shaw, Fort, 224
Sheridan, Philip, 17, 202

Sherman, William Tecumseh, 92, 202
Shiloh, Battle of, 95, 253
Shokoken, 137–38
Sickles, Daniel, 265
Sioux, 213
slaves, 59, 62, 73, 78, 95, 104, 144, 196
    emancipated, 225
    self-liberation of, 75–76, 188
Smith, Alfred, 44
Smith, Joseph (Commodore), 26, 39, 44,
    47, 80, 84, 117
Smith, Joseph (Lieutenant), 80, 93
Smith, Kirby, 113
Smith, Melancton, 171, 172, 174
Smith, Richard, 187
Smith, Roy C., 248–49
Smith Island, 146, 203, 212
Smithville, N.C., 223, 224, 270
    raid on, 143–45, 153, 156
Sommers, Rudolph, 187–88
South Atlantic Blockading Squadron,
    282
Southfield, 167–69, 188, 190, 196
Spain:
    in Cuba, 258–62, 267, 268, 270
    U.S. relations with, 265, 270
Spanish-American War, 218
spars, 180–81
Spear, Samuel, 98–100
Sphinx, see Stonewall
Spirited Years, The: A History of the Ante-
    bellum Naval Academy (Todorich),
    38
Staerkodder, see Stonewall
Stag, 225, 234
Stanton, Edwin, 83, 115, 163
Star of the West, 33–34
Steever, Charles L., 187, 234*n*
Stepping Stones, 119–21
Stewart, Charles, 36–37, 39, 275–76
Stockholm, Andrew, 181, 184
Stockton, Robert, 35
Stokes, Fort, 223

Stonewall (formerly *Sphinx, Staerkodder*,
    subsequently *Kotetsu*), 227, 228–29,
    248
Stotesbury, William, 187, 189, 234*n*
Stoughton, Edwin, 141
Stratton, Azariah, 134
Stringham, Silas, 56, 57, 61, 62–64, 69–71,
    94, 102, 109, 163
Strother, David (Porte Crayon), 99
Stuart, Jeb, 129, 141–42
submarines, 74
Suffolk, Va., 118–23, 125
Sugar Loaf, Fort, 223
Sumner, Edwin V. "Bull," 70, 93, 96, 97,
    114, 115–16
Sumter, Fort, *see* Fort Sumter
Supreme Court, U.S., 234*n*
Swan, Francis, 189, 234*n*
Swansborough, 103

Tarboro, N.C., 162
Tar River, 162
Taylor, Ezra, 92, 253
Taylor, Zachary, 165
Tecumseh, 181
Tenerife, 221
Tennessee, 161
Terry, Alfred, 213–15, 220
Thanks of Congress, 198, 201, 270, 282
Thanks of the Navy, 157
Tientsin, China, 246
Time, 278
Tonkin, Gulf of, 243
Tornado, 261
torpedo and spar device, 180–81
torpedoes (mines), 74, 161, 166, 172, 176, 178,
    180–81, 189, 192–93, 194, 211, 223, 226,
    229, 253
Toucy, Isaac, 38
Town Creek Battery, 223
Treasury Department, U.S., 55
Tredegar Iron Works, 75, 162
Trent affair, 158

Trinity Episcopal Church, 251
tuberculosis, 2, 92, 253, 258
    sciatic, 276
Tucson, Ariz., 254, 255
Tupper, Edward and Rachel Cushing,
    93
Tupper, Theodore, 93
Tyler, John, 35

Union League Club (Manhattan), 201
Union League of Philadelphia, 201

Valley City, 197, 229
Van Brunt, G. J., 70
Van Doren, Charles, 37–38
Varona, Bernabe, 262, 264
Vicksburg, Battle of, 127, 184, 206, 210, 227,
    256, 279
Victoria, Queen of England, 233, 248
Violet, 117
Virginia:
    blockade runners in, 76
    Civil War action in, 117–26
    secession of, 49–51, 78
    value to army of, 118
Virginia, CSS, see Merrimack
Virginia militia, 50, 51–53
Virginius affair, 261–62, 267, 270, 272

Wabash, 57, 63
War Is a Force That Gives Us Meaning
    (Hedges), 230
Warley, Alexander, 178, 192–93, 194, 200,
    270
    later years and death of, 281
War of 1812, 28, 56
War on the Waters (McPherson), 142
war prizes, monetary:
    awarded to WC, 198, 201, 233–34
    determining value of, 243n
Washington, D.C., 34, 35–36, 86, 198, 213,
    221, 250
    Alonzo in, 60–61, 116

as vulnerable to attack, 49–50, 55, 83, 113,
    128, 130
WC in, 25–26, 39, 44–45, 70, 109, 117,
    125, 138, 178, 207, 236, 257, 272–74
WC's funeral and burial in, 279–80
Washington, Treaty of, 261
Washington Navy Yard, 272
Webb, Alexander, 133
Webster, Milton, 197
Weitzel, Godfrey, 205, 209–10
Welles, Gideon:
    later years and death of, 281
    as Secretary of the Navy, 51–53, 74, 78,
        83–84, 86, 87, 95, 101, 117, 163, 185, 205,
        208, 213, 222n, 228, 236, 281
    WC rebuked by, 158–59, 185–86
    WC supported by, 44, 46–48, 53, 70–72,
        96, 97, 117–18, 125, 145, 148, 157, 179,
        199–200, 228, 229, 232, 236
Wessells, Henry, 168
Western Bar Channel, 143, 155
West Point, U.S. Military Academy at, 49,
    68, 73, 205
    Alonzo's education at, 25–26
    Confederte resignations at, 59–60
    Naval Academy compared to, 29
Wheelock, Sally, 241
Whetstone Mountains, 255
White, George, 186
White, William Alanson, 276
Whitehead, 98, 167, 172
white male supremacy, 238–39
Whiting, William H. C., 214, 221
Whitworths (cannons), 204
Wilderness, 208
Wilderness, Battle of the, 254
Wilkes, Henry, 187
Williamson, William, 74, 78
Wilmington, N.C., 147, 163, 226
    defenses of, 149–50, 223
    fall of, 227, 228
    Union blockade of, 52, 104, 108, 117, 143,
        157, 203, 213, 262

DISCARD

B CUSHING

Malanowski, Jamie.
Commander Will Cushing

METRO

R4001305966

METROPOLITAN
Atlanta-Fulton Public Library